ABSOLUTELY!

The Memoirs of Harry H. Briggs, Ph.D.

As told by the Paddlin' Professor
to
Letitia Sweitzer, M.Ed.

Copyright © 2011 Letitia Sweitzer   *   ISBN# 978-1-105-51467-8

Dedications

In loving memory of my wife and one true love, Lydia Briggs.

--Harry H. Briggs, Jr.

In gratitude to my parents Thomas Edward Lavender and Virginia Douglas Briggs Lavender, my grandparents Harry H. Briggs and Dora Douglas Briggs, and my great aunts Frances Douglas Pidgin (Our Ma) and Letitia Douglas Adams, M.D., for whom I was named, and to my Uncle Harry Briggs, one of the last with whom I can share vivid memories of these important people in our lives.

--Letitia Douglas Lavender Sweitzer

Acknowledgements

We want to acknowledge and express gratitude to some special people whose efforts and encouragement have helped move this memoir along, even made its publication possible, including Wadeen Hepworth for lending her scrapbook on Harry's Alaska years, James Underwood for proofreading, Doug Ireland for encouragement, Thomas Tilley for crucial production expertise, and Michael J. Cain for technical help, the cover design, and sharing his wisdom. Their enthusiasm and efforts for this project have been invaluable and are greatly appreciated.

My Early Inspiration

"I hungered for the romance of great mountains. From childhood I had dreamed of climbing Fujiyama and the Matterhorn, and had planned to charge Mount Olympus in order to visit the gods that dwelled there. I wanted to swim the Hellespont ... float down the Nile in a butterfly boat, make love to a pale Kashmiri maiden beside the Shalimar, dance to the castanets of Granada gypsies, commune in solitude with the moonlit Taj Mahal, hunt tigers in a Bengal jungle — try everything once."

Richard Halliburton, *The Royal Road to Romance*, 1925

FOREWORD

Every decade my Uncle Harry seemed to live several lives at one time, and he has so far lived nine full decades. He has been an athlete, a musician, a student pilot, a combat Marine, a journalist, a recreation director, a Ph.D., a professor, a college admissions director, a promoter, a public relations professional, a record setting marathon swimmer, a hotdog vendor, a publisher's rep, a landlord, an entrepreneur, a husband, an expert in Alaskan art and crafts, a haven for people who are down and out, an adventurer, a loner, and a man

about town—sometimes all at the same time. I think there have been whole years when he was every one of these occupations simultaneously. Moss never grew on him! Of all that, the one thing that he treasures and considers his mission in life was his marriage to Lydia. That was an adventure, too.

There was nothing in all this that could remotely be considered conventional. In fact, he was quoted by one journalist as saying, "Conventionality is an excellent trait—for bank clerks." In fact he knew a fair amount about bank clerks because his father was the vice president of the Second National Bank in Boston. While Harry seemed to purposely set out to rebel against the respectable, solid middle class upbringing his family imposed on him, he now, older and wiser, is honoring them by funding scholarships in memory of several family members he loved and admired. He has designated most of his modest savings to this endeavor, augmented by donations given on the occasion of his birthday swims.

While my Uncle Harry's entire childhood slipped by before I was born, he popped in and out of my childhood, teaching me the names and positions of all the Red Sox, how and when to steal a base, and when to expect a bunt. He once arrived from out of town in the middle of the night at my Aunt Letitia's house where I spent my summers, and, not wanting to disturb anyone by ringing the doorbell, he climbed in the kitchen window. I thought this is what considerate people did when they arrived in the middle of the night. And his arrival was always a delightful surprise.

I also heard about Uncle Harry's goings on from my mother, who was Harry's older sister, and from my great aunts who were his aunts, all of whom had different points of view. Several years ago, I wanted to put all the events and motivating forces of his life together in a memoir, his truth in his voice, and so I spent five days with him, as he talked pretty much nonstop in and around his current home in Leesville, Louisiana. As we went from Leesville to Toledo Bend Reservoir to Natchitoches, I scribbled as best I could, audio-recorded some to transcribe later, and typed on my MacBook whenever I had power and free hands.

Later I unscrambled the chronology with the help of some clues in the notes and voluminous newspaper clippings about his exploits. I connected it all in more or less the right order and sent him chapter by chapter the tales of his exploits in as much as possible his own words. He made short corrections and lengthy additions in his own all-caps handwriting. And then we did all that again for a final draft, racing against time until his 90th birthday celebration.

One word I heard him say repeatedly, especially when someone asked him if he was really going to undertake a certain new adventure, was "Absolutely!" That affirmation had to be the title of the book.

Letitia Sweitzer, M.Ed.   May, 2011

Chapter 1

Water

As we plunged, the walls of water rose up on either side, dark and angry, blocking the sky. We'd gone down in a valley in the shadow of death. Then, as if a whale lifted us, me and the boat, we rose up on a swell, looking out over the water of Cook Inlet as if we ruled it. And then down again, sucked down, helpless. All night, as we plunged and rose, I stayed at the wheel. The Flying Cossack was the investment that was going to make me, my wife, and two friends wealthy as we all deserved for all the hard work we had done and all the hard knocks we had taken. We were going to ride the Cossack to security if not riches by fishing for salmon. And now a decision I'd made to beat out a summer storm by crossing the bay instead of following the shore to a safe harbor threatened all that. The whole night I wrestled the wheel, turning the bow into the swells so we wouldn't be rolled over sideways. In case we capsized, I'd tied a pair of boots around my neck so that if I reached shore I could walk to a village. I feared the boat going down, bought only the month before. I feared the boat crashing against the cliffs. If it weren't for the boat, I did not fear the water. The water was like gentle arms that buoyed, even beckoned me. It had always been so.

My first memory was when I was about three and my family spent the summer on Cape Cod, right on the beach. I was playing at the water's edge, wading in the gentle waves. I lay down in the water as I'd seen others do and started to paddle. I was swimming! It felt exciting and rewarding until worried relatives pulled me out. My main desire after that was to return to the water, where I had discovered I could swim, naturally, instinctively, without fear. Water has defined my life. Even more my marriage has defined my life, but the lure of water came first…and last.

My mother Dora Darling Douglas, age 12, with her father Edward Foster Douglas about the time they moved from Nova Scotia to Massachusetts in the year her mother died.

Chapter 2

Family

My solidly middle class heritage and upbringing largely formed who I am, if only by my rebelling against it. No one in my family was prepared for the path I have taken, but I made a point of not asking for their participation or approval, and they still seemed to love me. I have led a life that is totally me. I've been true to myself or what they call today "authentic." And it's been okay. My life has had meaning, to me at least. Perhaps I can convey some of that meaning in this memoir.

My father was Harry Harper Briggs, born in Boston in 1884. His mother was born in Scotland, his father in England. In fact, his older brother Fred was born in England before the family immigrated to Massachusetts, where they had my father and his two brothers, Ralph and Roy.

My mother was Dora Darling Douglas Briggs, born in Nova Scotia in

Left to right: My oldest aunt Frances Fern Douglas, called Our Ma; my mother Dora Douglas, the youngest sister; my aunt Letitia Amelia Douglas. In back is Sarah Amanda Douglas, who stayed in Canada and raised a family.

1887 where her father managed lumbering camps. My mother's mother was from a French Huguenot family in Nova Scotia. In 1899, at age twelve, Dora followed her two older sisters Frances and Letitia to Boston. Her father may have come with her. So, with the exception of my Nova Scotia grandmother's French heritage, I am entirely Scottish and English.

My father Harry Harper Briggs about the time he married my mother.

My father Harry Briggs Sr. and his three brothers were raised on Beacon Hill in Boston. When grown, he got a job at the Second National Bank after some experience as an actor. He had a role in several plays in Boston. He appeared at the Shubert Theatre at least twice, and he had a good career ahead in theatre. However, at one point, he had to decide if he would pursue the acting career or that of a banker. He chose the more stable job to give my mother more security, but he remained a performer at heart. He was always the master of ceremonies at celebrations and family gatherings. He told jokes and was fantastic.

My older sister Virginia Douglas Briggs was born April 6, 1915, and was six years old when I was born on May 20, 1921. Until I was 16, my family lived at 99 Sargent Street in one of the oldest neighborhoods in Melrose, Massachusetts, near Boston. Later we moved to another house on Melrose's East side.

The house we owned on Sargent Street was full because, besides our immediate family, my mother's older sister Frances, the oldest sister and the first of the Douglas sisters to come to Boston from Nova Scotia, also lived with us, along with her much older husband Charles Pidgin. We called this aunt Our Ma because she had been like a mother to her younger sisters and other young people. Her husband, Uncle Charles, had been very prominent as a writer of bestselling novels, a playwright, an inventor, Head of the Bureau of Labor Statistics for the State of Massachusetts and, at one time, Commissioner of Education. In spite of being lame his whole life, he had been quite the man about town. By the time I was born he was old, frail, and penniless. He died at our house in 1923 when I was two, so I don't actually remember him.

And so I lived in a respectable middle class family in a comfortable home in a nice neighborhood. I soon began to create my own identity, exploring options, seeking passions that often took me outside of what my family considered acceptable.

My family spent a couple summers on Cape Cod where my family opened a restaurant for the season called The Red Parrot. Our Ma cooked while Mother and a family friend named Rena Withey waited tables. Friends came down and my father came down on weekends. They had other people to help so we had plenty of time to go to the beach. One day—I was about three—I sort of rolled into the water and found I could swim, dogpaddling. The family ran over to me because I was in the water unattended. They were not very happy with me, I remember, but that never stopped me from swimming in uncertain waters.

Apple harvest at my Aunt Letitia's farm in Plympton, Massachusetts. Then married to Frederick Adams, Letitia Douglas Adams, M.D., lived in an apartment in Boston, where she practiced medicine. On the left is Rena Withey, a family friend, then my mother.

Mother

My mother was greatly influenced by religion and poor health, which led to the religion. She never complained but was never really very well. I tried not to irritate her and I loved her very much. She was an extremely courageous woman.

My mother Dora Douglas Briggs about 1916, five years before I was born.

As I remember the story, my mother had tuberculosis in Nova Scotia. By that time, Aunt Letitia, my mother's sister several years older, was a practicing physician in Boston. Aunt Letitia sent my mother to a sanitarium in Massachusetts. Mother was in and out several different times. One time they brought her home, Aunt Letitia said she wasn't going to make it and let's make her as comfortable as possible. Someone suggested my mother try Christian Science. She did, and she got better. She often said, "I am alive because of Christian Science." So if you're given up for dead, and you try something different and you start to get better, are you going to stay with that religion? Absolutely. I'm glad I was brought up in her church and have those attitudes. Am I a Christian Scientist? Absolutely not.

When my mother had any kind of illness, she consulted her Christian Science practitioner. She even consulted him when her cats were ill. There was no medication involved ever. Physical examination to determine a treatment was never an option, let alone surgery. Mother had a huge egg-shaped lump on the top of her head, which she effectively covered with hair, but I knew it was there and I could tell that it was painful. She never sought treatment for it, unless perhaps she discussed it with her practitioner, but there was apparently no spiritual remedy forthcoming.

Here I am at about age six with my sister Virginia about age twelve.

My sister Virginia didn't like my mother and I don't know why. Maybe she was too strict. She was stricter with Virginia than with me. I don't know what the problem was. Every time I talked to my sister as an adult, she'd say, "Our mother favored you." But I wasn't aware of it.

Virginia's relationship with Mother worsened when she was heavily involved, while still in her teens, with Tom Lavender, the man she eventually married.

My dad did whatever Mother wanted. She had her way in bringing up the kids. My mother ran the house. However, Our Ma, who loved children and had none of her own, treated me like her own child. If my mother tried to discipline me, Our Ma would pat me on the head and say it was okay. She made it very hard on my mother. Our Ma finally left our house and went to live with Aunt Letitia, and I think that was the reason. I don't blame my mother. I knew Our Ma had placed her in a terrible situation. I accepted my mother's discipline. I'd do something bad and she'd punish me. Then after a while she'd say, "We'll forget about this." The reconciliation was fantastic. *My mother loves me again*, I thought. I couldn't ask for a better mother.

I gave her plenty of opportunity for the cycle of discipline and reconciliation throughout my elementary school days at first Whittier School and then Franklin School, both public elementary schools, and into my high school years at Melrose

High. She was called into all of these schools to deal with episodes of my misbehavior on top of the mischief I got into around home.

At Franklin School, a young teacher named Miss Barstow was the first female who really knocked my socks off. She was a gorgeous little brunette. I dreamed about her at night. Early on, she inspired me to something foolish in class to attract her attention. I then escaped into the boys' rest room at Franklin, which for my entire four years there was a stinking place with the odor spilling out into the corridor. No one should have to go in there. But Miss Barstow followed me in there and pulled me out by the scruff of the neck before I had the time to react. I had no remorse about the prank, but I felt terrible that I was the cause of the beautiful Miss Barstow having to endure the stench. At the same time, I admired her guts. Of course, my mother heard about that incident but not about my adoration of Miss Barstow. I even debated asking her if she would wait 25 years for me. I knew what the answer would be so I decided against it.

My mother was called in by the principal about the fights I got into in school, only the ones she knew about. I remember the playground bully named Tony Longo, in the class ahead of me. I was the biggest boy in my class, so he didn't bother me, although I was not as big as Tony. One day out on the playground, he started pushing some little person around. I'd had enough of this and decided to exert a leadership role. I held up a finger in his face and told him to quit. He must have thought, *Who is this guy a year younger?* But he didn't challenge me and backed away from the little guy he was pushing around. I was very pleased with my performance.

On the way home with a group of students, Joe Cairns, a boy in my class who had been watching me stand up to Tony, challenged me to a wrestling match to see if I was really tough. Joe was almost my size. So there on the grass in front of a neighbor's house, we struggled. It wasn't easy, but I finally pinned him. It was quite an exciting day. Was I competitive? Absolutely! And this day gave me quite a bit of physical confidence. Joe moved away soon after that, but would you believe that some 12 to 13 years later, during the war, I ran into him in the Pacific. There was a baseball game between campaigns, and he showed up with the visiting team. We remembered each other and had a great time. Of course, I didn't mention the much earlier fight because he was now over six feet tall and could easily have handled me.

Outside of school I also tried my mother's patience. One day I heard her remark that certain neighbors were "cheap." So I went down the street and I said, "My mother says you folks are cheap." And that person called my mother. Mother was embarrassed, of course, and she denied saying it. After they hung up, Dora scolded me, confessing only, "I may have said they were *ordinary.*" Ever since that unpleasant incident, I have always hated the word "cheap."

I also remember hiding behind some bushes and when Mrs. Bancroft, the elderly and sick woman who lived behind our house, came walking by, I jumped out and said, "You old shit." That woman called my mother while I was standing by the telephone. I said I hadn't called her that. The woman insisted on the word I had used. I said the woman had heard me wrong, that I'd called her "an old sheep."

Another thing I did later was really bad. I can't imagine I did it. It was Halloween and the people up the hill had a big Halloween party. I could see people dancing inside. A friend and I got a rock and I threw the rock right through the window. I was about 14 with a pretty good arm. You could hear the glass shattering. Right through the window! Then we were gone. The word was circulating that someone threw a rock through the Robbins' window. Did I admit to that? No. Nobody ever asked me. That could have seriously hurt somebody. That was dreadful. Why did I ever do that?

In high school, there were my car wrecks. I remember one when I was trying to outrun the police who were going to give me a ticket. I took a turn too fast on purpose, ran through a neighbor's hedge, crashed into their yard and out again. I managed to elude the police for then, but the car was scraped. Of course, I told my mother about the scrapes, not my father. I left it to her to tell my father, and she waited till he'd gone to work and called him on the telephone. She always protected me.

Dad

While I loved my mother dearly, I can't say I had the same feelings for my Dad. My mother painted my dad as a knight in shining armor, who could do no wrong.

Harry Harper Briggs

Totally trustworthy. I realized I had a lot to live up to, but I didn't relate to him. He was also fat. I thought, *My God, I would never allow myself to get like that.* Other dads were pushing their kids in sports. My dad wasn't. When people have asked why do I swim, I realized I had to do physical things to prove that I'm a man.

One summer my family rented a cottage in Annisquam, a town on Cape Ann on the north shore of Massachusetts, where the Annisquam River meets the Atlantic. The pilings that supported our cottage were actually out in the river. The people a few doors down had a Garwood speedboat, the Abbot family, even though my dad had a better job than the Abbot dad. My dad had what I called a putt putt, but I'd go ride in the Garwood with the Abbot twins. I didn't want to go with my dad. I thought of him as a little fat man. I was about 12, and you could say I didn't know any better.

One day I'd made a remark to put down the putt putt, and in addition he heard that I'd complained he wasn't in good shape. So one day he said, "Son, you get in this boat. I want to do something." Across the river, there was a bit of beach. He marked a line in the sand and went down a ways and drew another line and he said, "Start here and I'll race you to the other line." I thought I could handle him with ease, him with his big belly. He beat me by ten yards. I was really impressed. But instead of gaining respect for him, I thought if he were in shape he'd be a really good runner. What a waste of talent.

Looking back on it, I realize my mother and father were both very kind, generous people. They supported or contributed to many people who needed help. My dad and his brother Ralph supported their mother and their brother Roy and then the cousins who moved into their mother's house after her death. During the depression Dad was giving money to lots of people in the neighborhood who were having a hard time. Dad had his good job, but he never saved any money; he lived from paycheck to paycheck.

I think if my mother had been a driver, if my dad had married an aggressive lady and had given and attended the parties ambitious careers required, my father would have gone a lot farther in his career. My mother had some evening gowns and she was a very pretty woman but for her to go to a party in an evening gown was an ordeal.

Nevertheless, my father eventually became vice president of the Second National Bank. Well known in the banking world, he was on the board of the Boston Penny Savings Bank when he was offered the job of President. If I'd been in his position, I would have taken it, but he would have lost his Second National Bank pension, and he wanted to give my mother that security, so he turned the job down. At 65 he had his pension and Social Security and so, after a couple years, he took the job of manager of the Boston Clearing House so he had that salary also. He never built up savings and he was very, very generous to others. My mother was too. One of her specialties was taking in stray cats.

The reason my father and my uncle Ralph had to support our relatives was that they didn't do so well by themselves. Dad was doing well enough at the bank. Uncle Ralph had done very well in the manufacturing industry in several states, including furniture stores in North Carolina, and had started a business in Chicago, Briggs Textile, in 1930, and pretty soon was doing even better. The Briggs family still owns and operates Briggs Textile. Ralph was a very nice man. I liked him and his wife Helen a lot.

My uncle Ralph Briggs.

I saw the Boston relatives often and had pretty strong opinions about them. My impression is that my father's oldest brother, Uncle Fred, was a weak individual. His claim to fame was that he was organist at the very prominent Temple Street Church. Then we came into the Depression, and he had no more job. He didn't like to work, but he dressed as if he had a job to go to. He and his wife Aunt Agnes lived in a busted up apartment on Beacon Hill, and I think my dad and Uncle Ralph may have had to contribute to them. Agnes was a pretty woman. She had money in the beginning but ended up in poverty. After a while they moved into a dilapidated apartment in Newton.

Then my dad became interested in a travel agency. He went to a convention of travel agents as a representative of the bank. He liked to travel so much that he decided maybe he could start an agency himself. So he opened Briggs Travel Agency on the second floor of a building on the main street in downtown Portland, Maine. He put Uncle Fred in charge, so that was another way of helping his brother. The agency never made any money. If my Uncle Fred had had any drive that business would have probably made it. I remember once when Aunt Agnes found a $20 bill on the sidewalk in Deering, a nearby Portland suburb where they lived, and that saved them from starving that week.

My uncle Fred Briggs

Uncle Fred was depressing. He always complained about his health. He just sat there and did nothing. So how my first cousin Frederick Jr. came from that and did so well, I don't know.

Virginia and Our Ma used to say that I'm like Uncle Roy, that is, the black sheep of the family. I liked Uncle Roy. He was a short 5 foot 8 with a belly but strong and solid. We had the family Thanksgiving celebration every year on Sargent Street. Even Uncle Fred was invited. We usually had a football game. Roy had been a good athlete. He played for Boston English whose chief rival was Boston Latin, and later he played football at Boston University. I saw the clippings. People knew him from his exploits and BU. He was competitive even in our family Thanksgiving game. When I was about seven years old, he'd run over me. Bodies were flying. He cracked me once so I had blood all over me. He'd act like he'd won the state championship. He always liked me, said I was going to amount to something, not a likely prediction among others who knew me then.

Uncle Roy had a violent temper. My grandfather had established an insurance brokerage. Roy took over his dad's business, and, with money coming in, it went to his head. So he wasn't going to deal with minor stuff. He got very choosy. One time Roy was having a meeting with the head of a client company. Roy went into the man's office, and they had an argument. Roy destroyed this guy, hit him in the face, broke bones, and beat him when he was down. There was a lawsuit. After that, everything went downhill for the insurance brokerage. Then Roy was operating out of 72 Pinckney Street, his mother's house on Beacon Hill. Soon he became a soapbox orator on religious and political topics. I saw him once giving a political speech in the Boston Common. One night he was delivering an oration in the early morning hours. Our telephone rang and there was a problem. The police had dragged Roy to jail. Dad had to go down to the jail to get him out. This may have happened more than once.

We had to go to see my grandmother Mother Briggs every Sunday, after church, for a couple hours and give her a kiss. I hated it. She didn't necessarily want to be kissed but I had to do it. She was enormously fat. After the visit, we'd take Uncle Roy to see Edith Knowles, a girlfriend to whom he'd become devoted before she became an invalid. He was committed to her for the rest of her life though they didn't marry. Even when he was down, living in a single room in the house on Pinckney Street, he was always very upbeat with me.

My paternal grandmother Briggs, born Maria Susannah Harper, the only grandparent I ever knew.

Ultimately, Uncle Ralph and my father owned the house on Pinckney Street, but it wasn't a good deal for Dad because he was stuck with all the work. After their mother died, the Harpers moved in—my grandmother Briggs's youngest brother Will Harper and his wife Mildred—so we kept the house going for them. Ralph probably sent money to help the unsuccessful Uncle Will and Aunt Mildred, but the upkeep for the house was always Dad's problem. He finally sold his end to Uncle Ralph, and said, "This is your problem now."

I was not around Uncle Ralph, living in the Chicago area, but his family visited ours from time to time. My first cousin, Uncle Ralph's son Gordon, as a child once came to Pleasant Lake in New Hampshire while we were there. One time he insisted on going too far out in the lake

Left, my father Harry Briggs; center, his older brother Fred; his brother Ralph, at the wedding of Fred's son Frederick to Marjorie, September 1941.

where he got into trouble, not being a strong swimmer. I went out and pulled him in. He always gave me credit for saving his life. I was closer to Gordon's family years later when I spent time in the mid-West.

When I was in my teens, my dad sent money to my sister Virginia and her husband Tom Lavender when they needed something. When they wanted a fence, Virginia and Tom discussed it with my dad. He came back home and said, "They need a fence." My mother might say, "Yes, but we need this or that." But Virginia and Tom got the fence. I didn't want to depend on my parents like that and made up my mind early on to be independent.

I really never knew my dad when I was young, but I will forever be grateful that, after my mother died, we became very close and in the end I loved him as much as my mother. When I heard him swear a little bit and then have a drink before dinner, I thought, *Gee, that's great.* I thought he wasn't so dull as I'd thought. Well, dull wasn't the right word because he always had a wonderful sense of humor, but it was good to see him loosen up.

Virginia

My childhood recollection of my sister Virginia is very slight, but I can place her down at the cottage we rented at Annisquam. That summer she had invited her friend Lydia Barnes to stay with us. I wouldn't have thought those two would have been good friends, but they were very close. Lydia admired my sister's intelligence as much as Virginia admired Lydia's popularity. Lydia's family didn't have a lot of money so she was probably happy to have a nice summer vacation. Lydia was especially popular with guys, and so for me to have the great Lydia Barnes in the house was really wonderful. For some reason Virginia was upset the whole two weeks.

My sister Virginia when she was dating Tom Lavender..

Tom Lavender

My sister met the man who would become her husband when I was only nine. Tom Lavender was from Alabama and was at that time a graduate student at Harvard, so he didn't have any money. He was nine years older than Virginia, who met him when she was fifteen, when Our Ma, the matchmaker in the family, persuaded my father to take Tom and Virginia together to a Celtics game. In the following years he spent a lot of weekends at our house. I was still in high school when they married.

I always liked Tom. I remember once when we had a big snowstorm I took my sled to a big hill. Tom came over and he and I rode the sled down the hill. He enjoyed it, but his pants got caught under the runners and were ripped. We laughed all the way

home. Then the question was what are we going to do for pants for Tom. It was Saturday night and we couldn't get new pants and he didn't have any money anyway.

I thought he was really cool. He smoked Picayunes. He blew the smoke out and then inhaled it again directly up his nostrils. I asked him if I could try a Picayune once, and he gave me one. Wow, that was really strong. He had gotten them in Alabama and was just about out of them, so we went to the Coop in Harvard Square and asked for them. They had to order them from New Orleans where they were made. So the Coop supplied Tom with his Picayunes as long as he was at Harvard.

The relationship between my mother and my sister grew worse soon after she began dating Tom. My mother didn't want me to know all that juicy stuff, but there was apparently a bitter struggle going on. I think it concerned sex between Virginia and Tom.

My mother did not understand the power of sex. I'm quite sure that because of her early health problems, she never had much to do with sexual relations except to have children. Virginia's sexual relationship with Tom was too much for my mother to handle.

Sex was never discussed in my presence but of course it was often behind the scenes. I suspect—and Virginia has gleefully agreed with me—that something was going on. I don't think my father was a womanizer but my mother wasn't sexually going anywhere and most every man will cheat under those conditions.

My father went to Europe four or five times; he had relatives over in England. My parents kept things from me, but I was a wild kid so I found out a lot of stuff in the outside world while I didn't know so much about my own family. One day we went to see my father off to Europe and we went to his stateroom and there was a blonde woman sitting in his stateroom waiting for him. They got me out of that scene right away. It was sort of hilarious.

Chapter 3

Four Loves

After grammar school, I attended Roosevelt Junior High and then Melrose High School. In those days I had four loves: sports, romance, music and academics.

Sports

I played them all, street hockey, ice hockey, soccer, baseball, soccer, tennis, and of course swimming when we were at the shore. I was scrappy and skilled at all these sports, and I admired people who were good in sports. I was and am a sports nut, and I turned the many facets of sports into a career—or several careers.

Romance

I combined swimming and romance early on. The first experience I had with distance swimming was the two summers I'd spent at Pleasant Lake in New Hampshire. Our family spent our summers in various places. My father liked the mountains and my mother liked the water. So we split for the season, and I spent two whole summers in that lake. I was about thirteen. I swam across the cove where we were staying in a cabin. I had a little girl friend down the other end of the lake. The lake was about 1.75 miles long. So I'd swim down and back. We'd get complaints from boaters. My mother didn't want me to do that, but you can't hold back a kid. I loved being out on the lake. I loved looking at the shoreline. I'd stop and sit on a rock and look around. It was not about seeing how fast I could get there; it was just a love of swimming, swimming, swimming. I did the same thing the next summer, where this girl down the lake gave me my first taste of puppy love.

My first real romance was with Priscilla Hess in high school. I loved her and she loved me. We were a couple for most of our high school days. Everyone expected us to marry.

My family was happy about my relationship with Priscilla because they really liked her. Also, they were trying to save me from marrying someone unsuitable. The fact that her parents were both alcoholics didn't disqualify her. In fact my Aunt Letitia later paid for her to go to Simmons College because her family couldn't afford college. My mother, as a very loving person, did everything she could to shelter her son, which was a bad thing, in the hopes that I would marry a girl of British descent like us. She just didn't want a little Irish girl to get her hands on Junior. My mother said once, "You wouldn't date an Irish girl, would you?" Just because of that, I did date one a couple weeks later, Eileen Driscoll, the prettiest thing.

Music

By music, I don't mean music appreciation. To me music means going out and making some money at it. I watched Lawrence Welk and thought he was smaltzy, rooty tooty, but he had a fantastic band. I was part of a band in my early teens and beyond, and I carried my clarinet around with me as far as Japan and Alaska. I love jazz. Even now in good music I'd listen for those reeds and feel ecstasy.

Academics

Really academics weren't really a love but a major occupation. If I liked a class, I'd get an A. If I didn't like it, I'd get a C. I got good grades in what interested me. My parents were always getting after me to do my assignments. In the end I did discover a field of study that really turned me on for a lifetime. In the meantime, I was a thorn in the side of my teachers. First, I must say that my older sister Virginia was an excellent student. I remember everyone thought she was brilliant and I remember feeling that people were saying and thinking, "You will never be as smart as your sister."

The Latin teacher at Melrose High, Miss Kershaw, especially thought Virginia was just the most brilliant student ever. Miss Kershaw let me know she was disappointed in me. And I planned it that way. I couldn't live up to Virginia, so I decided to be bad. I did all kinds of tricks. I'd bang a book on the floor just when a teacher was about to make a good point, or I'd fall asleep and snore. Why I wasn't expelled I don't know.

Al Whitney, a big dumb looking fellow, taught math, I think it was. One day I started to ride Mr. Whitney. I'd ask him a question and I didn't like his answer so I got the whole class laughing. I thought, *I can destroy this guy and I'll see what he's made of.* I have people like that in the classes I teach now; I call them sharpshooters. Once I was wising off and Mr. Whitney grabbed me by my shirt and held me up in the air, so we were eyeball to eyeball until he let me go. I thought, *Man, how'd he do that to me?* After that I went to see the town baseball team play and discovered that Al Whitney played first base. And then I found out he'd played baseball at Harvard. I was ashamed I'd treated him that way. Years later, between my stints in the Coast Guard and the Marine Corps, I was in Washington, DC. Along came this guy walking sort of ding-toed down the street. I saw him walk and I said to myself, that's Mr. Whitney. I said, "Do you remember me?" He said, "I sure do." And I said, "Good, because I want to apologize."

Yes, I was a wild kid in high school. I got into a lot of trouble. I was belligerent and always wising off, mostly in a humorous vein. I was named Class Wit, and I was always showing off in front of Priscilla Hess.

The first time academics really engaged my interest was when I had a teacher at Melrose High named Eddie Loud, who was a veteran of World War I. He'd played for the Baltimore Orioles. You may say Baltimore didn't have a baseball team in those years. Actually, they did, but then they dropped baseball and got it back later and Mr. Loud played before the break. In the army he had been gassed, and he spent time in hospitals where doctors said he couldn't do anything physical or get upset. So he applied to teach at Melrose High School. Mr. Loud said to me, "Harry, you're coming in here with not the best reputation, but you have potential. So don't pull any of that stuff on me." I was impressed that he was that up-front. Then in class he talked about his own experiences, and he'd illustrate points of history with them. Everybody loved him. He was short, about my size, and he had a lot of muscle. He'd show his muscle when we asked him to. When class was over, I said, "Mr. Loud, I really enjoyed your class." Mr. Loud was really glad to hear that. I was a junior then, and, as a result of Mr. Loud, I took a lot of history and political science courses my senior year. He really influenced me. I took an interest in school after that. Who would have guessed that I would eventually end up with a Ph.D.!

"If you have enough determination…"

I only remember one time when my mother went to Europe because I went also. We went from New York to Southampton in England, then to Antwerp, Brussels, and Paris before heading to England, where my father would join us. The thing that stands out most for me about that trip, however, occurred on the ship going over.

It was 1937, when I was sixteen. I escorted my mother to Europe on the Westernland, one of the old Cunard Red Line ships. On board there was a small makeshift swimming pool, a heavy liner stretched over a frame. There was a very large lady who seemed to be in charge of the pool and someone told me she was Gertrude Ederle, a famous long distance swimmer. She was the first woman to swim the English Channel. She did it in 1926 in 14 hours and 39 minutes, a time two hours better than the fastest swim by the five men who had succeeded in swimming the Channel before her. She was so famous that a journalist of that era named her as one of the athletes, along with Bobby Jones and Babe Ruth, who made that era the golden age of sports.

Gertrude Ederle was just what I expected—solid. I said to my mother, "I'm going to speak to her." My mother said, "Go ahead." I presented myself and told her I was going to be a long distance swimmer. She said, "Have you ever done anything?" I said, "I've swum back and forth on Lake Pleasant, New Hampshire." She looked at me as if I had no idea how tough distance swimming was, which was the truth.

Then she smiled and said graciously, "If you have enough determination, you can do it." She didn't know, as I didn't yet know myself, just how much determination I had. I didn't do anything about my ambition for another twenty years. However, I did think of those words often, and finally put them to good use. Ederle was inducted into the International Marathon Swimming Hall of Fame in 1965, the first year that organization was founded as a division of the older International Swimming Hall of Fame. I am proud to have joined her in that prestigious list in 1997.

My mother and I went sightseeing briefly in England, in Antwerp and Brussels. My mother noted in her travel journal the stained-glass windows and the paintings. Then we went on to Paris by train, where she wrote about the bridges, the sunset, the tapestries, the palaces, and "the splendor of lights" in the evening. In one entry, she mentioned that "Harry is going to see the nightlife of Paris. It started at 9:45." Ah, yes, I remember the nightlife well. But in my memory, my mother was with me once and took me to the Club Lido, the famous nightclub. One of the flamboyantly and scantily dressed dancers came over and sat in my lap. I thought it was great. My mother nearly died of embarrassment. No wonder there was no mention of the occasion in my mother's very proper and limited journal.

After Paris, we went to London and, when Dad arrived, visited some of his relatives there and in Manchester, where we spent quite a few days. I got to go about as I liked once we were settled in a hotel; I went swimming, played tennis and golf, and went to movies after dinner. My parents even left me for nine days in Southport while they toured Scotland.

After graduation from Melrose High in 1939, I was eager to leave home for college and more intense experiences with sports, romance, music and academics. My newfound independence allowed me to engage in all of these with increased passion.

Chapter 4

On My Own: Two Degrees in Three Years

My first stop after graduating from high school in 1939 was Tilton School, then a junior college in Tilton, New Hampshire. I went there because I knew there was an excellent ice hockey program at Tilton. For my brief time there, I was selected for the school's athletics Hall of Fame. I didn't concentrate on academics my first and only semester. Even so, I thought I was ahead of other students academically, and I wanted to take on greater challenge. Even though my stay there was short, I still support a tennis scholarship there in memory of my wife Lydia, as I do for several colleges.

From Tilton, I applied to Tufts College (now Tufts University) in Somerville, Massachusetts, near Boston, but they turned down my midyear transfer. So I transferred from Tilton to Clark University in Worcester, Massachusetts, and did well there. It was a good little university. I succeeded in transferring to Tufts in the fall of 1940. After a semester at Tilton, a semester at Clark, two years at Tufts, and two summers at the University of Richmond plus a course at Harvard, I graduated from college in three years.

During the summers of 1941 and 1942, I was at the University of Richmond, where my brother-in-law Tom Lavender was a professor. He arranged for me to live in the Phi Kappa Sigma house, his fraternity from his University of Alabama days, while many of the students were away for the summer. He spent a lot of time with me there. We'd sit around with the guys in the frat house, and he and Virginia had me over to dinner at their house sometimes.

We summer residents in the Phi Kap house were involved in a few pranks. We sneaked onto the golf course at the Country Club of Virginia once and we were reported to the University. Tom thought it was kind of funny, but he said, "Watch your step because I have a reputation to keep." I really liked Tom Lavender.

I was a very independent youngster. I wanted to pay my own tuition. I'd become a lefty politically. The way I was brought up, I saw the struggle between the English Americans and the Irish Americans. In about the year 2000, the Boston Globe was talking about how the influx of Irish had been badly handled in Boston. To illustrate the point they reprinted an ad for employment at a bank that said, "Irish need not apply." It was the same treatment as the black people suffered. Both were second-class citizens, and this discrimination was going to fester and fester until ultimately it would bust open. I was no fan of the Kennedys, but Honey Fitz as mayor of Boston turned that city around. Harvard had always been a conservative bastion but, by the time I hit college, Harvard was very liberal.

So when I reached college I had very pronounced political beliefs, and I was very outspoken, which wasn't very polite. Aunt Letitia in particular didn't like it very much. I would preach the New Deal to anyone who would listen. Franklin Roosevelt was the greatest thing ever. Later, I used to spout off in the Marines, too. I can see why they said I was like Uncle Roy, who talked politics on a soapbox in the park.

So I wanted to pay my own tuition because I didn't feel I should spend my dad's money when he didn't approve of my opinions. I wanted to rely on my dad to the least amount possible to get through college. I couldn't quite do it, but I kept it to a minimum. After the war he offered to help me financially, and I said no. That hurt him but it was not for the reasons he thought. I was a man, and I just didn't want to rely on my dad.

At Clark College, a guy named George was on the baseball team with me. He'd been an iceman in his hometown on Long Island. He asked me if I'd like to join him that summer, and I agreed. George took me to meet the boss, and I became an iceman in Port Jefferson. New York. By taking all such work opportunities I pretty much paid my own way. I worked for a Howard Johnson restaurant evenings whenever I could. I also had a pretty good jazz band called The Rat Racers because there were rats in the dance hall, really, and they ran across the floor. I played with those guys for at least 4 years. While I was at Tufts we played at frat parties. I also got freelance assignments covering sports at the *Boston Traveler* where Arthur Siegel was the sports editor and the best-known sports writer in the city. I got to know Arthur Siegel really well. I asked him for a full time job. I told him that I needed the money to finish college. I didn't mention that my Dad was a bank officer. Siegel said he'd have a job for me when the war was over. However, he said I could probably do better in sports management. For decades, wherever I was, I reported on sports in newspapers, radio, and television, but it was never my main job. The sports management suggestion Siegel gave me, however, proved to be both prophetic and good advice.

I took the second summer semester at Harvard and I took summer courses at Boston University, and, based on these credits, I was admitted to BU grad school. Study, study, study, and with all this I graduated with a BA from Tufts in the summer of 1942 and received my masters degree in political science in December 1942.

While I was at Tufts, I played on the Tufts hockey team. In fact, in December 2009, an event that touched me a lot was described in a Northwestern State University (Louisiana) publication, as follows:

> *A ceremony was held at Tufts University in Medford, Mass., to retire the #9 jersey of Harry H. Briggs, Jr., Ph.D., who was a star player on the Tufts ice hockey team in 1941 and 1942. About playing ice hockey at Tufts, Dr. Briggs commented, "Although I played most positions, I liked right wing best. However, because back then goalies did not wear masks, most goalies didn't last very long in goal. I probably played goalie more than any other position."*

During my undergraduate years at Tufts, I was also coaching the team. My dad knew hockey, and he went to every game of mine. It was the only sport he helped me with. He also used to take me to the Bruins games. So he was very excited when I coached at Tufts. Every game when I coached, you could hear him yelling all over the arena. The guys all knew him. But my coaching days were about to end because I had been accepted into Officer Candidate School in the Coast Guard. I applied for an extension to finish out the hockey season but that didn't come through. So when I was leaving early in 1943, I said to the team, "What are we going to do for a coach?" and the team said, "Your dad!" So I went into the Coast Guard and my dad finished out the hockey season as Coach.

The experience of coaching with my dad in the stands was a step towards becoming closer to him. He wasn't an athlete, but he was there for me and it was perhaps the first time I really appreciated him.

Chapter 5

What'll It Be? RAF, Coast Guard, American Field Service, Or...

Before 1941, I wanted to be in England's Royal Air Force. We thought we'd be in the war eventually; why not get a head start. Some people said, if we knew aviation, we'd be ready to go to war. I decided to take flying lessons through a civilian course offered by Tufts, and, when I finished them, I'd go into the RAF and I'd be an ace and shoot some Germans out.

We were flying out near Revere, Massachusetts. I was a pretty cocky kid. I went to the base and met the instructor. I'd never been in a plane before. This guy figured he'd really be tough on me and wash me out. We went in a piper cub and he put me through barrel rolls, loop the loops, and stalls. Even as I was just coming off the ground I was sick. I was petrified and sick, and the guy knew it and so he was going to give me everything he had. He was a great pilot. "How did you like that, Briggs?" he'd say. It was terrible. *Forget about aviation*, I thought. I've been truly afraid four times in my life: I was afraid coming across Cook Inlet in the storm, climbing on the side of the Matterhorn, in WWII in the Pacific campaign, and that day in that plane.

Before leaving for home, he said, "See you tomorrow." And I thought, *Like hell he will.* Then I told myself: *You've started this, hang in there and get your license; you don't want to be a fighter pilot, but get the license.*

Next day in Bayside Airport, we did routine instruction. When you take off, you have to go into the wind, the instructor told us. That piper cub was nothing but one-by-twos covered with canvas. You're in this little box of canvas, so light if you want to turn to face the wind, you can pick up the rear end of the plane and move it around so it's facing the right way. Another guy turns the propeller and as it gets faster, you give it gas. Prehistoric. This was only 39 years after they got the plane off the beach at Kitty Hawk. Max speed was 75 mph. When you land, you do it against the wind. You have to slip it sometimes so it comes in diagonal, and you have to know when. One hour of this three days a week for a semester, and you got your license.

We had dual controls, and one day the instructor said, "Do you want to take it?" You had a stick, which was the steering wheel, a fuel gauge, and an altimeter, that's it. Boy, was it primitive. So I took it. Then after a while, the instructor said, "Do a stall." You put it upwards, and when there's not enough power to go further, it sputters and the front end goes into a stall and goes down. And you have to know what to do then. You have to turn it into a spin. The spin prevents it from crashing. "Do you want to do this?" No. Then he said, "You'll have to do it by yourself in a few days." So I did it, and I'm still here so I guess I did it right. Start with a stall, turn it into a spin, turn it three times, and you have to be high enough; when you come out of it you are about 500 feet in the air.

Except for that first day, the worst half hour of my life up to that point, it became enjoyable. I sometimes flew over Melrose where we lived. When I was 16, my family had moved to 96 Ardsmore Road, a little way out in the country in a more affluent area called the Eastside near Bellevue Country Club on Porter Street. Kiley's Farm, still under cultivation then, was to the other side of our house on Upham Street. When I got to fly solo, I'd tell my mother I'd be there at 1 o'clock and she'd be out there on the lawn waving. I'd come in a little lower than was legal and I'd dip my wings. Once I did more than dip my wings. I was flying from Bayside Airport in Revere when the weather became so bad that I landed on a pasture on Kiley's Farm and walked home to tell my mother what had happened. She called the airport and, per her instructions, somebody came and got the plane out of Kiley's pasture. It was quite an experience!

My instructor and I were good buddies by this time. I told him I'd wanted to go to the RAF, but not anymore. So he'd say, "Take 20 minutes and do whatever you want," and I'd go over my home and wherever I wanted. One time I flew across Cape Ann and I went over Little River in West Gloucester and the railroad and there was Aunt Letitia's camp between the two. I wasn't supposed to go over there, and I used up a little gas doing that.

The final flight was cross-country from Bayside to Portland, Maine, and then I had to do figure 8s around pylons. I only had so much gas and it was 100 miles up and 100 miles back. "If you have a tail wind, you're okay," he said. "But if you don't have the wind with you, go to Portsmouth (NH) airfield. I'll call them to expect you." So I went on to Portland. On the way back, I got pretty close to Portsmouth and the gauge was low. I forgot you have to go in to land against the wind. So I was coming in and there were three guys gesturing, No, no, no! I thought, *But I have to go in.* And then I saw the windsocks and realized I was coming in with the wind and would overshoot the runway. So I went up again and came in the other way. We talked about it; I said I just forgot and I hoped they wouldn't report me. I got my license and I've never taken a plane up since. That makes me a pioneer in the early days of aviation.

My flying "career" caused me to get the only F in my life. My flight instruction came at the same time as my class in physical education at Tufts. The PE instructor said if I took flight instruction, he would fail me in PE. I did and he did.

My Brief Coast Guard Career

Shortly after I got my pilot's license, I went into the Coast Guard OCS (Officer Candidate School). A candidate had to be five foot six. So the OCS guy said, "You're five six. Okay." So I was in. My mother was relieved I was not in danger. I didn't tell her those fast boats we had in the Coast Guard went on some pretty hairy missions. Much later I found out that Coast Guard personnel were the ones who made repeated trips from troop ships into the beaches of all the islands we took in the Pacific.

Soon after I was accepted for OCS, I took the physical. There was a line of guys against the wall, and then the line along the top of their heads dropped about six inches right where I was standing. They pulled me out of line and said, "You aren't five foot six," and I said, "Yes I am." They measured me and found I was five foot five and a half. Is that discrimination or what! I could whip every one of those guys. But I was not concerned. I was in, and I could do the job better than any one of those guys. I'd been around water all my life.

They tried to get rid of me. That was going to take some doing. It took three weeks for them to figure out how to get proper grounds for discharging me without admitting their mistake.

Regular academy guys were in one place and there were other barracks for the 90-day wonders like me, two people to a room. My roommate was studying for classes for new guys, but I wasn't because by that time I realized I was on my way out. So I was sitting there playing with a marble, one of those resin marbles, red, I can see it now, like a red bean but round. I was messing around, rolling the marble around my face, just a nervous gesture, and I got the marble a little bit into my nose. Rather than pushing it down from the top, I was pushing it up as I tried to reach it. I finally got it up so far that I could see a big lump was sticking out on the side of my nose. It hurt a bit and I went to sickbay and said, "I just pushed a marble up my nose." So they said, "Not only are you too short but ....," and they made a big joke of it: I'm the only person discharged in the history of the Coast Guard for having a marble up his nose.

Along with my discharge, I was given a little money. I said to myself, *I won't go home. I'll go down to Fort Lauderdale and surprise my sister Virginia.* Her husband Tom Lavender had taken leave from his job at the University and joined up as a naval officer and was stationed near there. I hitchhiked to Fort Lauderdale, got into downtown at midnight, and I was really whipped so I took a room on the sixth floor of a hotel. I was a chronic sleepwalker. This time I dreamed a train was bearing down on me. The train tracks really did come through downtown, and the cars were humping and bumping, and I thought the train was going to crash into me. Still asleep, I jumped out of bed, went over to the window and knocked the window out. I could see broken glass down there on the ground six floors below, so I didn't want to jump. Instead, reportedly without my under shorts, I ran down to the lobby and then outside. The guy at the desk said, "Holy smokes, I've never seen

Tom Lavender with Thomas Edward Lavender Jr., after Tom joined the Navy but before he went to the Pacific, about 1944.

this before." About that time, I woke up and said to myself, *Jeez, Harry, you're sleepwalking.* So I went back upstairs to bed.

But apparently I had a big gash on my arm from the broken glass that I hadn't paid any attention to. So there was a knock on the door and a guy from the Sheriff's department and the night clerk from the lobby were standing there. The clerk said, "He's the man," and there was the broken window and the blood on the bed. I told them, "Okay, I'll pay for it, but I don't have any money. I'll get a job tomorrow and bring you the money by the end of the week."

I went out to the beach and got a job as a lifeguard at the wonderful Olympic-sized pool on the beach at the Governor's Club, a fine hotel, which much later became the International Swimming Hall of Fame, to which I was eventually inducted. But at that time, I was a lowly lifeguard and not even that because my main job was to take care of the pool itself, now the centerpiece of the Hall of Fame.

After I got the job, I slept in a cemetery near my sister's duplex for a night or two. So then, when I had things under control, I thought, *Now I'll go drop in on them and give them a big surprise.* Well, the surprise was on me. They knew all about my breaking the window in the hotel. An account of the incident had been in the local newspaper with my name in it, and they had already called home. See, I hadn't told my parents I was out of the Coast Guard. So my dad had called the Admiral, and his office told Dad that I'd been discharged a week before.

Do you think at this point I've decided I'm going to play golf for the rest of the war just because I was kicked out of the Coast Guard? Just because I wasn't good enough for the Coast Guard doesn't mean I wasn't good enough for cannon fodder, so I was going to be drafted. I didn't like that. I wanted to go to war on my own terms. So, while I was staying with Virginia and Tom and working as a lifeguard that summer in 1943, I applied to the American Field Service and was accepted.

My Even Briefer American Field Service Career

After joining the Field Service. I went to New York to buy the uniform. At Fort Hamilton, where I had the physical, they said, "You have a bad case of varicose veins and we're going into the desert of North Africa. Sorry. We can't use you." It seems heat and varicose veins are not compatible.

Undeterred, I called Aunt Letitia, who had not been elected into the American College of Surgeons in 1926 for nothing, and said, "Can you handle varicose veins?" She said, "I know just what to do." She came over and slit my veins up near the crotch and tied them together, did that right in my bedroom. She gave me local anesthesia, didn't hurt a bit. That spring, I'd heard about heavy casualties in North Africa, where U.S. troops had taken a beating from the Germans at Kasserine Pass, and I said to myself, *I'd better get into this war because they're going to get me anyway.* Then I thought, *Get a hold of yourself, Harry,* because the Coast Guard busted me out and that lost me the chance to get into Officer Candidate School (OCS) with the Marine Corps or even with the Army.

U.S. Marine Corps

So in November 1943 I went down to the Marine Corps recruitment office and enlisted as a private. Boot camp at Camp Lejeune in North Carolina wasn't too bad. Marine drill sergeants tend to be high on filthy language and pushing recruits way past their ability to perform, then cussing them out for not performing. As time passed, however, they seemed to loosen up a bit. I happened to have a good Drill Instructor. Although his language was unnecessarily nasty, this DI did know something about psychology. One day I was in the lavatory area comparing notes on our training with other Marines when who should walk in but the Drill Instructor. Everyone thought, *Now what*? I don't know how long he'd been listening to us but he got over close to me and whispered, "Briggs, you're going to be a good Marine." Wow! Was that good for my morale! A little of that goes a long way towards making a good Marine.

You may have noticed that I never do just one thing at a time—one job, one school, one sport. In basic training, I was running what was supposed to be a money making venture taking recruits for R&R from Camp Lejeune to Washington, DC, the nearest big town where liquor was served. Sometimes, I'd stop in Richmond to visit my sister Virginia and her family while my fares were partying in DC.

Each trip I charged four recruits $25 a piece, which would have been good, but it ended up just paying to buy the next junk car. In about six runs to DC, I went through three cars. I started with a Plymouth convertible, which I already had. It soon gave out. Then I got a Buick convertible, and drove it to Parris Island. Three of us drove into Savannah, a town lively with Marines and sailors. I couldn't stay awake. I fell asleep with my foot on the gas and woke up headed for a tree at

My sister Virginia with her children Letitia and Thomas in front of their house in Richmond, Virginia, where I visited before going to the Pacific.

75 m.p.h. I swerved, rolled over, and skidded on the convertible roof. To our surprise, we survived. I took one more run to D.C. with this busted up Buick. Finally, I got an old taxi. It didn't make it back to camp from our first trip. We left it outside of

Wilson, North Carolina, and hitched rides back. We were an hour late returning to camp and everyone else was packed up. I threw my gear together and went with my unit to the train depot for a trip to Atlanta, from which we were headed to the west coast to ship out to the war in the Pacific. The highway patrol got in touch with my father and he had to pay to haul the abandoned taxi away. My father picked up a lot of pieces behind me!

Chapter 6

Island Hopping in the Pacific

I made it to Corporal real fast, right out of boot camp at Camp Lejeune. I'd taken training in combat intelligence and was one of only four who got Corporal stripes because of that. I pictured I'd be safe on a ship somewhere in the Pacific analyzing intelligence data collected by some unlucky Private who had to sneak through the bushes on his stomach to watch the enemy from a few yards away and then crawl back to make the report. But then Congress decided the guys in the action weren't getting Corporal for learning in the field so those back home shouldn't get Corporal either, and they made the change retroactive. So they took my stripes away, and I went to Saipan in June 1944 as a Private First Class to be one of those guys who sneak through the bushes on their stomachs to watch the enemy a few yards away and then crawl back.

We knew we were going to join the 2nd Marine division so I wrote my folks about that before we boarded a slow bucket to Pearl Harbor. Half of us were seasick and there was puke all over the floor. The trip from San Diego to Pearl took 12 days. Most troop ships had tiny cabins, a comparative luxury to ours, an old freighter. The hold was deep and ugly, with a ladder going down. Two companies were stacked four bunks high. We were below the water level, and we knew that if a torpedo hit us, there'd be a mad scramble for the ladder. In fact, they would have to seal that compartment off to save the ship. What a horrible way to go! So I stayed on deck as much as possible.

While we were on the way over, the Marine 2nd division hit the beach at Saipan on June 15. When you go on an amphibious invasion, you know a lot of people are going to be killed and the question is, will it be me. There were 2000 marines killed the first day. My parents were reading this in the newspaper pretty sure their only son was on the beach at Saipan. That took a real toll on my mother.

Saipan

Actually, I was among the replacements that came into Saipan after the first guys landed. They'd already taken the beaches so we didn't have to do that.

It was decided that it would take three divisions to defeat the Japanese at Saipan. Three divisions make up a corps. The Commander General of a Corps is a three-star General. The 4th Amphibious Corps was organized to consist of two Marine Corps divisions and one Army: the 2nd Marine Division, just recovering from the Tarawa campaign; the 4th Marine Division, just organized for the Saipan campaign; and the 27th Army Division. The Commanding General of the 4th

Amphibious Corps was a Marine, the famous General Holland "Howlin' Mad" Smith. He had three stars and was famous for getting the job done in WWI and in preparing our WWII amphibious invasion. The Major General (two stars) in command of the 27th Army Division was also named Smith. When the two-star Army General Smith refused to move his troops as fast as three-star General Smith wanted, "Howlin' Mad" earned his nickname again as he relieved the other Smith of his command. This incident created all kinds of problems between the Army and Marine Corps. In my opinion, Marines and Army should not fight together.

When my replacement battalion (approximately 1000 men) came ashore at Saipan, we were told that we had been assigned to the Fourth Marine Division (24th Marines, 4th Marine Division) instead of the Second Division as our orders said. There were no papers exchanged. I'm convinced that what happened was that some ambitious officer of the 4th Marine Division hijacked our replacement division as it came ashore. Although slated for the 2nd Marine Division, this officer just took it upon himself to send us up to the front where the 4th Marine Division was fighting.

We were herded onto trucks and driven to the front lines with Japanese snipers having a turkey shoot. For the next several weeks, I was with the 24th Marines as a combat intelligence scout, basically because I told the Battalion Commander that was what I was trained to do. Those first two to three weeks were probably as bad as I saw during the war. I experienced several close calls. I did my job as combat intelligence scout—sneaking ahead of my outfit, reporting back, moving forward with the others, securing an area, and repeating the process—and somehow made it through pretty much unscathed.

I did get hit by a nasty mosquito, and I scratched the bite down in a foxhole in the mud and it got infected. I kept on slogging along and by the time the campaign was over I was hobbling. When we were totally in control of Saipan, it was decided that the able bodied troops remaining with the Fourth Marine Division would be transferred into the Second Division and the walking wounded from the Second would go to the Fourth Marine Division, which went back to Maui to retrain for what eventually became the battle for Iwo Jima. I was among the able bodied, so I limped into the 2nd Division, where I'd originally supposed to be when I came to Saipan. A medic said, "What's wrong with you?" I said my ankle was infected where the top of my boot rubbed against the bite, and he said, "You're going to the naval hospital." There were people in that field hospital with arms and legs up in traction or their heads were held together with bandages, and I was there for a mosquito bite. I stayed for a week, got proper treatment, and got better. I had penicillin, a new drug used only by the military before it was available to civilians.

Then I went back to the First Battalion, Sixth Marines, 2nd Marine Division, where I contracted dengue fever and dysentery at the same time. I can't imagine being more sick.

By the time the Saipan campaign was over, there were replacements arriving every day. My papers came in with the new replacements, as if I had just arrived. I didn't pay any attention to this until I was discharged and found that I wasn't given credit for my service with the 24th Marines, Fourth Marine Division. If I hadn't made it out of Saipan, the official record I guess would have shown that I'd died in a campaign I wasn't even in!

With the exception of D-Day at Tinian, which came next and was ugly, my most vivid memories of the war took place the last few weeks of the Saipan campaign for which I was never given credit. The attack had begun June 15 and Allied troops occupied Saipan by July 9, with a loss of 16,500 casualties. Amazingly, I was not among them.

Saipan and Tinian, like other of the Mariana Islands, lay within long range bombing distance of Japan. We wanted air bases on these islands for our large B-29s, half again as long as the B-17s that were being used for bombing runs in Europe. So that was an important campaign. The Japanese knew it. Japan's loss of Saipan caused Premier Tojo to resign on July 18.

Since the end of WWI, Saipan had Japanese, Korean, and Okinawan residents because Japan controlled Korea and Okinawa. The indigenous people also worked in the sugar cane fields, and the Japanese treated them badly. Most of the civilian population, about 90%, survived the campaign for Saipan and gave the U.S. military its first taste of dealing with a Japanese civilian population in hostile territory.

However, when the Japanese emperor recognized that all was over for them in Saipan, he was afraid some civilians would defect to the U.S. Japanese civilians had been indoctrinated with tales of Allied savagery to conquered populations, but the emperor was afraid some civilians would discover their treatment by the Americans was benign and surrender to them.

So, in the last days of battle, the emperor issued an imperial order to promise Japanese civilians a favored place in heaven equal to those who died in combat if they would commit suicide rather than be captured. So more than 10,000 civilians committed suicide, many by leaping to their death off the 500-foot cliffs in Saipan. I did not see such suicides with my own eyes in Saipan, but I saw them later in Tinian.

After we occupied Saipan, I wrote Arthur Siegel, my friend and sports editor of the *Boston Traveler*, and told him about my war experience. He wrote an article about me for the paper, which didn't go over too well with my family. I'd been a very independent youngster, wanting to pay my own tuition, so for at least four years of college, I had a job as a sports writer at the *Traveler*. Siegel didn't quite understand that my dad could pay and was willing to pay my tuition. The article said something like, "Life has been tough for Harry Briggs. He's had a hard road..." He described how I'd sacrificed to get through school, and ended with something like, "now he's in Saipan, poor kid." My parents took pride in their solid middle class status, and they'd often helped out people who were struggling. It really smarted when they read that they hadn't helped their son get through school, and now he was in a foxhole in Saipan. I'm sorry that article was ever written.

Another thing I'm sorry was ever written was a certain letter from Our Ma. I'd been getting letters from home saying my mother had a few health problems, for example, she couldn't raise her arm at one time, but they said she was going to be okay. She was doing well. Then between Saipan, where I was lucky to survive, and the invasion of Tinian, which was going to be no picnic, I got a letter from Our Ma saying that those other health reports were all wrong and that my mother was very ill. What a terrible thing to say to someone who was stuck in the Pacific with no way to get home! I lost respect for Our Ma right then. And of course, I worried about my mother, just as I know she was worrying about me.

When I got out of the hospital, I went back to my unit battalion headquarters, 6th Marines, 2nd Marine Division, where shortly someone on the loud speaker announced that anyone who was a good swimmer should report in. I was a pretty good swimmer, I said. The guy said, "Are you *really* good?" I said I was. I was driven by jeep to a swimming hole to join about 50 other guys who thought they could swim.

Saipan is a gorgeous place if you're thinking about swimming instead of fighting. The cliffs go down the sea, and there are beautiful pools of clear water. The Sergeant in charge had us swim across the lagoon about 200 yards to a small island. Places in the distance are farther than they look so the tendency is to start out too fast. We watched 30 guys swim and none of them were any good; they gave out half way across and had to struggle back or be picked up.

So I said, "Let me go." I started slowly so I could pace myself, and I made the swim easily. The Sergeant said, "Step over there. You qualify." I said, "For what?" He said he couldn't tell me. I said, "I know we're going to Tinian, and I think maybe it's reconnaissance." Tinian is only a mile and a half from Saipan and the water rushes between the islands pretty fast. Tinian had a better airfield than Saipan so I knew we had to take Tinian. I had visions of going through the water with a knife in my teeth. A mile and a half and back is three miles and there's no one of those other guys who could do that. I myself would have to get in shape to do it. This was before I was a serious swimmer and swam 32 miles across Lake Erie. In the ocean you can swim for a long time, but you go around in circles if you don't have a guide boat. At night you'd have the stars, but In any case, getting to Tinian and back without being detected would be a challenge.

I went back to my Colonel and said, "I qualified for whatever." I never heard another thing about the duty for which I qualified. I'm guessing that they figured it out that their plan wasn't feasible. This episode lingered in my mind and helped keep the idea alive that I was meant to be a long-distance swimmer.

Tinian

I didn't swim to Tinian, but I soon reached the beach of that island in the usual way for which the Marines are famous.

We went in first in the bowels of a troop transport. We stopped about two miles out, to avoid the shelling and loaded onto the Higgins boats, piloted by Coast Guard personnel. Each boat held one platoon, 60 men. Then the Higgins zigzagged into shore with mortars falling all around. The pilot told me he had to make 15 more runs to the beach. His chances of surviving were about 50-50.

The Higgins boats couldn't go all the way in or they would get hung up on the coral reefs. So we jumped in the water a few yards from shore. The big guys were in up to their waists, but I was up to my armpits standing on my tiptoes, holding my rifle in the air to keep it dry. A couple guys were hit ahead of me, and when we got in we were held on the beach all night. The next morning, the Sergeant kicked me in the stomach, and said, "We're moving in." That's the last thing I remember about that day, for which I am probably fortunate.

The action generally followed the same pattern as my assignments on Saipan—the same scouting ahead, reporting back, moving forward, securing an area, and repeating the process. The particulars were diverse. I remember clearing an area all except for an igloo-shaped bunker. The commanding officer didn't want to leave the bunker with possible Japanese soldiers inside. We threw in grenades, and then, as part of my combat intel job, I crawled inside to see if anyone was still alive. Not fun. I did a lot of crawling in that war. My smaller than average size may have given me an advantage in this type of job.

We lost 25 or 30 out of 150 guys in my outfit in Tinian compared to Saipan where we'd lost half of our guys.

At Tinian we took only 1000 Japanese prisoners. I could see the Japanese soldiers there jumping off the rocks to their death rather than face surrender, as they had also done at Saipan. The cliffs are lower in Tinian, but still it was a chilling thing to watch even after all the death we'd seen in this war.

The taking of Tinian made possible the huge airfield from which our B-27s conducted the air raids on Japan. After Okinawa, the B-29 Enola Gay flew out of Tinian to drop the A-bomb on Hiroshima. Boch's Car flew from there, too, hitting Nagasaki. I would be dead if it weren't for those A-bombs. But before that happened we were in training for Okinawa. In the meantime, Allied forces took Guam, Leyte, Iwo Jima, and many other strategic footholds in our island-hopping campaign. At the end of March, my outfit headed for Okinawa, only 340 miles from mainland Japan.

Okinawa

Our troop ship arrived at Okinawa, and we were floating around about two miles off shore waiting for the invasion to start in a few days. One day I heard the whistles of the boatswain's pipe, and up the gangplank came this Lieutenant Commander, and I thought, *Jeez, he looks like my brother-in-law.* Then the loud speaker blared, "Would PFC Briggs come to the top deck." It was Tom Lavender. We were glad to see each other. He said something like "We've got a tough deal coming up here and we're going to do the best we can for you." He was in command of a squadron of minesweepers and he'd be sweeping into the beaches to clear the way for the Marine amphibious landings. He said, "Good luck," and we both knew it meant a lot more than that. It might be our last meeting. We saluted and he left. I thought, *There goes a good guy.*

Tom's was the first American outfit to go into the Japanese homeland (although the indigenous Okinawans wouldn't agree that their island was Japanese homeland). He could be proud that only one sweeper under his command was lost.

In the meantime, I was sent with a contingent of Marines in a troop ship with landing craft about 15 miles north of Hagushi Beach, where the Marines actually landed, to do a diversionary maneuver. The Japanese knew through their intel that we were the 2nd division and were going to attack in the area of the Motobu Hanot peninsula on the western side of the island of Okinawa, and they were preparing. So we put our Higgins boats into the water on the northern side of the peninsula and became active to draw a part of the Japanese forces up there until the real landing took place on the south side of the peninsula. We accomplished what we intended, a brilliant feint, and our forces landed successfully at Hagushi Beach. I got a combat ribbon but I don't deserve that; I was a mile out in the water while others went onto the beaches.

I was on a ship interpreting aerial photographs for the command, which was on a better-than-average troop ship with our destroyers all around us to fight off enemy aircraft, especially the hundreds of kamikazes that were now a major part of the Japanese defense. Once I was on deck and a kamikaze was coming right at our ship. I thought, *This is the end.* It was about a quarter mile away but it seemed like 5 feet away when one of our guys hit it. There was smoke and fire, and it plunged into the Pacific. Except for that, it was easy for me at Okinawa. Too easy, it seemed.

After that, I'm ashamed that I told my mother in a letter that I felt I wasn't doing a very important job and I wanted to go back on line to the Battalion as a combat intelligence scout. It was true, but I'm sorry I worried her. I was thinking of all those guys on the front lines who had wives and children, so many of them injured and dying, and here I was, a single guy, interpreting photographs at a desk on a ship, relatively safe. I asked for a transfer that would take me back into combat, and got it. I went through three campaigns and never was hurt except the mosquito bite infection, but I would have probably not survived in combat if they hadn't dropped the bomb on Hiroshima. Why did I have to tell my mother that I had asked for front line duty and got it?

By June 1945, there were another 20 miles of Japanese-held territory to take on Okinawa but we knew we'd take it. Then we were going to retrain to hit Japan in November. Back in Saipan and before the dropping of the atom bombs, I'd seen equipment and supplies being loaded on the docks at Chalan Kanoa to go into Japan. We'd had a long-range plan, but after the battle of Okinawa, where we had

49,151 American casualties of which 12,520 were killed, President Truman made the difficult decision to cut the war short with the atom bomb.

The Enola Gay took off from Tinian carrying an A bomb that fell on Hiroshima on August 6, 1945, and three days later Boch's Car took off for Nagasaki with the second bomb. The next day Japan opened peace negotiations, and on August 14, the Japanese accepted the Allies' terms of surrender. Oh, the joy when we heard the war was over! They couldn't control us; we went wild. Everyone got roaring drunk.

Chapter 7

Occupying Japan

Sailing to Nagasaki to occupy the defeated nation was exhilarating—until about five miles from shore we smelled the burning bodies of the victims of the A-bomb. We'd been enjoying the respite from killing and disposing of the dead, ours and theirs, for a couple months since the surrender, but when that stench hit us, our minds were brought back quickly to the horror of war.

However, a new era was opening for me and for the two countries concluding war. Rather than going into Nagasaki harbor with guns blazing, as we once imagined, we steamed in with basketballs and textbooks for the occupation. We weren't 100% sure we wouldn't have a little resistance. We were on Higgins boats, and mine pulled up beside a big British carrier. We were under the curve of the carrier and some Brits yelled down to us, "Go get 'em, Yanks." And I thought, *I don't know if I want to do this assignment.*

We landed at one of the Mitsubishi plants. It was smooth as silk. We marched down the streets. The Japanese had been told not to go out on the street, but we could see pairs of eyes peering out at us, and it was fun once we realized they weren't going to shoot at us.

The Americans began to help with sanitation and other immediate necessities, the worst of which was disposing of bodies. All in all, things were going pretty well. One day some of us took liberty and went into downtown Nagasaki. We were officially not allowed to go into the bombed area, but people began to go there. They told us the radiation in the area would last for 65,000 years, like forever, to keep us out. So I went in to see for myself. In the area where I went, here was nothing but smithereens except for a few Shinto shrine gates known as *torii*. I took a photograph of one sacred gate standing bravely in that rubble. I also kept some sand from there, but I lost it back in the States in a fire. Now at 90 years old, I am still here in spite of the radiation. They couldn't hold us back and they didn't try. How many people today can say they were in the bomb area within two months of the explosion? Not too many people who saw the actual bomb damage up close on the ground are still around.

One day a Japanese man, a college professor who spoke good English, singled me out. He said, "Would you mind coming with me and meet my family?" So I went with him. I took off my shoes before entering his house, and I had to bend down to get through the door. This was an educated man who wasn't totally sold on the idea that the Emperor was God. He admired Americans. There were all kinds of different attitudes among the Japanese.

Soon we moved from Nagasaki to Sasebo, a big Japanese air base. I was still a Private First Class when I was sent to Division Special Services training to learn how to run a Battalion Special Services section. There were four of us at the school, three Lieutenants and me. They posted the grades at the end of training and I got an A+, one Lieutenant got a B, and the rest were lower. My grade really impressed Colonel Strickland, who became my mentor. Soon I was running special services for the Battalion, which included education, sports, and all kinds of activities. I was given an aircraft hangar and six men to provide as good a recreation program as we could, which included getting a radio station going. I had a technician who knew how to do that. We were soon up and running with music and news. Then we started a little library and we got books. And you could take courses from the University of Hawaii and the guys who were headed back could go on and get college degrees. We were counseling people about these opportunities. And all of this was my responsibility. At some point, I was promoted to Corporal, for the second time, and Colonel Strickland started pushing me to go to Officer Training School.

The army had a big depot where we could get movies, but I was at a disadvantage because most of the people trying to get movies were Lieutenants for other special services outfits. However, I did come back with what our outfit wanted, and my Colonel noticed that.

Pretty soon I got out my clarinet, and a couple other guys and I formed a band. We brought girls in from a local dance hall. So I had an excuse to go into the town of Sasebo. I had all this stuff going on, and I had a jeep so I spent a lot of time in Sasebo. And quite a lot of it, I have to say, was personal. So I got to know the owner of the dance hall. He was a very nice Japanese fellow who spoke good English. We were not supposed to have any fraternization with the Japanese but that rule went by the boards.

One day this man said, "Do you want a girlfriend? I have a niece who lived up in Hokkaido." Hokkaido was the most northern of the three Japanese islands, like Siberia is to Russia or Alaska is to the States. She somehow made her way with her little girl by foot all the way from somewhere on Hokkaido to Sasebo, about 600 miles. She had to take a long ferry ride to cross the Tsugaru Strait to reach the main island of Honshu. Also, somehow she got through the five-mile railroad tunnel from Honshu to the southern island, where Sasebo is, to be with her uncle. He told me, "I think you will respect Kasuko, and you're the only one I've told about her." She wasn't in the dance hall; she had a little apartment up above. He took me up and introduced us. So I was very polite, and we talked. Apparently she liked me, and he discussed the situation with her because he was an honorable man. Then we became lovers.

And I was coming and going in Sasebo every day, and I danced with the girls downstairs, but I really liked Kasuko. When it came time to pull out and go up to Fukuoka, she was very disturbed, and I didn't want to leave her either.

Colonel Strickland said, "You really should be an officer, and I can give you the opportunity." I'd had the offer of officer training twice before, first after Saipan and Tinian, and then when we were on the way to Okinawa, and now this time. Colonel Strickland had arranged the deal—they had an Officer Candidate School (OCS) in Japan by that time—but he said there'd be four years in the Marine Corps after training. I said, no sir. I wanted to go back and finish my education. Col. Strickland and I were very close. He said, "I'm disappointed but it's your choice. You'd be a good officer." We were then at Fukuoka, and it was time to return to the States. He said, "Accept this deal, here in Japan, or go home." I said I'm going home.

He said he wanted to do one more thing for me before I left. He'd send me on leave for one week to Atami, the recreational place for all US forces not far from Mt. Fuji. It was the Japanese Riviera, where cliffs come down to sea. The resort was attractive with an old golf course. I got myself some clubs. Three of us went and shot a few balls off the cliff so we could say we played golf at Atami. The course wasn't at all in good shape at that time.

One night, the night before I left Atami, I had my clarinet with me, and I went into a club with a Japanese band that played stuff like Lawrence Welk, rooty-tooty stuff. I asked if I could sit in with them, playing American tunes. We'd influenced the Japanese enough already that they played American music and danced to it. So I played something like St. Louis Blues and they said, "Good, good," and were bowing to me. We went on playing and, when it was over, one of the dignitaries, said, "I'd like to reward you." There were always dignitaries everywhere you went, important people in Japanese communities. He said, "I have this lady over here. If you would like to, I'll make arrangements. There's a spa way up on the mountain, and they have a pool and nice rooms, if you'd like to take her up there for the evening." She was very pretty. I thought about Kasuko. I wasn't committed to her. She wanted me to marry her. I had thought seriously about it, but I was not committed.

So I said to the man that I'd do it. So I took this girl up there. We went on a long trail up the mountain. Man, it was hard. There had been a ski lift, but it had fallen into disrepair. At the top of the mountain we entered the spa. That's the only time I've gone into a bath where men and women were together. I was kind of timid, I'll tell you that, to go in there without any clothes even though nobody was paying any attention. So we were there that evening. She went down to the train station the next day and saw me off. And I went back south to Fukuoka. I'd told Kasuko I'd come see her again in Sasebo, but I didn't have time. The Colonel had just hit me with this— OCS or home—so I didn't have time.

I'd been in the Pacific almost two years to the day.

Chapter 8

Mother

When I left Japan in April 1946, I was taken to Fort Pendleton, where I was discharged and given $250. I thought I was rich. I hitchhiked to Spokane, Washington, to see a buddy of mine. Then I hit the road toward home, hitching rides. When I got to Minneapolis, I called home, and my dad answered. He said to come home as quickly as possible, so I bought a train ticket. When I arrived at South Station in Boston, crisp in my uniform and wearing my corporal stripes, I was striding along confidently. When Dad saw me, he cried. I tried not to cry and almost succeeded.

While I was away, my mother and dad had moved from the house in Melrose to an apartment on Arlington Street in Cambridge, apparently because of Mother's illness, which was worse than I'd realized. As we got closer to Arlington Street, Dad said, "Your mother is very ill, so prepare yourself. But she knows you are coming, so she's excited." Then the door opened and there stood a little old lady. I was shocked. I thought, *Did my letter telling her I was transferring to the front lines do this to her?* As we talked, she perked up.

After we'd talked a while, she said she had prepared my favorite meal. This was good news, although she shouldn't have been cooking for me in her state of health, but I knew she had wanted to do something special for me, and she was a wonderful cook.

Before the war, canned Spam had just hit the market, and I had tried some and told my mother it was great. So she always kept some Spam for me.

During the war we used K rations in the field, which were like bars of chocolate with white strings in them, probably coconut. We called these K rats. In each K rat packet they gave us four cigarettes, coffee and cream, biscuits, and a can of processed cheese or a "meat product." Not being a smoker, I traded my cigarettes for cheese.

So when we got back from the front where the food service was set up, what was it? C rations. Spam was the main feature. We were grateful at first. But then I ate Spam until I got to the point that the thought of it made me sick.

So there was Mother, beaming at me, saying she'd fixed my favorite meal. Spam. I ate the vegetables. I got halfway through the piece of Spam and stopped. She asked me, "Don't you like Spam?" I didn't want to disappoint her so I finished the piece with difficulty. I tell this story to my students who complain about spam in their e-mail. I ask them if they know why it's called Spam. They don't. I tell them it's something that you are so flooded with that you hate to see it coming, even though an occasional one is not bad.

Mother didn't want to talk about her health. As a Christian Scientist, she had different ideas about health than other people. In about three days after I got home, however, I heard her moaning in pain. My dad called an ambulance to take her to the New England Hospital for Women and Children, where Aunt Letitia practiced. In fact, she supervised her sister's exploratory surgery. They opened her up and found cancer all over her body, and there was nothing more they could do. Aunt Letitia said that three years before, if my mother had come for a medical examination, they could have taken care of the cancer simply. Within five or six days after my arrival, she died. I think she had been holding on until I got home. Once she saw me again safe and sound, she just let go.

During those last days, Virginia sent me a note for my mother, beautifully written, and asked me to read it to her. Virginia couldn't come but she wrote and gave our mother credit for being a wonderful person. I was so pleased with this reconciliation. As I was reading the letter to Mother, I busted up in the middle of it and cried. My mother said, "Harry, you're a Marine. I expect more of you than this. And remember, you will have to take care of your father."

Her religion was what sustained her and in my youth she hoped it would sustain me, and if not, my being a Marine should suffice.

I said to her, "Your religion has always been your greatest love." She said, "No, my family." And I realized that was true.

She was sedated for the last few days, and I stayed with her and held her hand. Once she became fully awake and said to me, "Harry, I want you to get a Ph.D." I promised I'd get one. Really that promise was the only reason I pursued a doctorate. And my dad wanted me to have one for the same reason, to fulfill my mother's last wish.

I was the last person left with my mother's body after she'd died. The others had left and the door was closed. I asked to see her one last time, and they let me back in. I was in my uniform. I gave her a Marine salute, the best salute I ever gave. That made me feel better.

Chapter 9

Grasping at Straws

My mother was right when she said I'd need to take care of my father. After her death he was devastated. He could hardly stand up at the funeral and had to lean on me. I spent the next few months with him, helping him with everything. He had been given several months off from his job during Mother's illness. He went back to work but I don't think he could handle it very well and soon retired.

In the summer following my mother's death, I felt the impact of my promise to get a Ph.D., and at the same time, I felt I needed to be in sports, and I wanted to have some fun, too.

I spent a lot of time with Dad. I also played for Jordan Marsh in the Metro Baseball League. I usually played second base. I was a good runner and hitter, but my arm was not so good. Our catcher missed a few games, and on those occasions I took over as catcher, where I called the pitches. I liked this responsibility, and I was good at it.

I was beginning to pick up where I was before the war, which meant continuing my passions, one by one, that had driven me in my youth, beginning with sports, and moving on quickly to romance and academics.

I experienced a sour note in the romance department when my Aunt Letitia made her only mistake in judgment towards me. She had always promoted my relationship with my high school sweetheart Priscilla Hess. Both her parents were alcoholics. Aunt Letitia had paid most of her tuition at Simmons College. I'd really loved Priscilla, and she really loved me. I'd chased her for so long until I finally fell out of love and began chasing other women outside of Melrose. I told her finally that I'd chased her long enough and I wanted to cool it, and I was dating others. Priscilla married just before I went overseas. She married a classmate whose parents had a lot of money. After a week she decided it was a big mistake. They must have had an annulment so when I came home she was single.

After my mother died, Aunt Letitia invited me to her home at 7 Village Lane in Arlington near Boston. I went, and who was there but Priscilla Hess! That was not a good thing. Coming down the stairs, I saw her and she didn't look any better to me then than when I'd decided not to keep on dating her. Priscilla told me I was the only one she'd ever loved though she'd dated others. I told her I'd felt the same thing but it was over. That was high school, this was now. I'd rather have a girl dump me than to tell a girl I don't love her any more. I resented Aunt Letitia's intrusion into my love life by springing that one on me. My next romance had to wait a while.

My father at his desk at the Second National Bank, very soon after my mother's death.

In the fall I took a step forward in academics: I started to study law at Suffolk University Law School in downtown Boston, where I also coached soccer, as well as law courses at Harvard. I guess I figured a J.D., a doctor of law degree, was close enough to a Ph.D. Or maybe I was just distracted by events. I was stopped by a local policeman in Stoneham, Massachusetts. He told me to stop, and I stopped. He blew his whistle and wised off a good bit, treating me as if I'd committed a crime and all for a disputable and minor traffic violation. Then he wrote me a ticket. As I took it, I said, "I'll see you in court." He was surprised. He expected me to pay the fine and that would be that. But I saw him in court and presented my case, talking as if the issue were the policeman's behavior rather than my ticket. After I got the ticket dismissed, the bailiff said to me, "You should be a lawyer."

You might say I was suggestible because I immediately enrolled in law school for the fall semester. I was also taking physical education at Boston University, which was a nothing program, and I was coaching and experimenting with different things. If I tried out a class and didn't like it, I just didn't go to class. I was just grasping at straws. Swimming had to wait for a while, and I also had to fit in earning a living.

Mexico

In this period of finding direction, I had the urge for adventure. I guess I have always been seeking adventure. It was never hard to find. I had always had a connection with the Boston newspapers, and so I pursued that avenue again. This time—in late summer, 1946—I went to Mexico to cover the Mexican Baseball League. At that time the Mexican league was luring away the best American baseball players, for example, Max Lanier, the three-time All Star pitcher, who had played in three World Series 1942, 43, and 44. The Mexican League paid him twice the salary that he was being paid by the St. Louis Cardinals. They even offered Ted Williams and Joe DiMaggio contracts, but these two refused. This issue seemed like a good topic for me to write about so I pitched it to the sports editor at the Boston Post, who liked the idea. The Post paid my expenses, and Aunt Letitia gave me $500 to help me do it.

First I interviewed the Pasquel brothers, the baseball moguls who were trying to make the Mexican League similar to the Major Leagues in the US. First they'd hired players from the U.S. Negro Leagues, and, when I was down there, they were causing a lot of resentment in the U.S. by hiring our big leaguers. I saw a truck out in front of Jorge Pasquel's walled home in the suburbs of Mexico City, and I cautiously parked two blocks away in case I had to make a quick getaway. I noticed an armed guard at the truck. As I left the house from the interview, I looked in the truck and saw boxes of rifles. As I started to take a photo, the guards jumped for me. I ran as fast as I could, got to my car and drove off without a photo. Back then it wasn't drugs and drug running but guns from the US that ended up in the hands of various banditos. I wrote the article about the Mexican League and the interview but I didn't tell about the guns. The pay was little but covered my expenses for the adventure.

Back in Boston in the fall of 1946, besides taking law classes at Suffolk University and Harvard Law Schools, I enrolled at Boston University, studying political science. That same fall I became the head hockey coach at Tufts, full time but temporary. The team improved so much during the season that I was expecting to be named permanent Head Coach.

There were no separate divisions then for the big schools or powerful schools, so Tufts, with its program in its infancy, played against powerhouses. We were trounced in the first few games, improved during the season losing by only a point or two, and then won our last two games. Thus it was a great improvement year. I could get these kids to play at a level over their heads, not always for the whole game, but they did very well.

Older coaches at big schools like Johnny Chase at Harvard and Harry Cleverly at BU were mentoring me. We would get together once a week and really have fun. I could see that, after a career as head coach, with my skill at organizing and with the Ph.D. I was going to get, I would eventually be Athletic Director. That same season, I was paid by the *Boston Post* to cover Tufts sports. I also had a job with Boston University as manager of their Newton dorms and their football facilities. I continued to be a comfort to my dad, living with him in Cambridge. The coaching and the sports reporting didn't bring in much money though, and I really needed a full time job.

New York City

In January 1947, I took a job with a big insurance company in New York City, while also taking courses at New York Law School because I liked law and I always thought I'd get a law degree after I got my Ph.D. From my job in New York, I went to Boston two days a week to coach Tufts hockey games till the end of the season. I had a girlfriend, Alice Hardy, a Tufts graduate, who lived in Beverly near Boston, and I came home every weekend to see her. I thought I'd marry her.

In my position as an insurance investigator, I found out how rotten those insurance companies were. An elderly guy who didn't have sight in one eye from birth had lost the sight in his good eye while working and ended up in Bellevue Hospital in New York. The insurance company wanted to get him off their rolls, so they sent me out, not to find out what the deal was but to find something wrong with the case so the insurance company's lawyers could terminate his claim. They sent me to Bellevue to see this man. Every other case I investigated, I found someone was ripping off the insurance company. This time, like always, I was supposed to get the person to sign some papers so the company could quit paying. The doctor said the patient would be happy to see me because he hadn't had any visitors for months and he'd just had an unsuccessful operation on his eye and would never see again. I went to see the poor fellow with one eye bandaged and both eyes blind. I went back to my boss with no papers signed because this guy deserved to have his claim paid. My boss said, "We pay you to get these papers." And I said, "You know what you can do with these papers." And that was the end of that job.

I'd been playing baseball for the Jordan Marsh team in the Boston Park League whenever I was home. Baseball has always played a big part in my life, almost as big as ice hockey. I followed many baseball players closely throughout their careers, interviewing many of them in my sports reporting career.

I paid special attention to Jackie Robinson, who, after a college career, military service, and a season with the Negro leagues, had signed in late 1945 with the Montreal Royals, a farm team for the Brooklyn Dodgers, thanks to Branch Rickey, the Dodgers General Manager. Robinson played the 1946 season with the Royals, banned in many places during spring training in Florida but welcomed enthusiastically in Montreal. He was the International League's Most Valuable Player that year with a .349 batting average and .985 fielding. He'd started at shortstop but, like me, he was moved to second base because his throwing arm wasn't great. His career was of particular interest to me not only because of his playing talent and determination, but because I cared a lot about giving a fair shake and social equality to people of all kinds. I admired Rickey for bringing Jackie Robinson into the minor leagues and grooming him for the Major Leagues, which up till then had no black players, not since the 1880s.

Anyway, I was going to use my severance pay from the insurance company to play baseball and go to law school in Boston. So the guy from the Boston office asked, "Instead of quitting our company, would you be interested in working for us in Boston." I decided I could put up with the company a bit longer to support myself while I took courses and continued my relationship with Alice. And I would be living with my dad, who was still lonely and enjoyed my company and going to my games.

I took a week off between jobs and didn't tell the man who'd hired me and showed up a week late. He was angry but kept me. I knew the routine; they'd give me the job to find the reasons to get rid of certain cases. They sent me to East Boston and I'd come back with 50 cases for which we could legitimately stop payment, or we had a good case and they'd have to take us to court to fight it and they didn't have the money. These were mostly bad people beating the insurance company. But one case was a Puerto Rican girl about 17 years old, who worked in a warehouse. The foreman was a shanty Irishman, a blowhard, and a tough guy. "If you can't handle the weight, you shouldn't be here," he said to the girl, who had lifted something and miscarried her baby and got workman's comp. When I talked to the foreman, I found he was anti-female and thought women were only good for having babies. She was a pathetic but nice girl, and she was forced to pick up something very heavy, and she miscarried. I did the same thing that I'd done in New York. I turned in her papers with no signature. I said, "I've given you 50 of what you want; give me this one." They wouldn't, so I quit.

Limerick

I'd always had the idea I'd like to have a place in the New England countryside. At the end of the summer in 1947, I found a very old house with no running water or electricity in Limerick, Maine, for sale for $3000. It had a two-seater outhouse connected to the house by an enclosed hallway, a nice big barn, 115 acres, and an ancient beaver hat in the closet. My aunt Our Ma loaned me the money to buy the farm. I really loved that place. I spent hours and hours scraping off old wallpaper from the walls and restoring the house. And I bought enough furniture to make the place comfortable for me and for visitors like my dad and my aunts, and once my niece Letitia, my sister Virginia's daughter—and my girlfriend.

By September 1947, there was a sports banquet for Tufts sports teams at a well-known business club near Copley Square. There were several hockey coaches there from the Boston Intercollegiate Hockey League. They gave me a trophy for being the Outstanding Coach of the Year for the previous season (1946-47) with the most improved team in the USA. In the nation! An article was written about me in the newspaper for that, and the coaches from the big hockey schools paid me a lot of attention. Pop Houston, Athletic Director at Tufts and president of the NCAA that year, said to me, "Come see me in a week." It was all coming together. I had recruited players for this season and was ready to get to work. In a week, when I saw Pop, he said, "Bad news. We've dropped hockey."

That was one of the biggest betrayals of my life, but I never blamed Pop Houston. It became clear to me that the school's basketball people were jealous of the publicity I'd gotten. Crowds came to the hockey games, much fewer to the basketball games, so they had gotten the powers-that-be to drop hockey to increase support for basketball.

I decided to recruit my own team. We'd play a season and then maybe we could be officially adopted back into the Tufts program. With the players I'd already recruited for Tufts I had a full team. But Tufts said I couldn't use the school's uniforms or names. Worse, I couldn't use their facilities. So I took the situation to the newspapers, and they ran stories about my efforts. In the end it didn't work out.

I don't remember my thought process in letting law school go or my application for work towards my Ph.D. in political science, but I have now in my possession a certificate for passing the foreign language requirement, in French, for the Ph.D. program at Boston University. But I had many irons in the fire and the great disappointment in the loss of the hockey team. I needed to get my head together, so

I decided it was time for another adventure and a change of location, while I figured a few things out. And I needed a job.

Chapter 10

Puerto Rico

In January 1948, I took a job in Puerto Rico as an assistant historian for the United States government. It provided a steady salary and a more exotic location than Boston. Alice and I had cooled our relationship, although I went back home to see her once from Puerto Rico, when she told me that I was still "the one." In fact, it was in April on one of those visits that I took her to my farm in Limerick, the only time she ever saw it. One thing my mother had taught me was to respect women. I took a girl out on a date three times before I even put my arm around her. I went slowly. However, I must have been moving too fast that weekend in Limerick because Alice felt pressured and wanted to leave. So we left, and that was pretty much the end of our courtship. So I was free to pursue romance elsewhere.

In fact, in Puerto Rico I experienced some high points in romance, sports, and academics, three of the passions that drove me.

While I was working in Puerto Rico, I'd arranged to be a stringer for the *Boston Post*. I'd been on their sports desk, not full time, but when they needed me. That spring, I was excited to hear that Jackie Robinson was coming to Puerto Rico with his team for an exhibition game. This was big news for me. The previous spring in April 1947, Robinson had played his first major league game for the Dodgers, the first black player on a Major League team. Even some of his teammates had objected to playing with a black man. I agreed with Leo Durocher, who responded to those players' objections by saying, "I don't care if the guy is yellow or black, or if he has stripes like a zebra. I'm the manager of this team and I say he plays." I admired Durocher and General Manager Rickey. I was interested in justice and also in what they call diversity today. In my youth, my family had been protecting me from diversity as much as possible, but I was my own man now.

Robinson would be coming with the Dodgers to Boston to play the Boston Braves during the regular season, but all the press would be there, and I wouldn't have a chance with him. But no one was in Puerto Rico to write him up but me.

So I got to the park in San Juan at 5 p.m. I had credentials and walked over to first base, where Jackie Robinson was shagging grounders. I was in awe of that guy and his achievements, so I approached him respectfully. I said, "Mr. Robinson, I'd like to do an interview." He said, "It's okay but you'll have to have permission from Leo."

Leo Durocher had just married film star Loraine Day and I could see them in the dugout. I was overly polite. I said, "Mr. Durocher, I'm with the *Boston Post*," and I showed him my credentials. Branch Rickey seemed interested nearby as Durocher started to chat with me. Remember that I was small and young looking, so all of a sudden Rickey entered our conversation with, "Say, does your mother know you are down here." I said, "Mr. Rickey, I have been in three Marine campaigns and do you want to know which ones? Saipan, Tinian, and Okinawa. Is that an appropriate question to ask me?" Rickey was very apologetic.

Unfortunately, I don't remember many details about my interview with Jackie Robinson. I do remember he wanted me to know that he had come to national prominence with only two years of play at UCLA whereas most athletes had three years to perform in a university that scouts and reporters were watching; before he came to UCLA, he'd played for a junior college. I wish I still had the article I wrote about Jackie Robinson. It was lost in a hurricane. Fortunately, I'd still had one more chance to interview Robinson years later.

Working for the government as a GS-3 ranked assistant historian down in the Caribbean was my first experience at working for the government. I was just there to get my mind together and ponder my course towards a Ph.D. I lived in barracks and ate in a dining room where I noticed this gorgeous girl named Eugenia Phillips. Her uncle, a Commanding General and a widower, had invited her to be his hostess for parties people of his rank had to give. She also had a job working for a military veterinarian and was a GS-6. G-3s didn't usually pal around with G-6s, so I had to figure out how I'd meet her. So I adopted a cat and I pretended it was sick. She examined the cat and I made my move. We hit it off and pretty soon were seriously dating.

There I was with this girlfriend, who was a GS-6, and my boss who was a GS-7, and I felt inferior. That emotional issue cost me months as I tried to improve my situation and be more desirable to her.

It happened, however, that a mid level government employee there, who became a friend of mine, had been hired as an assistant professor of political science at Western Reserve University in Cleveland, and was to leave soon for that job. Western Reserve (now Case Western Reserve) is a strange name, but I said I knew the origin of the name, and he was impressed. I asked him if he thought the political science department there needed any more help because I was sure interested in a paid position that would allow me to pursue a Ph.D. So my friend called the person who'd hired him, Dr. Earl Shoop, a very conservative political scientist who'd written a textbook used in over 200 universities. My friend mentioned to him that I was also a hockey coach. Dr. Shoop, apparently took an interest in hockey, and said that Western Reserve had a hockey team but it wasn't much good. Dr. Shoop said that he could have me put on as a hockey coach and as a teaching fellow in political science to help pay my way to graduate school. He was the faculty advisor to the Athletics Department and had much influence.

An incident that made this offer in Cleveland especially fortuitous occurred about the same time. One of my jobs as historian was to go to the Island of Vieques about ten miles off the shore of the main island. Once a year for two weeks, the Navy used the longer, middle portion of this 21-mile island as a bombing range and missile testing ground. The residents of Vieques, who lived on the ends of the island, on about a fourth of the land available, complained about these exercises for years. My job was to go to the site and see what was going on there and record it.

On the final day of the exercises in Vieques, when I was observing the loading of gear to go back to Puerto Rico, a crane overhead collapsed and drove a man right into the deck. I was standing 100 feet away. I went back and did my report, wherein I reported no casualties until the very end. I took it to the Colonel, a 50-page report, and he flipped through it. "We can't have this at the end." "Why not?" I asked. "The general won't like it." So I wanted to get out of that job.

I finally told my girlfriend, "Listen, Genie, I have a future but it's not here." I told her that, through my faculty advisor at Western Reserve, I had gotten a job offer as a hockey coach and a position as teaching fellow in political science. I thought those positions would offer her something better than what I had now. I asked her if she would go to Cleveland with me. She said yes, she'd come in a few weeks.

I brought the cat back to the States with me on an air charter with a lot of Puerto Ricans on the plane. A terrible storm brought us down on a farmer's field in North Carolina. The Puerto Ricans said it was because I had "el negro gato," the black cat, so I was made to feel responsible for this mishap. We continued the trip by bus to D.C. and then took a train to Boston.

I arrived at my father's apartment with my cat. He didn't know I was coming. I told him I had at job at Western Reserve to coach and teach and a girlfriend, Genie, still in Puerto Rico, who was joining me in Cleveland. A week after I got home, I got a Dear John letter from her. She'd taken up with an old boyfriend, she said. I took it hard. My dad was a very pleasant guy, and he got me out of a lot of trouble, but this time he didn't give me any comfort. I took the letter and went to his office all broken up. I was not quite crying but almost. I said, "I don't know what to do; I almost don't want to live." He said, "Son, you've been through a war, and this isn't the worst thing you will experience in your life, so be a man."

I resented his reaction a lot. But I pulled myself together and went to Cleveland to teach, coach, and get a Ph.D.

My Western Reserve yearbook picture 1949 as soccer coach.

Chapter 11

Cleveland, Limerick, and Norma

In the summer of 1948, I came home from Puerto Rico and was staying with my dad. I spent some time at my place in Limerick, and my dad came up on weekends. Our Ma had asked me if she could live in the house in Maine during the summer. I said, "Of course, you don't have to even ask. You loaned me the money to buy it. But it doesn't have any running water or electricity." She said, "I lived that way when I was a child; I can do it again." She had always longed for her own house. When I was a child, she had moved in with us along with her frail elderly husband, and then was widowed. She had

My aunt Frances, called Our Ma, dressed to go into town.

moved in with her sister, my Aunt Letitia, when I was a child, and was still there 20 years later. No doubt she wanted to have a place to herself, at least a few weeks a year, and she deserved to have her time in Limerick.

Cleveland Fall 1948-Summer 1949

In the fall 1948, I took up my positions at Western Reserve in Cleveland as Teaching Fellow in Political Science and hockey coach. I have to say the hockey program was a great disappointment. Western Reserve was trying to grow into a bigger player in the sports scene, but the support was nothing. We had irregular practices and had to scrounge for places to get ice time. I did my job and got paid for it, but it didn't amount to much. I found various ways to fill in. I organized the men's soccer team, which achieved varsity status in the fall of 1949, and was its first coach for at least one more year. I even coached freshman baseball through a couple of games and got paid for that. In addition, I found satisfaction in other sports activities.

I played hockey for the Euclid team; Euclid was a Cleveland suburb. I got involved with the Western Reserve football team as a sportscaster, and I started reporting Western Reserve sports for the *Cleveland Plain Dealer.* I'd always been connected with a newspaper. That university didn't even know how to do public relations and get their sports into the papers so I did it for them. Western Reserve used me any way they could. Dr. Shoop, as faculty advisor on athletics, relied on me for advice, and we became quite close.

In the academic area, however, Dr. Shoop and I didn't see eye to eye. He was a leading conservative in his field and I was much too liberal for him. After the first midterm exam in one of Dr. Shoop's classes, I expressed my liberal views, which he didn't care for. He told me, "If I'd known you thought these things, I wouldn't have hired you." At the end of the semester, he said about my final exam, "You did a pretty good job, but I have to give you a C for the course." Getting a C as a Ph.D. student wasn't going to cut it. Dr. Shoop assured me that he had a friend in another department, educational philosophy, named Dr. Robinson, to whom he would recommend me. Dr. Robinson, he said, had noticed me in my sports activities and was apparently pleased with my initiative. Dr. Shoop thought I'd be a better fit over there. But Dr. Shoop gave me two sections of political science to teach the next semester, which seemed contradictory to me. I wasn't good enough to get a Ph.D. in his department, but I was good enough to teach there. Believe me, I was glad to have my salary.

So the next semester, beginning in January 1949, I switched or rather I was switched to educational philosophy as a Ph.D. candidate while still teaching political science. I studied Aristotle and statistics in my new field. I could have handled political science much better than education, but I got almost all A's in education from the beginning.

Statistics was a hard course for me. Dr. Harry, a brilliant man and the educational statistics professor, said he'd seen me too often at sports events and not enough in the library. He was right, of course. As head coach for the Western Reserve soccer team and much other coaching experience, I had a long-range plan to become an athletics director so sports came first in my mind. I was getting a Ph.D. for my mother and, besides, I preferred political science to educational philosophy, so my heart wasn't always in my academics. Nevertheless, having a Ph.D. in any subject matter seemed a good credential for working for a university, even as an athletics director, so I journeyed on. I had to meet with my faculty advisors once a week, all four of them. Dr. Harry was one of them, and he never took me seriously as a Ph.D. candidate.

Norma

My second semester at Western Reserve I met Norma Maxwell. My political science students were always kidding me, "Do you have a girlfriend?" I said I'd just broken up with one in Puerto Rico. So one student said he knew a girl that was available and he'd like to fix us up. I was reluctant because I'd had blind dates before that didn't work out well, but I finally said I'd try it.

I went to Norma's house. She opened the door and I looked at her. Man! Was she ever cute! Not beautiful but cute. And she knew how to operate. She was the Midwest figure skating champion. Then she'd gone pro and skated in the Ice Capades and the Ice Follies. After a few years she'd decided to quit that circuit and go to the Cleveland School of Art, a degree-awarding school in the artsy and intellectual center of Cleveland. She'd enrolled in art school the same time I came to Western Reserve.

Norma was a petite brunette with a great figure, quite muscular. When I heard she was a figure skater, I told her I was a hockey player and suggested we go skating. She said she didn't like to go skating with guys because they couldn't skate as well. I assured her I could keep up with her, and she agreed and soon found out I could really skate. Her mother and stepfather, a prominent coroner always in the news for important cases, accepted me as worthy of their daughter because I was working towards a Ph. D.

So we hit it off. I wanted to take Norma to Boston in the spring to meet my Dad. Her mother said, "Don't go in that old car. Take mine." So we went off in her big Buick Roadmaster. Dad was living alone in Cambridge in his two-bedroom apartment. Dad had one bedroom and Gloria the other. I was on the sofa. When Dad went to work, you can be sure we took full advantage of the whole apartment.

I took Norma up to Limerick over spring break, and she liked my farmhouse. So we figured out how she could spend the summer in Maine and we could be together on weekends. She went to a camp not too far away where her little sister Roberta could go to camp, and she got a job there as a counselor for the summer.

Summer 1949

As usual between school years, I took a couple law classes at summer school at Harvard because law fascinated me and I thought that, after my Ph.D., I'd like to get a law degree. When I finished classes for the week and Norma had the weekend free, she'd come down to Limerick. It was a happy time but short-lived.

When the camp season was over and I'd finished the semester at Harvard, Norma's mother came to Maine to get Roberta. Then they all came down and spent the night at my farmhouse. My dad was expected to come up for the weekend, and we'd have a good time together. Norma loved my dad. All my girlfriends loved my dad.

My dad was getting in about 7 pm on Friday night on August 27, and we went over to Lake Winnipesauke to swim that afternoon, 30 miles away. On the way back from Winnipesauke I stopped at a store and I saw smoke in the distance. I said, "What's that smoke?" The clerk said, "That's the home of a young man who's studying law at Harvard University." We were in Norma's mother's car, and we tore off for the farm. When we got there, there was nothing left; only the ashes still smoldering. The volunteer firemen were spraying water from a stream about 150 feet away.

Everything I owned was gone, my house, the furnishings I'd recently bought as well as my mementos from the past, like some sand from the bomb site at Nagasaki, my Japanese flag and rifle, and my own M-1 from my wartime service that were stored in the basement. My barn was burned, and the older auto that I left at the farm was destroyed.

I didn't want to wait for my dad. I thought I could hurry back to Cambridge and head him off before he left home. I had no telephone. I was sickened by my loss. Norma's mother was more concerned with the fur stole she'd left in my house.

We left the house, while the fireman continued to fight the fire, and drove to my dad's apartment in Cambridge, but Dad had left early and we passed each other. He arrived and saw the burned house. My dad wasn't like steel. He got dizzy and was practically sick. At first, he may have feared I was in the house when it burned. A Catholic priest named Father Sheehy, the summer pastor for a church in Limerick, was there comforting my father. He said, "Come stay in the rectory because you are in no shape to travel." Norma and I and her mother were back in Cambridge and he was in Maine.

Father Sheehy called me in Cambridge and said, "I'm taking care of your father. He's upset, not stable. What do you want me to do?" I said I'd be up the next day to pick him up. He had his vehicle. Norma's mother and sister took off for Cleveland then. So we went back up to Limerick the next day in my Ford, a somewhat newer car than the one that had burned, and got Dad and met Father Sheehy, a big strong guy, very nice. I said to myself, there's one point for the Catholic Church.

Father Sheehy said he had occasional business in Boston and asked, "Would you take me down to Boston some time?" So we agreed to take him and have him as a guest at Dad's apartment.

Around that time, my aunt Our Ma had left Aunt Letitia's house and moved in with my father. I think it was because my father needed her to help with the household. Maybe it was a golden opportunity. It relieved me of worrying about my father who seemed so helpless and upset since my mother died. Our Ma had always been fond of my father.

So we arranged to bring Father Sheehy to Boston. Our Ma had led a sheltered life so the idea of a Catholic priest in the house was intriguing to Our Ma and maybe to Dad also. Their idea was that we'd always been a protestant nation. Our Ma and my dad were both unfriendly to the Catholic religion, but to have a priest in the house would be a diversion.

So one day in late summer I went to Maine and got Father Sheehy and brought him home to Cambridge. When my father came home from work at the bank, Our Ma had a nice dinner for us. It was exciting for her to entertain. We had two bedrooms in the apartment on Arlington Street. Both rooms had twin beds. So Father Sheehy and I had one room, and my dad and Our Ma were in the other. In the middle of the night someone was crawling gingerly into bed with me. I said, "Get the hell out of here!" and I pushed him with my feet onto the floor. "Don't you ever do this to me," I said. He said he was sorry. About two hours later, he had his hands all over me. I kicked him out again, and I said, "We're going back to Limerick first thing in the morning. We'll let my dad go to work first, and then you better be ready in the morning to go." Our Ma had breakfast ready and we rushed right by her without eating. For two hours in the car Father Sheehy said little. At the end of the trip, he said, "I hope you'll have compassion and not report me." I said, "I don't know what I'll do."

The population of Limerick was probably less than 200 in winter and 600 in summer so Father Sheehy was sent here for summer church. The rest of the year he'd be the chaplain at the University of Maine, and what a feast he was going to have there. I thought I should report him, but I had problems of my own.

I'd lost my house, Norma's mother was mad at my dad and me after the fire in Limerick. I didn't have money. I was on my own, but she thought my father had money and she wanted him to pay for the fur. Norma's mother, who had earlier supported our relationship, now put pressure on Norma to break up with me. Norma had been living at home while studying at the Art Institute, but now she escaped her mother's pressure by moving out of her parents' house and going back to skating. She was the star of a small show that played for elegant supper clubs in 5-star hotels. I returned to Western Reserve to start fall semester sports and academics, although Norma and I continued our romance when I visited her in Buffalo, Pittsburgh and Syracuse where she was performing.

1949-1950

I pursued my course work the next school year under the encouraging eye of Dr. Robinson and the scornful eye of Dr. Harry. Fortunately Robinson was the head of the department.

I was watching TV one night in early 1950 when a Marine major came in the screen, saying the Marines were offering commissions to World War II non-commissioned officers with a college degree and "meritorious service." I was coaching at Western Reserve at the time, and I went down to see if I qualified. I'd turned down several chances to go to Officer Candidate School (OCS) in Japan because I'd then owe four years of active duty, which I wasn't willing to do. So this easy avenue to becoming an officer piqued my interest. There was nothing to it. I qualified. I filled out some papers and was told to come back in a week to be sworn in. This had to be the worst program the Marines ever had. I certainly wasn't prepared. Never mind, I was now a 2nd Lieutenant and I'd have two weeks paid training every year.

I bought a uniform in order to go to my first training at Camp Lejeune in North Carolina and I decided since I was down that way I'd go by way of Jamaica first. I'd always wanted to go to Jamaica. I met a young lady in a hotel in Kingston. Her father was an Army major, and she wanted me to meet him, so I put on my uniform and went to meet him. He kept looking at me hard, sizing me up, as if I was some kind of phony. That's how I learned that I needed to wear my 2nd Lieutenant insignia bars. It took me a while to do this, but I did buy some bars for my shirt.

When I got to Camp Lejeune, I met a big guy, a bird colonel. I said, "I know you! You're Colonel Strickland." He remembered me from Japan. "You didn't go to OCS like I wanted you to," he said, "so how come you are an officer now?" I told him about this program. He said, "Come with me upstairs." There he told me that I needed bars on my shoulders, too. He said, "I'm glad to have you in the service." We had a good old time. And then I went out and bought some more bars. As usual I learned through experience and plenty of mistakes without any formal training.

Back north, I decided to join the Buffalo Reserve Marine Battalion. The officer in command, a hard-nosed guy named Witkowski, asked me, "Have you ever held a command?"

I said, "No."

"Do you know how to hold an inspection?"

I said, "No.

"He said, "Then what will I do with you?"

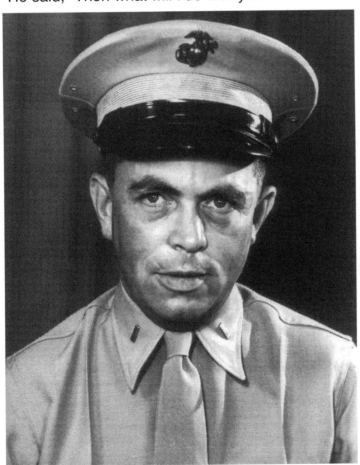

An officer at last, and with my Lieutenant's bars on my lapel.

I got to know Witkowsi quite well. He soon learned what to do with me. He valued my combat experience. When it came time for promotions, he nominated me for Captain along with two others, who had been through OCS programs. Our records were sent to Washington to be evaluated, and the other two got their promotions and I stayed a 1st Lieutenant. At that point I realized my career with the Marine Corps was not going anywhere. However, in time, my status as a Marine would serve me very well in surprising ways.

In the '49-'50 season, I played hockey with the local team, coached hockey and soccer, wrote for *The Plain Dealer*, and dated Norma. I also was a teacher at Brush High School in the spring semester, getting more deeply into the matter of education, and I was formulating my thesis topic, "The History of Teacher Training in Ohio." Before my research was over, I would visit every college that had an education department in the state; there were 45 of them, more than any other state in the nation. I guess you could say this topic combined my interest in history, which was my undergraduate major, with educational philosophy, the field into which I had recently stumbled.

Summer 1950

At the end of the academic year, I was headed back to Boston for the summer. I went into the office of Athletics Director Bill Counsel to say, "Goodbye, see you in the fall for soccer." Bill was on the phone. He said, "Hold on." He interrupted his phone conversation and said, "Do you want to be a camp director this summer?" I said, "No, not really." He held up his hand to signal me to stay as he went back and forth between me and his caller, who turned out to be Bill Townsend of the Easter Seals organization. Townsend wasn't satisfied with the first director he'd hired for a new camp that Easter Seals had started right here in Cleveland, and he was looking for a new director. I said, "What kind of camp?" He said, "A camp for crippled children." I said I wouldn't know how to handle crippled children. Townsend said the assistant director was a fine young man who didn't want to take over the responsibility of director but would be very helpful in acclimating me to the job. After about ten minutes back and forth, I said, "Well, all right."

I wanted to go home and see my dad for a couple weeks first. So I went and told Dad I was going to be the director of a camp for crippled children. He wondered if I could handle that. He also wondered how I kept coming up with these crazy things to do.

The first day the kids were arriving at Camp Cheerful. I was really nervous watching the buses come in and unload all the kids with crutches and wheelchairs and braces. By the end of the day I was carrying the kids on my back, putting them in the water, completely comfortable and having fun. I thought, *Am I ever glad I took this job!* I put everything I had into this job. I felt I was an outstanding director and it was wonderful work.

In the middle of the season, a public relations woman from the national organization in Chicago came down to visit us. Everyone was great, the counselors were great, Bill Townsend was great, the secretary was great. The PR lady said, "The morale in this camp is terrific. You really know what you're doing!"

I said, "Not really."

She came back later and took pictures and used them to raise money for the first crippled children's camp supported by the national Easter Seals organization, probably the first of any kind of camp for crippled children in the country.

Chapter 12

Dad and Alice, Gloria and Me

In January 1951, my dad retired from the Boston Clearing House, which he managed after his retirement from the Second National Bank. According to Aunt Letitia's diary, which is now available to me, my sister Virginia wrote Aunt Letitia at the end of January saying she was worried about Dad because she hadn't heard from him since Christmas. In fact, he took an extended trip to Vermont and Montreal. In March he took a vacation to Florida, returning tanned and happy. He'd always loved to travel and he deserved the pleasure, but there may have been more going on. In another entry from Aunt Letitia's diary, Aunt Letitia had received a letter from Virginia with "much news about her dad." As was her habit, Aunt Letitia only hinted at the most interesting things, so I don't know the news, but about that time Dad began seeing a woman, who was a vice president at John Hancock and lived in the same apartment building with my dad. They often had dinner together in the restaurant in that building. I found this lady wonderful and accomplished. She and my dad were fond of each other by all accounts, and I was happy he was not so lonely. I was distressed when I learned they had broken up. Next he started dating Alice.

If either of these ladies accompanied my dad on the first vacation trips of his retirement, he would not likely have told the family, especially not Our Ma, who was living with him and was probably not pleased with his absence, let alone his having a girlfriend. In fact, I wonder if Our Ma had something to do with my dad's split with the lady from John Hancock. Our Ma, 16 years older than her youngest sister Dora, my mother, had fostered the relationship of my father and mother, and, when Our Ma lived with us when I was a boy, she had tried to have more influence over him than my mother liked. Now that Our Ma was living with him, as a sort of mother figure (she wasn't called Our Ma for nothing) she had him to herself. She would not want to lose her position of prominence in his life.

On the occasion that I met Alice, I have to say I saw a father I had never known before. He was more fun loving than I'd ever seen him. He took an occasional drink, he told a few dirty jokes, and was terrific. Needless to say, he could not have done either of these things with my mother's knowledge. When my sister met Alice, our father's new girlfriend did not pass muster. She was crude, Virginia said. Her "whiskey baritone" and cigarettes didn't help. From my point of view, she was giving my dad a new lease on life, and I was happy to see it. Besides, I rather liked Alice. As much as I loved my mother, I was glad to see Dad have a few years with someone less virtuous and more a party girl.

In the meantime, from fall 1950 to spring 1951, besides my studies and coaching at Western Reserve, I went to Akron, about an hour south of Cleveland, to play pro-hockey for the Akron Stars in the Ohio Ontario Professional Hockey League. In my spare time, I tried to move my thesis along. It was slow going.

Summer 1951

I went home for a visit when the school year was over in June, and my father and Our Ma came to Aunt Letitia's home in Rockport, and so did I. Our Ma was thinner and pale. We were all together, but the subject of Alice didn't come up.

In the spring, I had been asked if I was coming back to direct Camp Cheerful again that summer. I said, "Absolutely." In my second year as Director, we repeated the success we'd had the first year, and I was very satisfied and happy with the work.

Fall 1951-Spring 1952

My Aunt Letitia at her retirement from her medical practice. She served on the Board of Directors of the New England Hospital for several years after that.

During the following school year, I was working on my thesis to be titled "The History of Education in Ohio," a record of the progression of teacher training programs. I visited all 45 of these programs, more than any other state in the nation.

For the Akron Stars 1951-52 hockey season, besides being a team member, playing often in the goal, I was bench coach, and I took over the management of the whole operation becoming GM of the Akron Stars as well as manager of the Iceland Arena where the Stars played. We took the Stars out of professional hockey and into the Cleveland Metro Hockey League, which meant that there was no payroll. While I was manager of the Arena, Norma came down here for ice time. And my dad came to see some of my games. It was like old times.

Not only was my father retired and free to come to games that spring, but also Our Ma had left his house. In January 1952, she'd had an attack of some sort. Aunt Letitia visited and noted that Our Ma was weak and weary. As a physician, she discussed her sister's case with the attending doctor. Our Ma's cardiogram said her heart was fine. Aunt Letitia wrote in her diary, "Believe it's nothing more than one of her spells." Our Ma had an attack she attributed to her heart when she was particularly upset about something. I would not be surprised if she was upset about my father dating.

In February, my father took Our Ma to Washington, Connecticut, to live with the Wheelers, old friends and neighbors from Melrose. Florence Wheeler was a widow about my parents' age and their daughter Janice had been a classmate of my sister Virginia. Janice was a schoolteacher in Connecticut and had bought a big old farmhouse there and was willing to care for Our Ma as well as her own mother. As much help as Our Ma had been to my dad, keeping house for him after my mother died, he must have relished his new privacy and freedom now that he was dating. I'd missed any drama associated with this transition and just enjoyed my father, now with more carefree time, coming to my games.

Hockey in Akron

My sports activities and my academic life intersected unfortunately when one night in Akron I was filling in at goal for a fellow who had been hit by a puck the night before. Keepers didn't wear facemasks in those days. So there I was in the goal, my defense was in front of me, blocking my view, when a puck came right at me like a bullet at close range and hit me in the face. I went down in a pool of blood. They took me out and cleaned up the ice. I let the team doctor stitch me up, and then, being raised by my Christian Scientist mother, I tried to get back in the game using mind over body, but I just couldn't.

That was on a Saturday, and on Wednesday I had a meeting in Cleveland with my faculty advisors. By this time Dr. Allen had replaced the frail Dr. Robinson as department head. But first I was on Bob Wiley's Monday night radio sports show, and Bob said, "You're gruesome. I'm putting you in the hospital." So he took me to the hospital where I got some more stitches under my right eye. The Cleveland newspaper picked up this story. So when I walked into Dr. Allen's office for the meeting, he took one look at me and said, "Mr. Briggs, I read about you in the newspaper. I have to get you out of here. Dr. Harry must not see you like this. I'll cancel the meeting." And he did. Dr. Allen was always looking out for my best interests, sometimes more than I was. Before he left, Dr. Robinson had made Dr. Allen promise that he'd see me through the Ph.D. program. I was grateful for that.

Another thing that happened that spring had a long-term effect on my career. I was playing for the Akron Stars and, at the same time, managing the Arena. Right before the last game of the play off championship in Akron, I was already in my skates ready to take the ice when there was a knock on the door. The lady selling the refreshments for the concession said she couldn't get the concession door open because the concessions manager had been drunk and failed to come in and unlock it. This was a dirty little concession run by Sportservice, a huge national company based in Buffalo with which we had a contract. In any case, concessions were big money and the stands were full. There was going to be trouble without the concessions sales. So I took my skates off and came out and tried various doors and methods and couldn't get in. So I finally found a hefty guy and asked him if he could break the door down. He did, and I went back and put my skates on again and went out and played the game. We lost the playoff championship. Was it because, instead of preparing mentally for the game, I'd been thinking too much about hot dogs?

It happened that the same two teams were again going to play for the Ohio State Amateur Athletic Association Hockey Championship in the Akron Arena. This was a bigger game than the one the week before. Before the championship game took place, I went to Buffalo to see the people at Sportservice. I wanted to get out of the contract with them and manage the concessions myself. I talked to a young guy at Sportservice about my plight, how I was a Ph.D. candidate and also a sports manager, and I needed to get a better handle on the concessions. The guy said he was himself working towards a master degree in Buffalo, and he understood. He said he couldn't let us out of the contract but he'd send me someone reliable to work the concessions for the state championship.

He went on to say, "Come work for us. You can have your pick of jobs. We need managers in San Diego, in Billings, Montana, or here in Buffalo." Buffalo is only 200 miles from Cleveland and long drives didn't bother me at all. I said, "I can be up there every other week." So I had an option for earning a living the next fall while pursuing my love of hockey. Going from being 50 miles away from my Ph.D. pursuit while in Akron to being 200 miles away while in Buffalo may have been a metaphor for distancing myself from my academic work, but I didn't think of it that way.

While I tried to keep up my relationship with Norma by visiting her in her performance locations, she had cooled on me. Actually the fire at my farm had changed things, and she ultimately informed me that she didn't want to wait for me to finish school. So she joined an international show, working in Hawaii, Australia, Singapore, and Japan—outside of my commuting range. That left me open to somebody or something new. We did apparently exchange contact information, as this was not the last time I'd see Norma.

Summer 1952: Gloria

That lady from the main office of the Easter Seals organization in Chicago—did she ever know what she was doing! She was always positive and the most diplomatic person. She said, "We just started a camp in Colorado and the first year management wasn't so good. I want you to come as director and get it going strong." She was offering a full time, year round job with an office. I'd be hiring people. The camp was in the mountains; I love the mountains. So I went to Stonehenge Handicamp—my second time to be the second director of a camp. And I had the same success there as I'd had in Cleveland.

It was at Stonehenge that I hired Gloria Bass, a student majoring in speech therapy. She was great with the kids; that young lady was absolutely dedicated to those kids. My dad came to Colorado to see me once that summer. I was glad to have him see me getting along so well in the job with the kids and with Gloria.

She was 11 years younger than I was, but we fell in love. She wanted me to stay in Colorado in that full-time job after the summer ended. I wanted to stay but staying wasn't that simple.

I didn't want to take a year round job far away from Cleveland because of my hopes of getting my Ph.D. If I stayed with Gloria in Colorado, I wouldn't get my Ph.D. So she went back to school and I went back to school, but we were in touch and in love and planned to be together soon.

I only had to work on my thesis this coming school year. Dr. Allen was now in charge, offering me support in contrast to Dr. Harry's continued skepticism. I had my meetings with them but my actual work on the thesis wasn't going too well. Dr. Allen kept telling me that I wasn't making sufficient progress.

Managing Buffalo: Fall 1952-Spring 1953

After camp in Colorado, I'd had to decide where I'd go to be working on my Ph.D. and at the same time have a job that I enjoyed, that earned me some money, and preferably kept me or led me on a career path. I wasn't actually thinking all that; I was just solving little dilemmas one after the other, and things worked out pretty well.

To be near enough to Western Reserve to check in with my advisors often and to pursue the topic of my thesis, as well as to play hockey and work, Akron seemed a good choice. I'd had as much fun with the Akron Stars as I've ever had anywhere and managing the Iceland Arena was a reasonable job, but it was a dirty little town.

Or I could go with the Buffalo Hockey Club, a team in the American Hockey League. How I'd gotten in with the concessions management outfit there the previous spring was one of those unpredictable little events that you can't plan but you have to know it when you see it, and I saw it.

Sportservice had concession units in almost two thousand venues. They owned some of the buildings; they owned some of the teams, as they still do. For example, they owned the magnificent new baseball stadium in Cleveland, home of the Indians. They named it Jacobs Field after Louis Jacobs, my boss at Sportservice in Buffalo. They also controlled concessions, sports facilities and the Convention Center in Cleveland. Today Sportservice owns the Boston Bruins and the concessions at the Boston Garden in my old stomping ground.

Louis Jacobs had bought the Buffalo Hockey Club several years before I took the job there. He also had the food concessions at the War Memorial Auditorium and the baseball park. In Buffalo, he bought the Hockey Club to use as the promotional arm of Sportservice in Buffalo; in other words, in addition to having a franchise in the American League, the Hockey Club promoted virtually every event that used the War Memorial. It had a monopoly—boxing, wrestling, hockey, a sports show, a flower show, RV show, home show, professional tennis, Ice Capades, Ice Follies, Holiday on Ice, the circus, indoor track meets. Then the Hockey Club, acting for Sportservice, bought the Buffalo Bills and their baseball park.

The Buffalo Hockey Club had a large wing of the Sportservice home office. The ticket office for all the events was at the Buffalo Hockey Club at North Delaware Avenue. This caused Sportservice ultimately to be called Delaware North, its current name. The company used me to go to corporations to sell season tickets or have special nights at individual promotional events. They also used me in PR. I would escort good-looking Ice Capades skaters to do TV shows. This meant that I got to know the best-known TV and radio people. And because of this job, for the first time, I could buy a new car, a great little maroon Studebaker convertible.

The company had treated me very well, but, as time went on, I wanted to be my own person and that would be impossible with Sportservice. I'd worked hard and learned a lot about concessions, promotions, and PR, all of which I would need in the not so distant future. In the meantime, there was not much time to work on my thesis.

On the Ice with Gloria

When I joined the Buffalo Hockey Club, I told them I would need a month off before and during the Christmas holidays in order to do two weeks training at the Naval Amphibious training facility in San Diego. They agreed. This gave Gloria something specific to plan for.

Gloria was still in school in Denver, but her family's home was in Houston. So in early December, I left for San Diego by way of Denver. I arrived in Denver, put on my Marine Corps uniform, which she had never seen before. We went to dinner in one of our favorite spots up in the mountains. She rather enjoyed the military approach. The next day she left for her family's home in Houston, and I took off for San Diego. After the two weeks in San Diego, I left for Houston and was on the road Christmas Day. The weather was terrible in the mountains and even in Texas. I arrived in Houston several days after Christmas and the two ladies, Gloria and her mother, were very pleased to see me. I'm sure Mrs. Bass believed that I would be her son-in-law, although I wasn't that much younger than she. She treated me wonderfully.

The first day was great, but then I suggested we go to an ice arena not too far away. At this point Gloria's attitude changed. I had never seen her in this mood. Her mother was very upset about that. Anyway, we finally went to the ice rink, where Gloria refused to go on the ice. She was simply impossible. There was a group of high school kids working out on the ice, and I asked if I could join them. So I grabbed a stick and went out on the ice and buzzed around with the kids. They thought it was great, to play with an American Hockey League player. I guess I was showing off, but I managed to impress the youngsters and I left feeling pretty good.

Gloria, however, continued to be hostile and the night before I was to leave, Mrs. Bass told me what the trouble was: Since Gloria knew that Norma had been a professional skater, and she felt inferior in comparison to Norma and didn't want to skate with me. I explained to her that I'd much prefer to teach her to skate than to be competitive with her as I'd often been with Norma. Gloria apologized for her behavior then. I thought Gloria was being childish—she was young—and I wondered how that would play out if we were married. Anyway, we patched it up and I left for Buffalo in a good mood.

Back East

Several weeks after my return to Buffalo, I flew to Cambridge to see my dad and drove to Rockport to see Aunt Letitia. I told them both I was in love with Gloria and that we'd probably be married, which Aunt Letitia duly noted in her diary.

In March, Gloria flew east to visit me during her spring break. I picked her up at the Buffalo airport in the evening, and we drove the 500 miles to Rockport, arriving at 6 o'clock in the morning. I then left her there with Aunt Letitia and drove back to Buffalo because they needed me for an important PR project. After two days in Buffalo, I returned to Rockport. In the meantime, Aunt Letitia showed Gloria around Cape Ann and generally entertained her, writing in her diary that Gloria was "a pretty, gentle girl." I was glad she had Aunt Letitia's approval, as she had my dad's.

When I got back, I took Gloria up into the White Mountains of New Hampshire to prove that we had mountains in the East. It was on this trip that she told me she had made up her mind about our future. She said, "I want to be married, I want kids." I said, "You'll have to wait. Can't you wait a year?" I was thinking about the time I'd take to finish my Ph.D. She said no, if I loved her, we'd get married that summer. I insisted I needed to finish my education first. She said she'd quit school and work to support us both until I got my Ph.D. I said, "No, I have to do this on my own." Having a woman support me was against my principles. While I hedged on this idea a few years later, I basically believed that a man should provide the money and the security the way the good Lord planned it, while the woman runs the household and is queen of the castle. World War II collapsed that way of life. We argued about this the whole trip to the mountains. Gloria went away saying, if I wouldn't marry her, she'd find a man who really wanted to be with her. She flew back to the University of Denver, where she was studying speech therapy, and soon was dating someone else. I was in despair.

Over the 1952-53 hockey season, I'd grown to dislike my job with Buffalo Sportservice, a national organization, which was and is the biggest sports facilities and concessions business in the world, owned by Louis Jacobs. Even though sometimes it seemed like a mistake to have taken this job, at the same time, I learned a lot about running concessions; sporting events and concessions were, in the coming years, to become an even bigger part of my life.

Because at the most immediate level I wanted to get out of the Buffalo deal, I thought of going east nearer my dad and the hockey leagues where I was known. Bates College in Lewiston, Maine, not only had the Dean of Students position open, but it had a pretty good hockey program and, of course, I pictured myself becoming a hockey coach there, too. I didn't get the job at Bates, but my mind was beginning to take me back to New England.

In June, reports came that Our Ma was not at all well. Aunt Letitia diagnosed it from a distance as her distress over my father's impending marriage to Alice. When the family started gathering, as Our Ma became seriously ill, she wrote in her diary, "But I believe that Harry's marriage may be the cause of this breakdown." Virginia and her son Thomas Jr. went down to Connecticut to see her. Two weeks later, Aunt Letitia and Letitia did the same. Aunt Letitia reported that Our Ma did not come down the stairs.

My father and Alice married quietly in August. After the wedding, Our Ma, in fact, recovered and lived twelve more years in quite good health until she fell on those same

Chapter 13

Boston Again, Norma Again, Gloria Again

Still reeling from losing Gloria, I began to think of how I could go far away to get my head together, as I often did when I was in despair or confusion. A faraway adventure promised to get me back on track. Early in 1954 I found a job opening for a civilian athletic consultant for the US military in Europe, and I applied and waited. And waited. I learned that the FBI called on Mrs. Harris, in whose house I lived when in Cleveland, to check on my character, all for a GS 3 level job.

In the meantime, Gloria went hiking in the mountains with the guy she was dating. She loved the mountains; maybe this guy didn't. She remembered how much I loved the mountains, she told me later, and she started thinking about me. She wasn't over me. So she agreed to give me one more chance.

She came to Cleveland to spend a week in late summer with me, while I finished up my work towards the Ph.D. I was still with the Buffalo Hockey Club going to Western Reserve one day every other week. Gloria said that she was coming for a week, so I took leave from the Hockey Club and met her in Cleveland. For the rest of the week, we went to Lake Chautauqua in New York, a beautiful resort area. While we were in a cabin there, she slept inside in the bed, and I slept on the porch for the sake of propriety. She was still very young and had been trying to hold out until marriage.

While Gloria and I were at Lake Chautauqua, we saw newspaper coverage of a swim by the head of physical education at New York University. Three times that summer, he'd tried to swim from Sandusky, Ohio, to Pelee Point, Ontario, on Lake Erie. That 32-mile swim had been tried and tried many times over years. Many swims had been tried unsuccessfully, for example, from Niagara Falls to Toronto on Lake Ontario, which is about 30 miles. At that time people figured that one couldn't be done. This fellow had just failed at his third attempt to swim Lake Erie. I told Gloria, "I can do this." She said, "No, you can't." That was before I'd tried to swim anything.

To show her what a good swimmer I was, I told her I'd swim across Lake Chautauqua, which was ten miles long and only about a mile across. So we got a boat and I swam across Chautauqua, and it was tough. That mile was hard, very hard, because I hadn't been swimming recently, but I acted as if it were easy. A guy on the shore said to his little girl, "How would you like to do that?" Showing off, I said, "Maybe I'll swim back." And I was hoping Gloria would say, "No, you ride back with me." She did, and I was pleased to accept that offer.

Then I told Gloria, "I'm going to do Erie." When I say I'm going to do something, I intend to do it. As with my Ph.D., it was just a matter of time.

At the end of that summer, I hadn't made as much progress on my thesis as I'd hoped. Gloria had given up on me marrying her any time soon, and she stuck to her ultimatum. When I took her to the railroad station, I said, "I guess this is goodbye, and I won't see you again," and she said it was. Goodbye.

Not long after this farewell, I left Buffalo for good. I loved Gloria so much. I tried hard to forget her, but it was hard.

My Father and Alice

In early September 1953, soon after my father's wedding to Alice in late August, I was in Rockport having dinner at Aunt Letitia's with my dad and Alice as well as my sister Virginia, her husband Tom Lavender, and Aunt Letitia's friends Carl and Ruth Swanson, whom I never did like. It was a nice dinner like all the many dinners my

aunt's long time housekeeper Mary Baker had served us over the decades. After dinner, we were sitting around the living room and Virginia had something she wanted to get off her chest so she started an attack on Alice about what she called an intrusion into our family. She questioned Alice's motives. She said Alice wasn't good enough for her dad. It was terrible. I felt sorry for Alice. She must have been shocked and did nothing to defend herself.

I was equally shocked and disappointed that my father did not come to Alice's defense and tell Virginia he would not tolerate her talking that way. I thought, *Won't someone help this woman?* Not Aunt Letitia who was the hostess. Not my Dad, who was her husband. So I finally said to Alice, "I think we need to get out of there." Alice and I got in my car and we drove around Cape Ann, which is very picturesque, a tourist destination, for about two hours.

Mary Baker, Aunt Letitia's housekeeper for many years until Aunt Letitia died in 1964, was like part of my family. She fed me many meals and cared for me.

I said to Alice, "I'm really embarrassed about my family. Please forgive us." I don't know why my Aunt Letitia didn't stick up for her even if she didn't like her because Virginia's tirade was so rude. I guess my dad was afraid Aunt Letitia wouldn't like it if he argued with Virginia. I'll always be sad that my dad did nothing to defend his wife.

Alice said, "I love your dad but I can see that I'm not popular with your family." I told her the situation wouldn't change and Dad would have to distance himself from the family. Alice really liked me. I didn't care if I liked her or not if she made my father happy.

All Aunt Letitia said about that incident in her diary was, "A very strained evening."

In November, when I was back in Rockport, Aunt Letitia had a long talk with me in which she tried to make me understand Virginia's point of view. Regardless of her view, my sister's disrespect was way out of bounds. I was on Alice's side because she was making our father happy.

Hockey Season 1953-1954

I'd come to Boston because I'd wanted to get out of the Buffalo deal. I soon got a job as assistant manager of the Boston Arena.

How I did I walk into that job? Clark Hodder, who had been my mentor when I was at Tufts and was then the coach of the Harvard hockey club, was now a big Republican supporter and so had been appointed manager of the Boston Arena Authority by Republican Governor Leverett Saltonstall. Hodder was a coach by trade, not a facility manager. When I approached him, he said to me, "I suppose you know how to make ice?" and I said, "Absolutely." Hodder didn't know how to do anything with the facility himself but he was a big name in hockey. So I did all the work. Pretty soon Hodder had a heart attack and couldn't continue in his job, so I went from Assistant Manager to Acting Manager of the Boston Arena to finish the season.

In Boston, I didn't live with my father because, when he had married, he converted his two bedrooms into one larger one. He and Alice wanted the place to themselves. When I went to work at the Arena, I asked permission to live in a room in the loft of the facility. I threw down a mattress there, and that was my home. My dad came down to visit me sometimes but he couldn't get up the ladder to my loft. It was kind of funny. My dad and I had become very close, and I will be eternally grateful for that.

To have the Boston pro hockey team, the Bruins, train at the Arena would be a step forward for us. I contacted an old friend in the Bruins' front office, who had preceded me in Tilton School hockey and later at Tufts, a very talented guy. We both ended up in the Tilton School Sports Hall of Fame. He put me in touch with Herb Ralby.

Herb had worked for the Boston papers and was sufficiently experienced to hold down the public relations job for the Bruins. I had known him when I was at Tufts. Herb told me that the Bruins needed a place to work out, but the Boston Bruins players and fans were largely Irish and Jewish, that is, Democrats. Herb knew the Arena was Republican run so he didn't expect he could get much space with us. I told him, "Don't worry, I'll make it work." If the Bruins called and asked if they could work out there at 4 pm, I said, "Absolutely." Then I'd change the time of some high school, because the Bruins, as a pro team, took precedence over a high school.

But we had plenty of high school games there and several high school leagues. When a new league was formed south of Boston, they wanted to have their games at the Arena. So I gave them 7 to 9 Friday night. The very first time the South Shore League showed up, I had a couple of premier referees working the games to be sure we got a good start; one was Smokey Kelleher and the other one's name I forgot. For years Smokey had officiated the Bruins' games as well as numerous high school and college games. He was a quality ref. Pretty soon the games were in full swing and the crowd started shouting obscenities at the refs. The fans were crowding at the railing and about to riot. I was in the press box with my dad. He said, "This could really be trouble. Somebody's going to get hurt." I grabbed a bullhorn and went down there. I told them loud and clear, "I'm the boss here; I run this place. If you don't settle down, you're going to ruin hockey for South Boston forever. So back off...." I started walking towards them, backing them up and backing them up, and I got them back in their seats.

Dad said, "How did you do that?" I said, "With a little bit of luck." He said, "That was wonderful." He was so proud. Dad and I had some good times together, and that was one of them.

There was a restaurant in the building where Dad and Alice lived, and they used to go down there and eat and I'd join them occasionally. One time we were down there and Smokey Kelleher and his buddy came in and spoke to me. They'd thrown me off the ice a few times when I was a player and also as a coach, so we knew each other. My father had followed hockey enthusiastically for many years, but he'd never met these refs. Smokey went up to my dad and said, "Are you Mr. Briggs?" And he went on to say, "I wanted to tell you that your son is really doing great things for hockey in Boston." My dad practically cried he was so proud.

So here I was in a world I loved, but I had a promise to keep so in the spring 1954, at the end of the hockey season in Boston, I began to go back and forth between Boston and Cleveland determined to give my thesis three months of concentrated hard work. And I did. I worked at Aunt Letitia's house in Rockport, for days or even a week at a time, returned to

On one of my many visits to Aunt Letitia's home in Rockport, Massachusetts, I posed with her Pekinese, Honey, about 1954 when I was finishing up my Ph.D.

Cleveland, worked some more there, back and forth through mid June. I was finally focused.

Norma Again

One day there was a knock at the door of Mrs. Harris's house in Cleveland where I lived off and on. I opened it and there was Norma Maxwell back in town. She'd just given up her skating job that had taken her around the world as far as Japan and Australia. She'd had a boyfriend but they'd just split so she was looking me up. We started dating again. Two weeks later I got a letter from Gloria saying she wanted me back. So it was goodbye Norma, hello again Gloria.

I finished my thesis early that summer of 1954 and had to defend it before a committee. Dr. Harry still didn't like me and didn't take my work seriously, so I was worried about my prospects. After I'd defended my thesis for four grueling hours, I went out of the room while the faculty discussed whether they'd accept my thesis. Dr. Allen found me afterwards and said, "I can't shake your hand now because it's not official, but you made it." I ran all the way to a telephone booth and called my dad at the bank. The woman who answered the phone recognized my voice, and said, "All right, Junior, I'll get your dad." Dad came to the phone. I told him I'd made it. I cried and he cried. I'm crying now as I'm telling this. It was the culmination of eight years of trying to keep my promise to my mother, and I'd done it.

On July 2, I had my degree.

Summer 1954

Three great things happened to me in early summer of 1954. First, I got my PhD. Second, after long months of waiting, I got the job in Europe, the one I applied for, in part, to help me get over Gloria. Third, Gloria called and said she'd broken up with her boyfriend John and she had always wanted me. She said, "I really miss you. Can we start over where we left off?" I said, "Absolutely! And I have a job in Europe!" She'd always wanted to go to Europe. It was perfect. Now that I had my Ph.D. and a job, I was ready to marry. Europe could be our honeymoon. She said, "Come to Denver right away!"

In a couple weeks, however, I had to go for two weeks training with the Marine Reserves, and settle a few things in Boston, so I said I'd be in Denver with her in a month. When I got out to Colorado, she said she'd changed her mind again. Her mother, who liked me a lot, couldn't believe it! Neither could I. Let me tell you, I was depressed.

Gloria lived with a lady in Denver named Mrs. Billings, whom I had hired as a cook at Stonehenge Handicamp. She knew all about our romance and was distressed to see it end, particularly after I had driven all the way out to Denver. After Gloria said she'd changed her mind, I drove Mrs. Billings up to Wyoming where she had a cabin in the mountains. I spent several days with Mrs. Billings, who was lonely in her old age. I asked her, if I went back to Denver to try again with Gloria, did she think I had a chance. She said it might be worth a try, so I drove the 400 miles back to Denver and I found Gloria at Mrs. Billings' house. I asked Gloria to go back up into the mountains with me. The mountains had always been a special connection for us. She came with me but to no avail. I finally gave up and took her back to Denver.

When I left her in Denver for the very last time, she told me she loved me and that letting me go was a decision she'd probably always regret making. To say I was upset would be a gross understatement. The experience had taken a toll on me physically, and a few miles into my trip home I became ill. I stopped the car, curled up in the back seat of my car and slept for ten hours. When I woke up, I felt better. Nevertheless, the 1500-mile trip back to Boston was not very pleasant.

Looking back on this experience with Gloria now, I suspect she was pregnant and tried to get me back right away, then, seeing I was slow to get there, she returned to her boyfriend.

Gloria ended up marrying John that August. Aunt Letitia mentioned several times in her diary how depressed I seemed at the time of her wedding. I had real trouble getting over Gloria, but Europe lay ahead. I packed my bags at Aunt Letitia's house and cleared out a space in her garage to leave my car. She took me to the train station the evening of September 24 to board a train to New York and begin my journey to Frankfort, Germany.

Between my train trip to New York and boarding my ship to Frankfort, I managed to contact Norma Maxwell, who was working in Manhattan. I found her at Ohrbach's, an upscale store on Fifth Avenue next to Lord & Taylor. She'd been hired to paint murals on the walls of the store's first floor. When I walked in, there she was standing on a scaffold. We were really pleased to see each other, but we only had few minutes together. That was my last contact with Norma. She was an exceptionally talented lady. I'm sure she did well.

Chapter 14

Europe and My First Marathon Swim

Besides my heartbreak, what prompted me to sign up for a two-year job as a recreation consultant with the Army in Germany was my idea that now was my chance to become a long distance swimmer. It was a ridiculous concept because I had no idea how hard it was to do that. I thought it wouldn't be that difficult. The only experience I had was the two summers I'd spent on Pleasant Lake in New Hampshire, the few hundred yards I swam at Saipan as a trial for swimming to Tinian, and the mile across Lake Chautauqua to impress Gloria.

I was assigned as a civilian employee to the Special Services of the USAR-EUR, the US Army in Europe. The USAR-EUR headquarters was in Heidelberg and its Special Services headquarters were in Nuremberg, where I went for two weeks of training. I had a little office in the Palace of Justice, where Hermann Goering and other high-ranking Nazis were tried by military tribunal after the war. After that was over, the U.S. Army kept the Palace of Justice. It was fun for me to have a little office in this castle-like building for two weeks.

I soon learned, as I had noted in Puerto Rico, that working for the Army as a civilian GS-3 is like being a Chinese coolie. I was nobody. The Captain in the athletics office at Leighton Barracks in Wurzburg, where I'd been assigned after my training, heard I was coming to help. He said, "I don't need help. Stay over there in your office and mind your own business."

Nevertheless, I was always looking for useful things I could do for our guys in uniform, and I found, devised, or was occasionally called to do various things from time to time. For example, a black guy from New Orleans, Charlie Joseph, who after his service became the sixth ranked middleweight boxer in the nation, approached me about setting up a boxing program. I said I'd like to, but when I took the idea to the Captain he didn't want any such thing. He said something like, "Briggs, I told you to mind your own business. I'm retiring in a few months and I don't want to be bothered before then."

Once I got called to Frankfort to help organize a sports event just before Christmas. A black tie dinner was held to which the Argentine ambassador was invited. He wanted an escort for his daughter and inquired at the officers' barracks for a volunteer. There were no takers there so I was asked to go. I went to the dinner with the ambassador and his daughter who was kind of cute. For most of my assignments, there was some fun involved.

However, the assignments were spasmodic, and I often ended up just driving around Europe and enjoying myself. So, to fill the time and supplement my meager income, I turned to academics; I got a part time teaching job at an extension of the University of Maryland five miles away at Kitzingen.

When Special Services called me back to Nuremberg, I decided to work out with the Nuremberg ice hockey team in the Germany Hockey League. I went out on the ice and knocked a few people down. They weren't used to that American style of hockey, so they asked if I would teach them our kind of checking. I could have put together a USA hockey team that could challenge Russia, where the national hockey team was also a military program. I presented my plan. "We don't want hockey, Briggs," said my superiors in the USAR-EUR Athletics Office.

So I did what I could where I could. I organized a boxing tournament. I ran a USAR-EUR ladies' basketball tournament in which the Marine Corps had a team, which didn't do very well.

I traveled around on weekends. I went to remote Andorra, for example, because Richard Halliburton had been there when the roads were all dirt. In my youth I'd read this adventurer's famous book, *The Royal Road to Romance*, and fancied myself following in his footsteps. I was also chalking up my own adventures. When I traveled through East Germany to get to Berlin, I was really worried when the train stopped and the commies wanted to see my papers. However, worry didn't keep me from pushing my luck. I once walked down the main street of East Berlin and then slipped off on a side street and came back to West Berlin, all just to say I was in East Berlin during that period. Richard Halliburton would have been proud.

All this time, I was toying with the idea of trying to swim the English Channel. I was in my mid 30s and I knew my hockey days were numbered as a player. Hockey requires youthful reflexes, especially in goal. I preferred right wing, but probably played in goal more often. That puck in the face back in Akron was a sort of warning. I wanted to stay active so I said now's the time to try that long distance swimming. I thought the English Channel was the thing to do. I'd taken this job in Europe partially to find out what you have to do to swim the Channel. I figured you don't have to be an exceptional swimmer. It only takes 14 or 15 hours. So I went over to Calais and looked into it. I had no credentials, just an idea. My main claim to fame was I'd met Gertrude Ederle. I hadn't tried a swim of any significant distance ever.

I was very naïve. I found you couldn't just do the Channel, you had to have money to hire guide boats and there was paperwork to get permission; not just anybody is allowed to do it. The water was cold, too, and the feat would require a lot of training, which would cost money for lodging, food, and training facilities. I found that to get the right kind of support it would cost $50,000 to make the attempt.

I also didn't know how tough the swim itself was. I found that you have to have a good escort who knows the currents. The fastest you can swim over a long period of time is not over two miles an hour. And if you do your best at 2 miles an hour, and you're against a current going 3 miles an hour, you swim for an hour and you've lost a mile. So you have to know the currents and you can't go all the way with a favorable current, so the first thing you do is start out on an outgoing tide and then in an hour, if you have it right, you could be 7 or 8 miles out there. I saw on TV a Channel swimmer, who got within a half mile of the English coast and the tide had turned. An hour later, he was a mile and a half from the shore, and after that he was so far out the only way he could possibly make it was to stay afloat till the next incoming tide. Even so, the next time the tide came in, the necessary current might not be exactly in that area.

How many people have crossed the Channel? More than 800 people, and now it's a race to see who can do it the fastest. If you don't have the right guidance, you don't have a chance in the world. When I learned what the Channel was all about, I was discouraged.

But I hadn't given up. By summer, the German hockey league season was over, and I quit my job with the USAR-EUR and took a full time position with the University of Maryland. I was sent to teach political science at the Air Force base in Chateauroux, France. I found the French didn't like Americans at all. Certainly, in the summer of 1955, we were not popular in Chateauroux.

In late June, I went into Paris looking for information about a Channel swim. I had no contacts, so I walked into the offices of the Paris edition of the New York *Herald Tribune* and asked for the sports editor. It happened that the sports editor was a young fellow from Boston University, and we found we had a lot in common. We went for a long walk and talked a long time, and, based on that talk, he wrote a piece about my determination for his paper. He said he couldn't help me with the Channel. There was a group of captains who had taken over guiding swimmers across and these captains charge a lot. But he had an idea: The *Herald Tribune* had run a story on a French fishing boat with three men aboard that capsized between Corsica and Sardinia. When the men were in the water, a shark took a bite out of one of them, and his leg had to be amputated. We found there had been many unsuccessful attempts to go from Corsica to Sardinia across the Strait of Bonifacio. The editor said, "Even if you are good, you have no resume. But if you go down there and make that swim, I'll make sure you get wire service coverage." So I committed to do this and he was behind me all the way. A student named Phil Proctor at the University of Maryland at Chateauroux, a big good-looking tennis player, wanted to go along on this venture. He was from California, a nice young fellow, so he was in.

I started to work out. I hadn't swum a mile since Chautauqua. I was huffing and puffing after a quarter mile, and I thought, *Gee, why did I ever think of doing this?* And I began to put some distances together and get some pacing and I made a 3-mile swim several times on a nice lake at Chateauroux. I got some helpful publicity for that swimming.

The Matterhorn

Two weeks before I tackled the Strait of Bonifacio, however, I made a big mistake. I decided I'd toughen up my legs—and this was ridiculous—I'd go climb the Matterhorn, the almost 15,000 foot high Alpine peak on the border between Switzerland and Italy. There was another reason I had this idea; Richard Halliburton had done this. Climbing the Matterhorn was one of the adventures he described in the book that had long inspired me, and I wanted that under my belt. As for swims, Halliburton had crossed the Hellespont, but that was no more than a mile across, so I was going to best him in the swimming department.

I was guided up the mountain by a professional guide from Switzerland. We walked the 13 miles from Zurmatt to the base camp, where we spent the night. The base camp had a few crawl-in compartments in addition to the main room for eating and discussing one's mountain exploits. We were up early the next morning. My guide, who had been a member of the Olympic ski team, gave me instructions, such as, "Don't make a move until I climb up ahead and secure myself." He would then hold the rope to which I was attached below. Only then could I move. You can bet I promised to follow all his directions.

The climb up the steep, snow-capped mountain was thrilling and terrifying. The ascent to the peak took two hours and the descent to the base camp again took four hours, then the 13 miles back to Zurmatt. I was satisfied and proud that I had done it. However, it was the worse thing I could have done before a swim. It tightened up my muscles badly. My toenails were black from coming down the 13 miles from the base camp to Zurmatt. That adventure practically crippled me. Dumb, dumb, dumb, but what did I know.

You see, I never had a coach or a teacher like kids today. Everything I learned I got from experience. Climbing the Matterhorn before a 16-mile swim I learned was not a good idea. Wiser, I hobbled on.

The Strait of Bonifacio

Two weeks later, Phil and I headed down to Corsica, a French province. Was that ever primitive! We flew into the capital city Ajacio, a dirty little city, the only city really, about 75 miles from the sea. Napoleon was born there. Except for Ajacio, the island looked totally undeveloped, just as described in "The Count of Monte Cristo." We got on a 20-year-old bus with people and chickens and rode to Bonifacio, a town on the Strait of Bonifacio where high cliffs drop straight down into the sea.

Phil thought this whole thing was quite the adventure. We had a game plan. We knew there were sharks in the Strait, and we tried to get a gun but couldn't. Instead, we had a long stick with a knife on it. We needed an escort. We arranged for one finally, an old fellow who had a really old sailboat, a small one, 16 feet long, which he claimed was the smallest boat that had ever crossed the Atlantic. He was a world-class adventurer without any money. I asked him to escort us in his motorboat. He agreed. I didn't have much money and so I asked, "How much?" He hesitated and I said, "How about $25?" and he jumped at it. It was big money to him.

I remembered the article about the fishermen and a photo of the capsized boat and the shark that got the guy's leg. So we had a plan: The old man would be driving the boat while Phil would be looking for sharks. If one appeared, I'd retreat but wasn't going to be hauled up on the boat. I was going to swim to the boat and get my back up against the boat while Phil was going to ram the spear down the shark's throat. That was the best thing we could figure. We also had a shark repellant that the Air Force used; it was purple and left a purple wake. Years later I heard that it was proved not only that it doesn't work but it actually attracts sharks.

So the next day we started out from a spot on the shore a little way from town. The local townspeople knew we were going to do the 16-mile swim and they were very interested, but they didn't come to see us off because the shore is lined with huge cliffs and there was no room on the shore for spectators. As for proof that we had made the swim across the Strait, we'd taken care of that. There was a lighthouse in Sardinia and we notified the keeper that we were coming, and he could see our arrival.

We did the first three miles easy enough as in practice in France, but I began to weaken at five or six miles. I thought I couldn't finish. See, I didn't know how far you could go even when you're tired. I didn't know what it was like to be tired. Half way across I was extremely tired and I kept on going. Then I seemed to have a second wind at about eight miles, five miles further than I had ever been in my life.

Just then, the old man's engine conked out. I had a decision to make: to give up and lose my resume or go without escort. So I decided to keep on going. I tried not to think about sharks; I had to think about nothing. A mile from shore Phil and the old man caught up with me. They'd got the engine going. Boy, was I glad to see them. But there was only a mile to go.

Nearer the shore, there were huge swells, not waves, big and long swells, and they didn't crash on rocks, they just slid a couple feet up on the rocks and then they slipped off. Finally, one swell just planted me on the rocks on my feet. As in Corsica, the cliffs in Sardinia came down to the sea. A couple guys on the cliffs were dancing and waving, the lighthouse keepers! They wired back to Bonifacio that we'd made it.

Upon our return to Bonifacio, a lot of people had gathered to greet us. They threw a party in a beer hall in the hotel and the talk was all about the swim. I was totally whipped and had gone straight to my room but about midnight I finally had to come down and have a few beers with them. It was great fun. The celebration lasted until dawn.

So that was the first swim, my first credential as a long distance swimmer. The editor in Paris did a great job for me. He contacted a Herald Tribune stringer in a little town half way between Bonifacio and Ajaccio—dirt streets, no paving but a town. The stringer there came aboard the bus and took pictures. An article with photos hit all the wire services including AP, UPI, and INS.

I heard later that an article with the picture of me and of the cliffs of Bonifacio appeared in the Boston paper. The headline called me "Swimming Savant." My dad didn't know anything about this adventure. I'd written him that I was returning home in a few weeks after "a little swim." He didn't have the faintest idea I was going to do something like this; he didn't even know I had a desire to do it. He was at his desk at the bank when one of the guys came to him with the paper saying, "Have you seen this?" My dad said, "My god, crazy kid." He couldn't quite figure me out.

Music and Romance

Of course, I didn't spend a year in Europe without indulging in romance and music. In France after the war, women were desperate for male companionship, and I was invited home for dinner by women I'd barely met, many hoping for a long-term partner to help them manage financially. Music poured out of clubs frequented by locals and servicemen. At Chateauroux I used to go down to the USO to listen to jazz. I even asked if I could play with the band and my clarinet got a little action. The Ida Tunis Quartet used to perform there, a very good group that sang sultry ballads. Ida Tunis was a nice looking Scottish singer, and we hit it off.

At that time, I was receiving publicity in Chateauroux for my swimming. Ida asked me if she could come with me for some of my three-mile training swims. She'd sit on the boat sunning herself. We held hands a few times. We really liked each other, but I wasn't pushing the relationship.

After my swim across Bonifacio Strait, I returned to Chateauroux and went down to the USO. I stood just inside the door at the other end of the dance floor, listening to her sing, and I waited. When she saw me, she turned to the band and told them what to play. Then she looked straight across the room at me and sang "I've Got a Crush on You," a song Frank Sinatra used to sing. So we were off and running. I was soon feeling serious about Ida.

All too soon after my return, Ida's mother came down to the USO and yanked her out of there, and she was gone. I never saw or heard from her again. You might say I was unlucky in love.

At this point, I'd decided the Channel had already been done, and being the first to swim a body of water was a lot more satisfying. I decided, as I had predicted to Gloria once before, that I'd be the first person to swim across Lake Erie.

Alternately, I thought, *Don't be such a wise guy, you had a hard time doing the sixteen miles*, and then I said to myself, *Who knows?* By then I realized I didn't know so much. You don't know how much stuff you have in your body until you go out and try it.

So I arrived back in the States in mid-August. I stayed in Boston mostly, visiting my father and Aunt Letitia. Then, in mid-September, I picked up my car and left for my new job in Kansas.

On the way, I went by Washington, DC, because I had another exciting idea.

In August 1955, I posed at Old Garden Beach, a small rocky beach down the hill from Aunt Letitia's house on Dean Road in Rockport, so my niece Letitia could take pictures that I might use for publicizing the swims I planned to make.

Chapter 15

Kansas and Lake Erie

On my way to the College of Emporia in Emporia, Kansas, to take on my job as Associate Professor and Admissions Director for the 1955-56 school year, I took a short detour. I was still in the Marine Reserves, and I had an idea that the Marine Corps might support my swim across Lake Erie as a public relations event, now that I had a record as a distance swimmer. So I went into the Marine headquarters in Washington. I talked to a Lieutenant Colonel there and showed him my clippings about my swim across the Bonifacio Strait a few weeks before. He seemed very interested. He said, "What do you want from us?" I said, "I'd like to swim across Lake Erie. I'm a Lieutenant in the Marine Reserves, and I'd like to have you sponsor me." He was interested in my proposal because it would bring positive attention to the Marine Corps. However, he didn't think his boss, a full Colonel, would be interested.

He was right. The Colonel was very nice, but said, "We're really not in the swimming business." I said, "I know that, Colonel, but I thought it wouldn't hurt to ask." He shrugged. "Sorry, better luck with somebody else."

So I went out to my job in Emporia figuring I had plenty of time to work on getting a sponsor for my swim the next summer. In the meantime, I began swimming every day as soon as I got to the college. The school was excited about my swimming role and looking forward to any publicity generated by my activities.

Emporia College was a Presbyterian school. When I was recruited for the job, I was told, "We'd like to say you are a Presbyterian." I said I wasn't and not to say any such thing. Soon after that, my hiring was announced in the local newspaper. The article said I was a member of the First Presbyterian Church in Emporia. When someone from this church arrived to welcome me, a very stiff fellow, he said, "We're expecting you…." Soon after, a more personable fellow came from the Second Presbyterian Church, saying, "Any chance you'd come to Second Presbyterian?" I said, "Absolutely. I won't be a member, but I'll come occasionally," and I went a few times.

The main job of Emporia College President Luther Sharpe was to raise funds for the college, and he was great at it. He went to almost every Presbyterian congregation in the state and usually got some money. I followed right behind him identifying prospective students and visiting them in their homes. I enjoyed this job. President Sharpe and I were a terrific team and we became close friends.

I'd been in my new job about two weeks when my office telephone rang. "Is this Lt. Briggs? I'm Colonel So and So. Do you remember me?" I said, "Yes sir." He said, "Are you still interested in that swim across Lake Erie?" I said, "Absolutely!"

The explanation for the Colonel's change of heart was that a young Marine recruit in basic training at Parris Island had just drowned during the 30-mile march through a swamp, the final challenge near the end of training. I can picture this because I've been through it. The recruit is struggling, he calls for help, the Sergeant says, "Come on, keep it up." The Sergeant was tough because he was supposed to be. Most of the time this works to turn these guys into the best amphibious landing troops in the world. But this time the Sergeant didn't realize what serious trouble the recruit was in. This guy gave out in the swamp, sank down in the water and drowned. It turned out the guy couldn't swim, not so unusual then, but not what you expect of a Marine. So there was a public outcry about the lack of preparedness of the recruits and the negligence of the Sergeant who would take a guy who couldn't swim into water with a full pack on and not pay sufficient attention to his cries for help. He said that because of the terrible publicity, people were thinking, is this what we do to our young men, kill them in the swamp?

The result of this disaster was the call I got from the Colonel in Washington who wasn't in the business of swimming. Anything the Marines could do to get the heat off, especially something in the water would be valuable. Well, I could sure show them a Marine can handle a challenge in water. So we began to design a PR campaign that would demonstrate that Marines do swim and that also met my need for a sponsor for swimming Lake Erie.

The Colonel asked me when I'd be able to do this swim and I told him in the summer when my school year was over and the water would be warmer.

So he said, "We have a battalion at Toledo, Ohio, at the western end of Lake Erie. When you're ready for active duty, take your training at the Toledo Battalion. We'll really be sending you over there to swim."

I said, "Maybe we can do something before that. I'm already scheduled to do two weeks Marine training at Coronado Beach at San Diego amphibious assault school during my holiday break. Maybe we could start this collaboration with a swim in San Diego." The Colonel got back to me saying that I could do the swim when my two weeks training was up and he'd get with the San Diego Chamber of Commerce to help plan and publicize a swim across the San Diego Harbor.

A Good Swim for a Seal

It was winter. A lot of people had gone across the San Diego harbor in summer when the water temperature goes up to 68. In my opinion, the west coast is too cold for swimming. I can swim easily in 68-degree water, but I don't do it for fun. However, nobody had ever crossed the harbor in winter because the temperature drops to about 60 degrees.

The thing that beats a long distance swimmer is loss of body heat. The water sucks the heat right out of you. Your body will eventually reach the temperature of the water in which it's immersed. Even in 85-degree water after a long time you lose body heat. Once you lose body heat you start to shiver. It's a terrible feeling to be shivering. You ask yourself, *Can I stand this for another 15 hours?* Usually the answer is *No. I can't stand it for even 3 more hours.* This is where you separate the men from the boys and the women from the girls. Most swims are not successful because of the loss of body heat.

In the long swims I made, this became the issue. Once my mind forced my body to go on even when my temp was down to 90 degrees. It's a mind game. One section of your mind says, *Keep on,* and the other says, *I don't care if you fail or not, I can't stand it any more.* After a few hours, that's the problem in anything under 70 degrees. I can do a long swim at 70 degrees, at 68 I can't. At San Diego it was 60 degrees but only five miles and I was strong.

When I went for my two weeks of Marine Corps amphibious training in San Diego, I had permission to work out in the pool there, and word got around about my plan for eventually swimming across Erie. The five-star Coronado Beach Hotel joined the effort to give me a local swim and provided me with a room for three days. Between the hotel, the Chamber of Commerce, and the Marines, they concocted a five-mile swim for me across the mouth of San Diego Harbor from Coronado Beach Hotel to Marpi Point on the North shore. I did my two weeks training for the Marines, and then I made my swim. Did I mention, the water was really cold? It was a tough swim and I had started to shiver, but I made it. The crew told me later that a harbor seal followed me most of the way across. It was just a Sunday afternoon stroll for the seal.

Two members of the media greeted me when I touched down, and came with us on the boat ride back, but most of the media was at the hotel. That night I went to a favorite bar in downtown San Diego where they knew about the swim from advance publicity and where I met up with a very nice young lady I'd met there before. We had a very good time.

The Marine Corps was pleased with my performance and got us some pretty good publicity. The Marines were probably now thinking, *He really might make it across Lake Erie.* The lake had been tried dozens and dozens of times without success, I told them, most recently by the Chairman of the physical education department at New York University. They asked, "What makes you think you can do it?" I said, "I just have a feeling I can." So they assigned me to two weeks at the Toledo Battalion for the following summer. I went back to Kansas for my job and was swimming in various pools—at the College, the YMCA in Wichita, the Kansas City Athletic Club—which I arranged to coincide with my recruiting trips. The Toledo Battalion Marine Reserves were going to give me all the support I needed, and they did. I began making long swims in preparation for the big one.

The toughest swim of my life may have been at Lake Kannapolis on April 1. That was April Fool's Day, and maybe that was a message for me. I'd arranged with the Corps of Engineers to swim just 1.5 miles along the levee. The press was there. We were getting a lot of publicity for Emporia College because there aren't a lot of distance swimmers in Kansas. I was unique in that state.

I hadn't expected the water to be so cold in April. It was in the low 50s. As soon as I put my foot in Lake Kannapolis, I thought, *What a mistake this is.* I went in anyway. I felt an initial shock and I said to myself, I don't think I'm going to do this. In maybe 20 seconds, however, my body adapted to it. It was a strange feeling, like I was in limbo. I wasn't cold, I wasn't hot, just nothing. I started to swim, thinking I'd better make this as fast as I can but not swim so fast that I don't make it all the way. It was a little over a mile; that's a long way to swim in cold water, I don't care what anyone says. And we made it, in 35 or 40 minutes. I did the distance at the fastest pace I'd ever done a swim. I wanted to get out of that water!

When I got to the end, there were quite a few people there. I have pictures of me coming out of the water, my favorite pictures. I looked very triumphant then.

Within minutes after I came out, they put me in a warm-up place with hot air blasting on me. I began to shake uncontrollably for about ten minutes. I think, just as you can't bring a sea diver up to the surface too fast or he gets the bends, similarly you can't warm somebody up too fast like that. I just shook for about 15 minutes. I've never had that happen before and I hope I never have it happen again. My mind was all right but I couldn't control my body. It was frightening.

The Ribbon Creek Incident

Something happened later that week that intensified my Marine sponsors' desire to publicize my feats in the water and everyone's attention.

On April 8, 1956, at Camp Lejeune, Staff Sergeant Matthew McKeon had marched a platoon of recruits into the swamp behind the rifle range at Parris Island at night. This was not the 30-mile march all recruits did near the end of training. This one was a disciplinary measure. The Sergeant said later he'd heard that this punishment had been done before in that location. However, he didn't realize how deep Ribbon Creek, the tidal creek that ran through the swamp, could get and how swift the current was. He did know, however, that some of the recruits couldn't swim. Panic broke out as recruits struggled in the fast flowing water to save themselves and others. When the march finished, six men were missing, all drowned; their bodies were recovered by divers two days later.

There was an even greater public outcry than on the last such occurrence about negligence on the part of the Sergeant, who was court martialed, and the lack of preparedness of the recruits. Even though their boots and gear would have been hindrance in any case, surely Marines, who were the ones to hit the beaches in amphibious landings, should all know how to swim and be able to handle a current. Immediately following the Ribbon Creek tragedy, the Marine commanders at Parris Island and Lejeune were changed, training was lengthened, and more oversight and transparency were built into the programs. Today Marine basic training includes combat-oriented swimming. The rest of the year, people frequently asked me what I thought about Sgt. McKeon and the Ribbon Creek incident. The need for a dramatic swimming feat by a Marine motivated the Marine Reserves to support me generously in my upcoming swim.

I waited about two weeks after my short swim at Lake Kannapolis, where I'd gotten the shakes, and I went back and swam the length of Lake Kannapolis, which was about five miles. It was kind of dumb to do that while it was still cold, but I wanted to conquer that lake that had caused me such a fright. Two weeks later, I went to Oklahoma, where I did a three-mile swim and, the next weekend, a five-miler, and the third weekend, a twelve-mile swim, the longest swim I'd ever made, on a lake right outside of Tulsa. As a Marine lieutenant, I got lots of valuable publicity there for me and for the Marines.

A man named Ed Wright owned a fishing camp in Oklahoma for which he wanted some publicity. He told me, "Forget Lake Erie. If you swim the thirty-mile length of the Ft. Gibson Reservoir, I'll give you $5000." That was a lot of money at that time, and I'd get nothing for swimming more than 30 miles across Erie. Nevertheless, I stayed with the Marine Corps plan, and ultimately it was the right decision.

I made one more swim to get ready for Lake Erie. That was on Grand Lake, 12,000 feet high in the mountains of Colorado. It's 5 miles long, gorgeous water, with 1000 feet of glaciers above the lake. Quite a few attempts had been made to swim across it without success. The water was 52 degrees in midsummer.

We'd announced we were going to do this swim about a month in advance. I got a letter from two elderly ladies, the Cairnes sisters, who had lived on the lake their whole lives. They said, "Please don't try it, Mr. Briggs. Too many people have tried it, and they ended up in bad shape." I wrote back, "I appreciate your concern but I really think I can do it. And I'm going to try." They wrote again, saying, "Please don't try it." I didn't mind their warning. It gave me even more incentive. After the San Diego Harbor and the Lake Kannapolis experiences, the cold of Grand Lake wasn't quite such a shock. The swim was very smooth and took about three and a half hours.

Quite a few people were there at the landing where I came out of the water. There were tourist attractions all around and a nice hotel. A rope across the entrance to the pier kept people from going out there during my swim, except a young woman, privileged because she was lying down on the pier sunbathing in a bathing suit. And I remember walking by her after my swim. She looked up and said, "You made it look easy." And I thought, *Okay! I made it look easy! Fan-tastic!*

The Cairnes sisters were at the landing at the finish also, and I took care not to be an I-told-you-so. They invited me to their home and attended the banquet staged by the hotel that evening.

Erie

By mid-summer I felt ready for Lake Erie. The Marine Reserves had arranged for me to be sent to the Toledo Marine Battalion as my two weeks reserve training, the only way I could get paid while training.

Marines manned the flotilla that accompanied me out on the lake. We had a big yacht and about ten other boats, and we had a Colonel from Washington, DC, aboard plus about half the battalion. They also had a PR person from Washington, DC, on board. A Marine plane was sent from Cherry Point Air Force Base to take me to New York for public appearances, if I made it across—a nice touch but ridiculous. If you swim 30 miles you come out of the water with your eyes swollen shut and you can hardly walk and you're not ready for prime time. For me to fly into New York for PR purposes in that condition would be a disaster.

We left from Pelee Point, Ontario, at about ten in the morning, headed for Cedar Point, Ohio. I was really in shape and everything went well. About midnight, 14 hours later and about halfway into the swim, a bad thunderstorm came up with lots of lightning. Lieutenant Robert J. Hookey was going to make decisions. He and I had come to the agreement early on that he would be the manager. He'd keep me in the water if I wanted to quit and he thought I could go on—this never actually happened—or pull me out if necessary. When I stopped for nourishment, without touching him or the boat, I talked to him alone. I didn't want to talk to a bunch of different people because that tends to cause confusion.

When this terrible storm came up, it didn't bother me a bit. I went up with the big waves and then down but I could always see the big yacht, now above me, now below me, as the swells lifted and lowered it. The small boats were scattered all over the place and the Colonel gave them a signal to stop so Lt. Hookey and I could talk. I said, "They have a lot of these storms on the Great Lakes that don't last long and maybe that's what we have here. Probably this will blow over." Lt. Hookey was listening to me, but the Colonel had already told him we have to abort because there were 30 Marines out there, and if we lost any Marines on Lake Erie, we'd really be in trouble. The people would say we lost them so a guy could make a swim. Terrible! I wanted to argue some more, and he said, "Briggs, that's it. If you want to continue, we'll leave you out here by yourself. " Of course, he wouldn't do that. I had to follow orders; after all, this was military service! So they pulled me out of the water.

I was so unhappy because I was going so well. So well! The people in New York were waiting for the big story. We'd gone about 18 miles. I was really upbeat. I was confident. I thought, *Once I get through the night and have the sun on my shoulders...* But now it was all over. I went back to Kansas. People said I just didn't make it. Yeah, but I would have if only... Nobody was interested.

Before I left Lake Erie, I'd asked the Marines if they could support me if I came back in a month to try again. I couldn't be on active duty and they couldn't do it officially but they could have Marines out there on the lake on their own time to support a buddy. They said, "We believe in you. We're sure you can do it." They said, "We'll support you." I thought that once I was in that beautiful shape, that I could maintain that shape for months. I thought, since I'd completed 18 miles, feeling good, I'd be ready for the next swim with no problem. Wrong. I'd only been in this business for a year and there was a lot I didn't know.

I went back to Emporia and did my job as admissions director and associate professor and didn't swim at all except one day, when I swam a few lengths of President Sharpe's private pool, until my second attempt at Erie.

On September 3, we went back to Lake Erie where the water temperature had gone down four degrees lower than on my first attempt to swim it; it was now 68 degrees. We left from the same place at Pelee Point, Ontario. About ten miles out I was shivering. By twenty miles out, I was almost unconscious, and they had to take me out of the water before I drowned. It was all over.

I was so disheartened, so down on myself, so depressed. I began to analyze my performance. Why did I do so poorly? And the answer was that I didn't stay in shape. I also realize, in retrospect, that it had something to do with the four degrees difference in temperature.

In any case, I was a disgrace to myself, to my family, and to the Marine Corps. I was so despondent I decided I was going up to Alaska, the last frontier, to get my head together and figure out who I am and what I want to do. So I called the college. The people there said, "We heard you didn't make it." That time they could legitimately say, you're not that good. So I told them I'm quitting. Then I wrote a letter resigning my positions as associate professor and director of admissions.

At that time, I knew my dad was in the hospital and it was a few days after an operation for prostate trouble, maybe cancer. Alice was there caring for him. I went to Boston to see him. I told Dad, "I hate myself. I don't count for very much. I have to get away to get my mind together." Dad said, "Come on, it isn't that important." "Well, it is to me," I said. So he said, "You're going to do what you're going to do."

When I left my Dad, he was feeling beautiful, his recuperation was going well, and Alice was pleased she was not going to lose him. The family was together. I told myself as I told my dad, *I am the best distance swimmer in the world, but I hate myself for failing so I'm going to Alaska.*

Chapter 16

Alaska!

I had no idea what I was going to do in Alaska. When I'm in distress, I seem to go somewhere new and far away to get my head together, as I did when going to Puerto Rico or Europe, but then at least I had a job waiting. Now in Alaska I stepped into a new world with no idea of what lay ahead. I just knew this was the last frontier, and that sounded good to me.

I'd driven to Seattle, left my car there, and taken a plane to Juneau, the capital of the Territory of Alaska. While I was waiting for my plane to Anchorage, I got into a conversation with a lady from the Alaska Crippled Children's Association. I told her I'd been a director of two Crippled Children's camps. She said there was a position open as executive director of the state Easter Seals Association, which was known in Alaska as the Alaska Crippled Children's Association. I said, "I could do that."

That was a Friday; the board was deciding on a director on Monday. This woman said, "I have enough influence I can make it happen. Do you want it?" I said, "Absolutely."

On Monday, I was in the Parsons Hotel in Anchorage. The board met on Monday and I got the job. So now I had the dream job Gloria had wanted for me, directing Easter Seals activities for the rehabilitation of handicapped children. And Gloria had always liked the idea of Alaska with its amazing terrain. The next year, when I got a cocker spaniel puppy, I named her Gloria.

Dad

After I'd accepted the new job, my immediate problem was that my vehicle was in Seattle. So I flew there and drove back. I couldn't be reached for the five days I was driving. When I reached Anchorage, I was told my dad had passed away. The funeral had already taken place. I didn't get to say goodbye to my dad, to tell him again that I loved him, to give him a Marine salute. I walked to the end of 4th Avenue and stood looking across Cook's Inlet at the mountains Dad would have loved, and I cried. I was all alone. I still miss him.

Settling In

When I first came to Anchorage, I lived in a nice basement apartment in a home. The people who owned it were very nice and treated me almost like a son. They also had strict rules. One was that no women were allowed in my apartment. Once a young lady was visiting me from out of town and I was showing her around. I took her to my apartment just to show it to her for a few minutes. The folks upstairs weren't home, but they found out and really gave me a lecture. But the fuss blew over. They were in the office cleaning business and I actually got them a job cleaning the offices where I worked at Alaska Crippled Children's Association. In May 1957, I bought a 4-plex. I moved into one apartment and rented the other three out.

The Plumbers

After I'd started my job with the Crippled Children's Association, as always, I got involved in the first of my perennial passions: sports.

Hockey came first. In early November 1956, I noticed in the *Anchorage Times* a call for anyone interested in hockey to go to the city skating rink. I went to the meeting and determined early on that there was little leadership. By the end of the meeting, I had been selected as manager, coach, defenseman, and anything else that might apply, including publicity director.

The first thing I did in my new roles was go to both papers, the Times and the News, asking them to run a piece requesting sponsors for the team. The next day I had a call from the manager of the Hohn Plumbing and Heating Company, Joe Belinsky. He said that he would give us $500 for exclusive rights to the team functions, including naming the team the Hohn Plumbers. I accepted this offer, but we needed money for hockey sticks and other equipment. $500 wouldn't normally come close to providing uniforms. I lucked out on these. I had met a member of the Anchorage Elks, who had come up from Tacoma, Washington, where he had been an officer with the Tacoma Elks. During his last year in Tacoma, somehow the Elks had acquired 18 brand new hockey uniforms to be worn by the Tacoma Rockets of the Western Hockey League. For whatever reason, the Rockets went bankrupt, ceased to exist, and somehow the Elks ended up with the uniforms to settle a debt. My Elks friend negotiated a deal, and within a week I went down to Tacoma and picked up the uniforms. All we had to do was take the name Tacoma Rockets off the sweaters and replace it with Hohn Plumbers. A local tailor volunteered to do this for us. When we took the ice for the first game, our new green uniforms made us look like we were in the National Hockey League.

Up to this point, a local Anchorage team had never beaten a team from the military—Fort Richardson or Elmendorf Air Force Base. In our first game against the Fort Rich team, although we had great uniforms, we looked rather terrible as a team and lost by a big score. Games in Anchorage in the past had been played on a skating rink without boards. You really can't play a proper game without boards, so I prevailed on Alice Moffet, director of the Anchorage Parks and Recreation Department, to install boards around the entire rink, a quite expensive improvement not in her budget. I won her over by playing my position as Director of the Crippled Children's Association to the hilt. By this time, I also had the two local newspapers and Channel 2 TV on my side, and Hohn was getting a lot of publicity. I wrote most of the pieces for the papers and appeared on Channel 2 myself.

When the snow was taken off the ice, which was done quite frequently, it was thrown over the boards so that spectators stood on the snow as high as or higher than the boards. We had four skaters each holding the corners of a blanket, into which the spectators threw money between the first and second periods. Even at the first game, which we lost to the Fort Richardson Pioneers by a big score, we collected over $100. Later, during the state tournament, we took in over $300 per game.

After the first game, we began to get more players, some pretty good former high school and college players, for example, Dave Benson, who had been an all-American at the University of Minnesota, a great hockey school.

After several games downtown, the Plumbers went out to Fort Richardson. At the end of the first period, we were tied 1 to 1. Midway through the second period with the score still tied, "Goose" Gosselin, the best player for Fort Rich, turned and lifted a backhand right into my face. The puck had only gone a few feet when it caught me just a little bit lower than the puck had hit me when I played for the Akron Stars. I went down in a heap spilling blood all over the ice. I had broken bones in the right side of my face. I was immediately taken to the hospital at Fort Rich, where I had X-rays made and got more stitches. This incident apparently unnerved the Plumbers, and I learned the next day that we lost 12 to 2. Nevertheless, I remembered that great first period and I was convinced—and I convinced the Plumbers—that we could play at least even with Fort Rich or Elmendorf.

There were no helmets or goalie masks back in those days but we managed to apply some rubberized metal strips to a football helmet, much like football helmets today, and I got back in the line-up for the next game.

As I had hoped, the Plumbers were flying when we took on the Pioneers in the next game downtown. The locals were standing three deep all around the rink. We beat the Pioneers 5 to 3 in this game. Was this ever great! We now had a fan base for the rest of the season. The games were close. We took the Plumbers up to Fairbanks where we beat the two town teams and broke even with the University of Alaska.

I then organized the state AAU Hockey Tournament for Alaska, consisting of the three Anchorage teams and the three from Fairbanks. In that double elimination tournament, we faced the University in the final game for the championship. Although our level of hockey in Alaska wasn't quite as good as in Akron, I played the game of my life. I was on the ice most of the game, concentrating on defense. I had announced that it was the last game of my "career" and the crowd was with me. We won 2 to 1. Great! Great! Great! What a way to go out!

Baseball

Based on my organization and publicity efforts for hockey, the Anchorage Baseball League came to me in the spring of 1957, asking me to do the same for baseball. Baseball was one of my big loves, too, so I got on board. I wrote articles for the newspaper about the games, and I publicized the League on station KENI radio reports, which I did often. Each of the two newspapers only had one sports writer so of course not every baseball game was covered. Any article I wrote and slipped onto the sports desk was likely to appear in the paper the next day. For my PR efforts for baseball I got paid a portion of the hot dog sales at the games.

KENI Radio and Television

Since the Hohn Plumbers took the ice, I'd been doing sports broadcasts for the local radio station KENI and Channel 2 television. The Plumbers' fans appreciated my reporting. Some wrote letters to the station complimenting my coverage as "accurate and entertaining" and sometimes enclosed a dollar bill or two for the hockey organization. One said, "This would have gone into the blanket had we been there."

While I'd always been in sports reporting from my college days when I wrote for the Boston newspapers, I never imagined I'd ever be reporting on camera. In fact, looking back, in 1948 I resented TV. *Who's going to watch it?* I wondered. *Radio is good enough.* When my Aunt Letitia bought a big television in a mahogany console, I learned something about who would watch it. About 1950 I conceded that TV was here to stay.

In Anchorage, TV wasn't too well established until 1955. There were two TV stations, KENI and KTVA; the latter was not on a regular schedule while KENI was on about five hours a day. KENI didn't have enough money to subscribe to a network so programming was all local, as it had been in the States a few years earlier. In Anchorage when I came in, local TV was low cost stuff. The technology was primitive. At first, I did 15 minutes of sports on Saturday for KENI. So Alaska and I were both getting a late start in TV. That was what was great about it; I was there almost from the beginning in another kind of frontier.

We finally had an hour of daily news like big networks: "The Big 60" had news, sports, and weather. Our newscaster was Ty Clark, the Cronkite of the North. Bill Stewart sold ads and liked to be on camera, where he was really terrible. Darrell Comstock was behind the controls, and his son was handling the camera. One day when Ty Clark was off for the weekend, the guy who was to do the news didn't show up, so Darrell was going to do the news. He was pretty good but he had on a tee shirt and wasn't prepared. I had a suit. Someone else took over the controls. I did my piece and quickly I handed my coat to him. He was a tall skinny guy. The sleeves of my coat barely covered his elbows, but we managed to get through. We got a few calls from people who were amused that we had only one jacket between us, a little large for me and much too small for Darrell.

Besides my 15-minute Saturday show, I often did longer pieces as needed, all live. Over the years, I'd also tape pieces for the station when I was on the road, based on interviews with some nationally well-known sports figures including Ted Williams, Vince Skully, and Billy Martin. I once reported on an All Star game in Boston. There were about 50 tapes in all, sent in by airmail from the lower 48, but my coverage mainly featured Alaska sports.

KENI radio and Channel 2 sometimes did simulcasts. When we did TV alone, I was more nervous. When I finally realized you have to talk to that camera like a friend, I relaxed.

Guys and Dolls

Along with my sports interests, of course, I was on the lookout for female companionship and hanging out in clubs where there was music. I went downtown to a club called Guys and Dolls one night. This gorgeous brunette came slithering down the bar. She asked me to buy her a drink.

Drinks were four dollars each, and you had to buy one for her and one for yourself. Now I knew this whole routine well from the old days going to the Majestic Ballroom in New York City near Times Square, when I was a student and also worked for the insurance company. So I bought us two drinks; her "whiskey" was tea of course, and I didn't drink alcohol. But I went along with the ritual and we talked. When she said, "Honey, do you want to go to the Blue Room?" I said, "No. I know the system."

According to the system in the Blue Room, where the lights are blue and dim, you have to buy a bottle of cheap champagne for $40. Not only that, the B-girl would sit down for a bit and then excuse herself to go to the ladies room. As she stood up and turned to go, she'd knock the champagne bottle with her elbow and spill it, and you'd have to buy another bottle.

So I declined the Blue Room and bought us drinks as necessary. I liked her and so I said, "I'll meet you at 4 a.m. at the Anchorage Westwood Hotel. I know you won't be there, but I'll be there." That was part of the system, too. A guy asks a girl to meet him later at a hotel. She agrees and so he spends more on her. The management doesn't want the girls to go. They don't want to lose their best girls to outside action. The good ones don't go.

I gave her twenty dollars for agreeing to meet me. I went home to bed and got up in time to be at the hotel at 4 a.m. just in case she came and because when I say I'll be somewhere, I'm there. As I expected, Lily didn't come. She was one of the good ones.

But we met again at Guys and Dolls. I asked the piano player Wendy Williamson about this beautiful girl who for working purposes went by the name of Lily, the Silver Serpent. Wendy said, "Oh, that big guy over there in the corner is her husband."

She was the most successful B-girl in the place because, besides being beautiful and having an intriguing accent from her native Germany, she was in it for the business. She got guys to buy drink after drink and to take her into the Blue Room. She was successful there, too, limiting the business to champagne and flirting, unlike some of the girls.

She must have been the most successful B-girl in Alaska. In nine months there, as I learned later, she'd moved into a luxurious apartment, bought a new Thunderbird, and a fur coat and saved $60,000. Then she wanted to go back to Germany to open a small hotel in the mountains. So she and her husband left Anchorage, taking the Thunderbird with them. But she was not to be out of my life forever.

Earning a Living

Academics came into the mix soon after I arrived in Anchorage, when I took a position of Assistant Professor of political science at the University of Alaska branch at Elmendorf Air Force Base. I don't think I've ever had just one job at a time. I held this one at the University until 1965.

My job with Alaska Crippled Children's Association was disappointing in that I had to manage the organization and especially to raise funds, but rarely came in contact with the children we served. Being with the kids had been the main joy of working for the camps in Cleveland and Colorado, and I missed that opportunity. One exception stands out. We conducted a mercy flight to bring in a native Alaskan child from Dillingham, a small town on Bristol Bay, who needed treatment at the Alaska Native Services Hospital in Anchorage. I flew out to get her and accompanied her to the hospital. I used to have a photo of me with this little girl. Providing treatment for her was a gratifying experience for me. I managed to secure from the U.S. government an old building downtown, which we turned into a treatment clinic. Otherwise, fundraising and bureaucracy were not how I wanted to spend my time.

In the process of setting up the flight to Dillingham, I got to know Major Dawson, publicity director for the Alaska Air Command. He was a graduate of Boston College, so we had a lot in common. He said that the Alaska Air Command historian had committed suicide and they hadn't found anyone to fill the job. He asked me if I'd take it. I decided to quit my job with the ACCA in May 1957, if Major Dawson would permit me to take the job with the Air Command in October. He agreed and that gave me the summer off for swimming.

Erie Again

Somebody had said to me, "Why don't you try Erie again? You're in Alaska now, you have to think big." I said, "Naw…" But pretty soon I was hooked. So I called my Marine buddy Bob Hookey in Toledo, who had been with me for both previous attempts at Erie. I said, "Bobby, I want to try it again. Will you back me one more time?" He said, "I'll talk to the guys and I think they'll do it one more time, but you better be in shape." I said, "Don't worry. I'll be in shape."

So in the spring of 1957, I announced on KENI my intention to swim across Lake Erie. I started to train in pretty cold water in Anchorage. I swam Sand Lake many times, a 78-acre lake in southwest Anchorage. I continued to train with daily workouts, short swims on Sand Lake, long swims up and down on Goose Lake, which is about three miles long, and an Alaskan record long distance swim on Big Lake near Wasilla. Big Lake is about 15 miles across at its widest point, but my crossing point was only 5.5 miles. Even that distance was the longest swim ever made in Alaska up until that time; that record may still stand.

So I was in good shape again, as I'd promised, when I went down to Ohio and hooked up with my Marine buddies. Bob Hookey, who had been in the nearest boat during my first attempts at Erie, was at my side again. Johnson Outboard Motor Dealers Association had also joined in, promising boats and motors. But we weren't getting the attention we had before because this was my third attempt. I told everyone that, if I got within five miles of my objective, nothing would stop me from finishing my swim. I was determined that this swim would be The One.

I began the swim on Saturday, August 17, 1957, from Marblehead on the tip of a promontory sticking out into Lake Erie near Port Clinton, Ohio, with

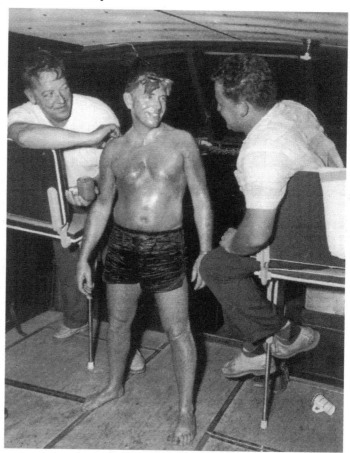

Just before going into the water for an Erie swim.

two guide boats, an anchor boat, and a supply boat, manned by a total of 13 men. We didn't have a yacht as we'd had before, but about a mile out a private cruiser came along and the folks aboard asked what was going on. When they heard about the swim, they asked if they could accompany us. So now we had a yacht out front again. It was a blessing.

About a mile and a half out, I remember a terrible stink of a dead fish that was about a mile up ahead and it must have been huge because the air smelled bad for miles. Breathing that stuff was a hard way to begin, but I eventually passed it. Pollution was always an issue too, and it really smarted my eyes.

At about mile ten, I'd been swimming toward the yacht, and it was always moving away. So at one of my stops I asked Bob Hookey to tell the people on the yacht, if they could stop every half hour and let me catch up to them, I'd have a feeling of accomplishment. So they did and each time I got to the cruiser, they'd be clapping for me and that helped a lot.

About four miles from the Canadian shore, at about 9 on Sunday morning, the wind picked up to 25 m.p.h. and four-foot waves developed.

Bob Hookey, promoted to Captain since my previous swim, was again my primary support guy. When Bob had gone to rest and a replacement was out there, I asked how far did we have to go. This person said three miles. I always want the truth. I count on it. Anyway, I swam for another hour until Bob came back, and I asked him how far now. He said about 3.25 miles, so I'd swum for an hour and lost a quarter mile. That was discouraging. But I was in a do-or-die mode, so I just went on. The final four miles of the swim took me ten and a half hours to complete out of a total of 34 hours and 55 minutes. Man, those last miles were tough; I almost gave up but I had a lot of encouragement from the guys on the boats accompanying me.

The folks on the yacht had decided that, about a quarter mile from shore, they would blow their horn to see me in. This plan had slipped my mind. I just knew the sound was very annoying and I didn't know what it was about. And then all the little boats that had begun to accompany us and the people who were gathering began to blow their horns. Then I remembered what that meant. A quarter mile to go! It was almost 8 pm, twilight, and the horns were blowing and it was really something!

All you have to do is touch your foot to the bottom of the lake on the far shore. So I remember the moment when I felt my foot hit the bottom. I'd done it! I'd completed 32 miles in 34 hours 55 minutes. When I got in a little further and tried to stand up, I couldn't. Two Canadian lifeguards pulled me out. They said later that my body was just like jelly. My eyes were swollen, and I was near collapse.

A doctor on the Canadian side said my body temperature had dropped to 87 degrees. He instructed my people to get me aboard the yacht immediately, wrap me in blankets, and not to move me. They put me in one of the two staterooms on the yacht and sailed back to the public dock in Sandusky where we spent the night. I don't remember too much about that except that I was only half asleep because I was aware that I had lost too much body heat and that I had to regain it as fast as possible. I didn't move a muscle the whole night. I'm not sure I was aware of him, but Bob Hookey spent the entire night beside me. I didn't get up until the next afternoon. I was wobbly but managed to walk off the yacht to Bob's car. He drove me back to the Toledo Battalion Armory, where there was a cot ready for me. I slept soundly from about 6 p.m. to the next morning. When I got up, I felt pretty good since my body heat had been restored and my eyes were coming along well. A victory banquet was held at the Armory that evening, which was a lot of fun.

We still hadn't heard from Johnson Motors; their people didn't know where to find me. I don't remember if they located us that Tuesday night or Wednesday morning, but Thursday morning they had me on a plane leaving Toledo and headed for LaGuardia. By this time, I was just about back to normal. Johnson Motors flew me to New York, and that's where the fun began. I was invited to be on the Ed Sullivan show, and now famous writer Gay Talese wrote an article about me for the *New York Times*. Also *Sports Illustrated* interviewed me and ran an article in the issue with the great black tennis player Althea Gibson on the cover.

The *Sports Illustrated* article included lots of detail about my swim other than what I have just related, so I'm adding here some paragraphs from that interview written up the same week that I made the swim:

> *I'd arranged for the people in the guide boat to give me a wigwag signal every 15 minutes, meaning that I should change [breathing] from one side to the other. I figured I would make the trip in 30 hours and so would see this signal 120 times. I decided to keep track: one down and 119 to go; two down and 118 to go and so on. And I did keep track as far as 80 down and 40 to go. Then my right arm went bad and I could swim only on my left side, and there was no more need for signals.*

> *I also occupied my mind by working out simple mathematical problems, and all the way across I kept reminding myself: when you get near the shore you must remember to ask for your swim trunks and put them on.*

Distance swimmers don't always wear trunks during marathon swims because of likely constriction and chafing. They are protected by nothing but a coat of lanolin. I don't now remember anything about my trunks on that swim and, in any case, I would not have been able to put them on without assistance at the end.

> *Every hour I took some nourishment. I drank a lot of tangerine juice with dextrose added and once, treading water, I ate a Clark bar. I needed something hot, and for that I had one of the Gerber baby foods—strained chicken, mixed with something to make it liquid so I could drink it from a Coke bottle. It helped a lot.*

The yacht made it possible to heat the liquid. I don't think we could have made it without the yacht. My hands never touched the boats or the hands of the crew or I would have been disqualified.

> *After about three hours, the water begins to affect your eyes and your vision gets cloudy. I threw away my goggles after the first 20 minutes because they leaked. Toward the end, I couldn't see the small boat beside me and had to guide myself by the big cruiser where they had the galley. The blurred vision didn't worry me; it has happened before on other long swims. It clears up in a day or so.*

Once, early Sunday morning, they let me pull alongside the boat up ahead, just for the psychological lift. It's tough to keep swimming hour after hour and never catch up...

I kept thinking of that cruiser, and the bunk in the cabin, and getting into the bunk and going to sleep. Also I imagined myself climbing out on the bank and beginning to cry because it was finally over, and the idea was so real that I began to cry right there in the water, with miles yet to swim.

When the horn on the cruiser began to blow, and blow, and blow, I was in a kind of delirium, but I heard it and knew we were nearly there and that I was going to make it. Then my foot touched the bottom... My eyesight was just about gone by that time. I couldn't see the people on the bank.... But I heard them cheering.

Not only was I the first person to cross the 32 miles of Lake Erie but also, according to the *Anchorage Daily News* and others, mine was "believed to be the longest distance swim in history, excluding river swims which make use of strong currents."

Telegrams of congratulations arrived from Anchorage Mayor Anton Anderson, my colleagues in Alaska, the Marines back in Toledo, and many others.

J. Walter Thompson, a New York PR firm hired by Johnson Outboard Motors, was putting out press releases about my swim and someone was listening. Henry Holt approached me for a book right after the swim. They definitely wanted a book but it had to follow certain specifications: I was to select seven great historical adventures like climbing Mount Everest or Lindbergh's flight and then compare these to what I've just done. They said it had to be stories told by someone who had experienced something like that and what I'd done qualified. I had the swimming experience, yes, but researching these other feats was not what I wanted to do right then. I also remembered the long process of writing my thesis, and I didn't want to repeat that.

However, I also didn't want to give up the opportunity, so I called Bill Joseph, my former boss at Sportservice when I was with the Buffalo Hockey Club. He'd heard the news of the swimmer who had crossed Lake Erie and was amazed that I was the one. He said, "Back then, I didn't know you were a long distance swimmer." Back then, I wasn't! I asked Bill if he could arrange an appointment with Charlie Young, the sports editor for the Buffalo newspaper. He got me the appointment. Charlie said, "I can handle that book for you but I'm too busy now. Wait six months until I retire." I went back to the publisher who said they wanted the book right away or not at all. End of story.

In the beginning of October 1957, after my swim across Lake Erie, I went to work for Elmendorf AFB, as I'd arranged the previous spring. The historian of a major command like the one in Alaska calls for a G.S. 12, which was the second highest pay grade in civil service. However, in Alaska it was a G.S. 13 because the government found it hard to keep personnel there with the cold weather and high cost of living. What a difference to go from a G.S. 3 in Puerto Rico to a G.S. 13 in Alaska!

In December 1957, the Hohn Plumbers, the Fort Richardson Buckners, the Fort Richardson Pioneers, and the Elmendorf AFB Rockets became the original members of the Anchorage Hockey League with me as president. Our board included Gene Williams for the city team, Don Loewen for Elmendorf, and Lt. Webster for the Fort Richardson Pioneers. The Anchorage Hockey League started its season on January 5, 1958. Now that my playing days were over, I could devote more time to the Hockey League.

And, as spring 1958 came on, I began to envision my next big swim.

Chapter 17

Lydia

In the spring of 1958, after I took the job as Civilian Historian, GS 13, Alaska Air Command, Elmendorf AFB, I left that job. If I'd stayed, I'd have an excellent retirement now. However, after nine months, I thought I could do better on my own. I was an incurable entrepreneur. I continued to teach evening classes in political science at the University of Alaska at Elmendorf, for the pleasure of teaching and a bit of income.

That spring, I was also promoting the Alaska Speedway through my sports reporting. I was trying to do the same thing for car racing as I did for hockey and baseball, and, as was said in the *Anchorage Daily Times*, "If Briggs magic holds, the Speedway will continue to be 'the place to race' in Alaska." Racing had some characters involved with names like Dirty Bud Borders and Lead Foot Johnny Deloges; the latter towed abandoned cars away for the city. If car racing was a sport, I was going to promote it. The Alaska Speedway job paid me quite well.

However, I also had more than my share of nonpaying jobs in 1958. I remained President of the Anchorage Hockey League, for which I organized a clinic for officials to iron out some inconsistencies, scheduled games, recruited players, and wrote articles for the newspaper for publicity. Then I was elected Alaska's representative to the Amateur Hockey Association, U.S., holding that position through 1967, as long as I was in Alaska.

An additional nonpaying job came my way in 1958. Since I'd come to Alaska, I had become quite friendly with Alice Moffett, manager of the Anchorage Parks and Recreation Department, serving the almost 200,000 residents. She had helped me with the hockey facilities from the beginning of the organization of the Plumbers and with the baseball facilities. When a spot on the Parks and Recreation Commission opened up, she made sure I got that job. I was actually the best qualified candidate for the supervision of the Anchorage Sports programs. For this appointment, Alice had to work through the commission, which in turn made recommendations to the City Council.

Once on the Commission, I got to work with Norman Brown, the owner and publisher of the Anchorage Daily News. He and I put together a deal to move the city beach from Lake Hood, where there were too many private planes, to Goose Lake. This was almost a million dollar project, which entailed bringing tons of sand to Goose Lake. We put up a state of the art facility with boat storage, bathhouse, food concession, and tennis courts. I got one paying opportunity out of this volunteer effort when I was awarded the food concessions contract in return for providing expert advice on what a swimming facility should be. Also, when I was there at the concessions, they'd have two lifeguards at the beach instead of just one.

I happened to be out at Goose Lake in the latter capacity after the beach had closed and the lifeguard was taking care of closing duties. I heard a commotion and went outside to find that a young man, a black college student, had disappeared under the water. I jumped in and began to go back and forth over the water with deep strokes until in a few minutes my hand, at the bottom of a stroke, struck his body. I managed to get him to shore, but it was too late. I was shocked to have this loss in our new facility. The young man's mother, who was a lawyer and on the City Council, expressed gratitude for my efforts in spite of her grief.

Also that spring, along with some other leaders in sports promotion, I was involved in organizing a group called "Alaska Sports, Unlimited." With swimming, speedway racing, hockey, and baseball, I guess I felt too limited! Our first endeavor was to bring famous tennis star Jack Kramer along with three other prominent tour players to Alaska to lend prestige to a tournament we devised, the winner of which would be crowned "Alaska Tennis Champion." Big names like Kramer didn't come to Alaska, but I was determined to change that. We raised a few thousand dollars from sponsors, and I put in a few thousand myself to get started and staged the tournament in May. Pancho Segura was the winner and we were the losers. I lost $3000 myself; the sponsors lost plenty also. The tournament was played in such gorgeous weather that I think the citizens of Anchorage went out into the wilderness to enjoy the scenery that weekend. Anchorage was just not a tennis town.

Funny thing, tennis ended up changing my life for the better in a v very important way, much later. At the time, it was just another sports promotion adventure.

While I was always pursuing my passions rather than thinking of security, my passions were costing me money. I had to begin to seek bigger moneymaking ventures, too.

The Log Cabin

I figured the best way to make money in Anchorage, long term, was to buy real estate. Money wasn't my chief goal, as I guess is obvious because everything

important I'd done up to that point in life seemed to lose money. But hope springs eternal. I found a log cabin in downtown Anchorage, built early in the century on land once used as a dairy farm, now surrounded by modern buildings. I thought its history, solidity, and quaint character just cried out for someone to make it into something special. I bought it with the idea of turning it into the premier Alaskan gift shop and earning me some money.

Lydia

I was in the Guys and Dolls one night that spring of 1958, when I saw this beautiful girl with bright orange hair. I asked Wendy Williams, the pianist, who she was. "You know her," Wendy said. "It's Lily, the Silver Serpent." Indeed it was. The hair color had thrown me off. She was just as beautiful as I remembered her from the previous year. I soon learned that, after she and her husband went to Germany, he gambled his way through $40,000 of the money she'd saved from her earnings here at Guys and Dolls. So she left him and the Thunderbird in Germany and returned to Anchorage to her old job.

Her first time in town, she'd brought over some German girlfriends to work, who'd stayed at the Guys and Dolls while she was gone. Once she was back in Anchorage, she moved in with one of them, an attractive girl named Margit.

Lily, whom I'd come to know by her real name—Lydia—came to me and suggested we do something together on a certain day, and I said I couldn't because I had a date for a swim that day with Margit. "Not anymore," Lydia said. She was very direct. And so Lydia and I went swimming. In fact, we swam together five times a week as I trained for my next swim. Soon we became serious about each other.

I'd take my little dog Gloria to the lake. She'd go in first and I'd catch up to her. She'd swim on and on and—I swear she knew what I was saying to her—I'd say, "Now you keep going, and I'll see you on the way back." I'd swim on past her and then I'd find her on the way back. She'd be huffing and puffing. She was just a puppy weighing only seven or eight pounds. I'd hold her up in the air while I treaded water to give her a rest, and then I'd stay close to her all the way back to see that she was all right. Gloria, Lydia, and I often swam together. It was a wonderful time.

Over the next few months of dating, I learned a lot about Lydia's history. She was born in Germany and was a child during World War II. Her mother was a prostitute and Lydia didn't know which of two men was her father. Her mother, who was part Jewish, left the country, fleeing the Nazis, and came to the U.S. around 1934. Her mother was what was known as a "kept woman" in New York City. Lydia was not fond of her mother, who was in truth not a nice woman and, in addition, seemed to be jealous of Lydia's good looks. Lydia herself came to the U.S. in 1947. She told me about how she felt as her ship passed by the Statue of Liberty and how alone she felt in the city of New York. Her mother had a job waiting for her as a maid in a wealthy man's house, but Lydia didn't want to take that job. As soon as she arrived, she and her mother got into an argument about that, and Lydia left her home.

Her first night in the U.S, as Lydia was walking on 82nd Street in the German section of the city, an older man said to her, "You look like you need some help." Lydia's English wasn't very good, but he spoke German. He offered to take her to his home until she could get her life organized. He said she could trust his intent because he was old and a doctor. She took a chance and went with him. She stayed for six weeks. She first got a job as a hat check girl at Longchamps, an upscale restaurant, and soon learned that girls as pretty as she was could make a lot of money at the Majestic, where guys paid 10 cents a dance and bought drinks.

Lydia became very good at hustling drinks, and, in addition, she met many interesting people, often rich. She was particular, but if she did like a guy, she would move in with him. These episodes usually lasted about six months. One guy was an interior decorator from Santo Domingo, where Trujillo was dictator. He went down to decorate Trujillo's palace and took Lydia with him. They stayed in the palace. However, this boyfriend fell in with some of the people who were trying to overthrow the dictator. The result was that one day they had to get out suddenly. They drove to the nearest part of the Haitian border with government forces in hot pursuit. At the border, they jumped out of the car and made a run into Haiti, where they disappeared into a cane field.

Lydia had also met a Russian prince. In the wake of the Bolshevik revolution, a lot of princes had escaped to the U.S. One time the prince told Lydia that his wife was going abroad for six months and Lydia could move in with him for that period of time and he'd treat her like a princess. So for six months, they lived together in his brownstone near Washington Square in New York.

Some of her boyfriends were Mafia, who came to New York City for their evil work and went home to New Jersey at night. Then she met the gambler in New York, with whom she first came out to Anchorage.

One thing I came to understand about Lydia was that she didn't want to be in the business of hustling in a nightclub. An illegitimate child, she wanted legitimacy. In trouble with the Gestapo, she wanted safety. Depending on lovers, she wanted to own something of her own, to be somebody substantial, to have a normal life. I was very well regarded in Anchorage, considered "Mr. Clean," and she thought I could perhaps give her the life she wanted. And besides, she liked me. She wanted to make our relationship permanent.

Lydia was soon living with me in my apartment. She had moved her belongings into the apartment one weekend when I was out of town. Not being married to her, I was concerned with what my tenants in the building and others were thinking. I was trying to continue being regarded as an upright guy, in a time when living together was not done openly by proper couples.

The Eskimo Shop and KENI

In April 1958, I opened the Eskimo Shop at 612 E. Third Avenue in the log cabin, located across from the Alaska Native Services Hospital. At first the business was an investment; the shop was run by Martha Carr, the former manager of another shop named the Gilded Cage, but she left after two months because the shop wasn't producing enough income for her and her three children. So in June 1958, Lydia and I moved into an apartment behind the shop so I could better manage it.

My job as reporter and later Sports Director for KENI was never a paid job, but it was always rewarding. I enjoyed six years of glory with one sponsor for my sports program. Almost from the beginning of the "Big 60" news, weather, and sports show, a bank in Palmer called the Matanuska Valley Bank, which extended into Anchorage, sponsored me. That bank sponsored everything I ever did there. Boy, did they treat me well! The Matanuska Valley was the most beautiful valley, surrounded by snow-capped mountains, where farmers could grow the most beautiful, huge vegetables. Alaska had a short season but more sun than the Lower 48 and, as a result, our vegetables were huge and delicious and our local meat, eggs, and milk were fresh and healthy. A big competition developed between Alaska and Seattle. Everything came through Seattle, so if anything was slow, it was Seattle's fault. Seattle used to run vicious advertisements that said big vegetables weren't as nutritious as the smaller Seattle vegetables. It was a touchy subject because the media was caught between wanting to support local products and also accepting advertising money from the bigger Seattle suppliers. I was rooting for Matanuska vegetables and that bank in the Valley.

I became quite friendly with Paul Coombs. I don't know how much the bank paid for the sponsorship because apparently the owner of the station, Al Bramstad, didn't want me to know and Paul honored that wish. I know I didn't get any of the sponsorship money, but I got a good deal that met my needs. I used the Matanuska Bank-sponsored airtime with KENI to publicize the sports events that I was promoting. And I got two 50-second commercials a day on KENI's TV Channel 2 and six commercials a day on the radio. I'd say, "And now a message from the Eskimo Shop, located right across the street from the Alaskan Native Hospital." The shop was only one block from the downtown commercial area, but it was on a residential street and therefore off the beaten path. But the advertisements brought people to us. It's not the number of people you have come into a shop, it's how many are serious customers who will buy. The people who took the trouble to find us were better quality customers than browsers who just happen to walk by. So the Eskimo Shop did pretty well largely because of KENI. Later I similarly promoted other businesses through KENI. The Matanuska Valley Bank backed me even when I went off to the Lower 48, right down till I left Alaska for good.

I had mixed feelings about the celebrity I achieved because of my reporting on KENI. My sign off slogan was well known around town: "Well, that puts us around third and we're heading for home..." On the way home I'd go into the Club Paris. Jack, the Club's owner would have a ginger ale waiting for me, and he'd have the TV on above the bar. He'd say, "Hey, you did alright tonight." After that, I'd just sit and not really talk to anyone else. Then some big drunk would come over and put his arm around me and say, "Hey, Harry." I didn't like that. Several occasions I'd be walking along 4th Avenue when a mother and kid would see me. "Look, Ma. There he is," the kid would say, and he'd come up to me. I enjoyed that. But some guy would come up—I have one particularly persistent guy in mind—and he wanted to be buddies. To be a public figure, you have to be nice to everybody, and I just wanted to be left alone. I'm basically a loner.

The Helms Award

On May 10, 1958, I was given the first annual award of the Helms Athletic Foundation's Outstanding Anchorage Amateur Athlete of 1957, the year I completed the swim across Erie. An article in the Anchorage paper cited that swim as my main qualification for the award but also mentioned my other contributions to Anchorage sports, for example, they mentioned my Speedway and my hockey promotion efforts, saying, "His work as president, general manager, publicity chairman, writer, and public relations netted him only a feeling of accomplishment and the undying friendship of sixty hockey players, but he earned the title of 'Mr. Hockey' from the many who follow the winter sport here." I have to say that I was quite pleased by this recognition.

Lake Michigan

While we got the Eskimo Shop going, I was training for a swim a bit longer than the one on Lake Erie, the 34-mile stretch between Michigan City, Indiana, and Jackson Park in Chicago. No one had ever made a swim across Lake Michigan, and I planned to be the first.

To make the swim in August, I had to take several weeks for the final training and the swim itself. During that time, I got Lydia to transfer to the Fairbanks nightclub, which was owned by the same company that employed her at Guys and Dolls. I wanted to maintain my squeaky clean reputation in Anchorage while I was gone, and I didn't know who Lydia might bring into my apartment. Her girl friends could be pretty wild and the men they might bring around also would not be good for my reputation. So she went up there to Fairbanks as a B-girl and was as successful as she was in Anchorage.

We had managed to line up the Chicago Battalion of the Marine Corps Reserves as sponsors just as we had used the Toledo Battalion for the three Erie swims. However, my old friend Capt. Bob Hookey from Toledo came up to supervise the Marines.

Our other sponsors, Johnson Motors, provided the escort boats with drivers. Johnson Motors had me lodged at Lake Forest College near the Great Lakes Navy Station during my final training. My cousin Gordon Briggs' wife loaned me her convertible so that I and a couple Marines could go to the lakes to swim for four or five hours each day. It was good to see my cousins the times when I went to Chicago. Gordon's son Robie and daughter Pam were just little kids, rather excited to see their old Uncle Harry.

On August 30, 1958, I began my swim across Lake Michigan, starting out at Michigan City, Indiana, with Bob Hookey beside me in the nearest guide boat. The weather was calm, the water temperature was reasonably warm. I felt good; I was well prepared.

I'd decided to further protect myself from heat loss not just by my accustomed lanolin coating all over my body but by gobs and gobs of lanolin. We used five or six jars of it. Thick layers of the stuff were piled up on my shoulders and arms and coated even my eyelashes. When I went in the water at 8 a.m. and began to swim, my arms felt heavy. I could hardly drag them through the water. I thought I knew what was the matter. At my first hourly break, we decided to stop the swim and go back to the starting point and scrape that lanolin off. We lost several hours and added a full hour to the swim by this choice, but what a relief! It was like swinging a bat with a metal doughnut or swinging two bats and then stepping up to the plate; the one regular bat feels light as a feather. When I went in the water for the second time, my arms felt so light! The removal of the lanolin coating gave me a real lift. I never used lanolin or had any kind of grease for swims after that.

I went into the water for my second start in near calm. About 18 miles into the swim, which I'd done in about 12 hours, a storm came up at twilight. It went from calm to four-foot waves and the wind was very strong. We couldn't make much progress against the waves, and, when the wind hit the side of a support boat, it would blow 50 feet away and I had no guidance. I was zigzagging. I felt very strong, but we were discouraged.

Bob Hookey was in his guide boat about 10 feet away from me. By the time he and I stopped and talked a bit about the situation, the wind was blowing his boat fast towards me. If I touched the boat I'd be disqualified. So I thought, *What I'll do is go to the other side of the boat so that it will be blowing away from me instead of toward me.* It was a 20-foot outboard, no problem. I said, "I'll dive under the boat and we'll talk on the other side." Bob was looking down at me when I disappeared beneath the surface of the water, but apparently in the wind he hadn't heard what I said. So he began frantically looking for me. It was twilight and the boats were bouncing all over the place. At that slow speed it's hard for a boat to maintain direction. Everyone panicked because they couldn't see me. I yelled, "I'm here," but they couldn't hear me and were going off in the wrong direction looking for me.

We were about three miles from Gary, Indiana. I could see factory lights and city lights. I was thinking, *I'll have no trouble making it to Gary; I'll go slowly and take about five hours.* However, I wasn't familiar with the shore, and I had nothing but a pair of trunks on. Lucky for that because I don't always wear trunks once I'm in the water. Even so, if I walked into a diner on shore dripping wet, they might call the cops. I was more worried about that than the swim to shore.

When the boats finally started coming back toward me, I'd been missing about a half hour. Gee, were they relieved to see me! There was no question of resuming the swim in the high wind and waves, so they whizzed me into the city to the Hotel Knickerbocker. It was 10 or 11 at night; I was tired and cold, and they had blankets around me. Media was there. It was a downer that I didn't make it, but there was booze for the media and a party. I answered questions for about a half hour. I finally said I had to go to bed.

We'd covered a lot of water so I didn't consider the swim a failure, but it was very disappointing. The press treated it as a success, and my supporters were great. I got telegrams saying things like this one from Elmendorf Air Force Base in Anchorage: "CONGRATULATIONS ON A MAGNIFICENT TRY LAKE MICHIGAN…YOUR AIR FORCE ROOTERS."

The phone had also been ringing. The governor of Alaska was calling, and the mayor of Anchorage was calling the hometown guy. I said, "I'll talk to them tomorrow; I'm tired." But then someone came and told me Ted Williams was on the phone and wanted to talk to me. Now that's someone I really cared about.

I was getting more press in Boston than I knew; the press in my hometown was picking up stuff on the wire service that was printed about me in Chicago. So Boston was hearing about this Marine lieutenant who was a long distance swimmer. Because I'm a big sports fan, particularly a Red Sox fan, I knew Ted Williams had a virus and hadn't gone to the coast with the team. Back in Boston he was watching TV and saw on the news that this Marine had failed to complete the swim with no explanation much. Williams was just as intense about his Marine Corps duty as a fighter pilot as he was about baseball. He went from one obsession to another. We were both Marine reserve officers, we shared the Boston connection, and so he decided he'd call me. I didn't take the calls from the Mayor of Anchorage or the Governor, but this one I took. Williams was known for his terrible temper, and he was nasty with the press. If he made an error in the field and the crowd booed him, he turned and gave them the finger. He had a tremendous fan base but he was Terrible Teddy to the press. He was super nice to me. He said, "You didn't make it this time, Buddy, but…" Ted Williams commiserated with me and it meant a lot that he called when I was down, not in victory.

He knew how to inflate my ego. So the sports reporter in me said, "Let's talk about you." We talked about ten minutes. He finally asked if I had influence with Johnson Outboard. I said I had a little bit. He said he would like a sponsor to go to Alaska for fishing. Fishing was another of his passions. He later got a Sears sponsorship, which lasted for the rest of his life. Ted finally said, "Are you going to try to cross Michigan next year?" I said, "Absolutely." He wished me best of luck for next year. One paper described our relationship accurately; the other said, "his good friend Ted Williams." In any case, I valued this exchange between us, and I was committed to trying Michigan again.

The first Michigan swim that summer had marked the end of an era of swimming with the Marines. Of course, I didn't know what was going on with the team, but I have a feeling that the military guys didn't mix too well with the Johnson people. The Marines and I had officially come together in the San Diego Harbor swim in the winter of 1955-56 and went on together through swims in Kansas, Oklahoma, Grand Lake in Colorado, two failed Erie swims, success at Lake Erie in 1957, and then this first try at Michigan. I am forever grateful for the support of the Marines in helping me achieve my dream of becoming a marathon swimmer and the first to cross Lake

Erie. In particular, I'm grateful for the friendship and assistance of Bob Hookey, who continued to accompany me on my swims on his own time.

In the September 1958 issue of *Alaska Magazine*, writer James Doherty dubbed me the "Paddling Professor" in the title. This sobriquet appealed to reporters and PR professionals, and ever since, I've been known as the Paddlin' Professor wherever I swim. Doherty also made frequent reference to what he called my "squat frame," saying, "At five feet, five inches, Harry is roughly the height of the average parking meter." Doherty also quoted me in this article as saying I would next swim the tricky waters between Nantucket and Cape Cod, a 25-mile stretch not yet crossed by any swimmer. That had been long in the back of my mind but it was not to be my next marathon swim.

Harry Briggs Alaskan Associates

The attention my swimming brought to me also brought national attention to Alaska, which was only a remote territory in the minds of most Americans. Alaskans loved it whenever Alaska was even mentioned in the national news, and I got Alaska in the Chicago newspapers by training and swimming there. I wanted to ride that wave of publicity as far as it would go.

When I got back from Chicago and the swim, I was pretty well known. Though I didn't accomplish my goal, my swim was reported as a record setting marathon swim. Now seemed the time to use that public image. I formed a company as Harry Briggs Alaskan Associates through which I wanted to promote tourism. I felt that, with statehood pending, there'd be a flood of tourists wanting to experience the wonders of Alaska. I wanted to be a part of that excitement that I've always felt being in a movement from its earliest days. Also, having invested in property and a gift shop in this new frontier, I expected my work in tourism to ultimately bring me a very good income. Everything seemed to be coming together.

I wanted to go to New York City to get some help for my dream from national PR firms. My money was in real estate, so I needed some cash to go to New York. Lydia offered me $3000 to do this out of something like $15,000 she had made at the club in Fairbanks. I wanted to be my own person; I didn't want to take this offer. Lydia and I weren't married and I was beginning to have second thoughts about the relationship. I'll admit, I love the chase, but I have doubts during long relationships that follow. However, I needed the money, swallowed my pride, and took the $3000 to New York.

I met with some Madison Avenue bigwigs and tried to sell them on my vision. Things didn't go well. I didn't succeed in finding anyone interested and at a reasonable fee. I'd spent the money on the trip and I was coming back empty handed.

While I was in the East, I had an idea about how to make up for that loss. I knew that state boards of education approved the purchase of textbooks, and I knew a lot about education and textbooks. My Ph.D. was not for nothing! I'd heard about some educational publishers located not far away. I went down from New York City to Philadelphia to talk to J. B. Lippincott Publishing Co. and was successful in getting a contract to represent their line of textbooks in Alaska. Pleased with that deal, I decided to go back to Alaska via Chicago where I would spend a couple days visiting Rowe Peterson and American Book Company, also big textbook publishers. I was successful in getting a super deal with Rowe Peterson; I would get 10% of all sales made in Alaska even if they were called in by phone. The other companies paid me only for the sales I personally initiated and closed. The subjects of the three lines of books were different, so I wasn't representing competing books.

I had a misunderstanding with American Book Company about prices; the price list I was working with did not include my commission, which I was supposed to have added on. I sold thousands of dollars worth of American Book's texts. I'd signed the deals and there was no recourse. Even worse, that load of books was in a truck that rolled over on the Alaska Highway. I owed the Department of Education all those books, I lost the books, and I wasn't getting a commission for them. It took forever for the insurance to pay for the loss. That episode ended my relationship with American Book Company. However, when I got my first check from Rowe Peterson in about April 1959, it was for every book sold in Alaska for the whole year of 1958, over $1000, and I hadn't yet made a sale. The good Lord was smiling on me then. He must have known I had spent Lydia's money in New York for nothing.

The Worst Mistake of My Life

When I went back to Alaska via Chicago to make the book deals, I decided I'd stop by one of the clubs I used to visit when I was there training for swims during the years that Johnson Outboard Motors had sponsored me. I'd go back to the same hotel Johnson Motors had provided and was in bed by 10 p.m. However, I had trouble going to sleep so early. I'd always been a night owl. So about midnight I'd get up and go out to one club or another. I'd do a lot of looking, a little bit of talking, and then I'd be able to go back to the hotel and actually sleep. So this time I spent two nights in Chicago making book deals and in the evening I dropped by one of the clubs. I chatted with the bartender a bit and then I bumped into Little Tina, one of the girls I remembered from earlier times. She remembered me, too, and so we talked, caught up. It was fun. More fun than it should have been.

On top of some other misgivings, I thought, *If I can get excited by Little Tina, I really shouldn't marry Lydia*. I hated myself for this, but that's the way it was.

I'd told Tina about something we called black diamonds in Alaska. It's hematite, not expensive. Tina said she'd like to have a black diamond ring. She said she was headed to Florida in January. I said, "Somehow I'll meet you there." I planned to bring her a hematite ring. So I told Little Tina that I would meet her at such and such a time and place in Florida in January.

So in my mind, it was all over with Lydia, but to be honest I did have to wait to tell her before I had a fling with Tina. So I planned to go home and tell Lydia it was over.

When I got back to Anchorage, Lydia said, "When are we going to get married?" I said, "Wait a minute," and I waited and waited and didn't have the courage to tell her it was all over. I told myself, she was a fine woman and I'd just have to face it. So we finally talked turkey. Lydia brought her friend Margit in to persuade me. All her friends were behind her. She gave me two weeks to agree to marry her or else she was leaving me.

I was thinking, *I've slept with her so much, I don't get excited any more. Maybe this is what marriage is like, what life is like. I owe it to her to marry her.* I ended up saying, "We'll get married but I prefer not now."

While I was in New York, Lydia had already gone back to Germany and told her husband that she wanted a divorce because she was marrying somebody else. Before she came home, she'd settled all the divorce arrangements. There was no stopping her now.

In December, I got a letter from Little Tina saying she'd be there in Miami on the date in January that we'd arranged. Here's where I made a crucial mistake. I put the letter in the pocket of my coat and later hung it in the closet.

The Best Thing I Ever Did

I married Lydia on December 31, 1958, in Wasilla, a town near Anchorage recently made famous by former governor and vice presidential candidate Sarah Palin. There aren't too many people alive who were married in the Territory of Alaska. Congress had already approved statehood, and on January 3, 1959, Alaska officially became a new state as I began life in my new state as a married man.

When we got back to the cabin from Wasilla and we woke up in the morning on our first day married, Lydia looked around and said, "I never dreamed that I would own anything this wonderful." The cabin was pretty nice, but it wasn't most women's dream. I thought, *Harry, when you married her, you did something really good.* I was proud of myself.

Chapter 18

Promoting the New State

Alaska officially became a state on January 3, 1959. When we'd voted for statehood, people had come to persuade me to take Alaskan items to various shows in the Lower 48. People told me the rest of the country was eager to buy anything Alaskan. With my business in the Eskimo Shop likely to gain from such marketing, I pursued the idea.

We were beginning an experiment in publicizing Alaska at sports shows, learning as we went. I was combining my background in sports and selling things at sports venues with my new profession as trader in Alaskan crafts. In anticipation of statehood and the interest I expected from tourists, I booked three sports shows in quick succession in Kansas City, Chicago, and Minneapolis. The promoters of the shows told me what great opportunities the shows offered. Crowds would come, sales would be great, and people in the Lower 48 would buy anything that came from this new state. I took with me to the first two shows a Native Alaskan artist named Robert Mayokok along with some of his art. He did little sketches of Eskimo life right there at the booth, as people watched, and sold them for a dollar. The rest of the time he worked at carving, and each day completed about one walrus ivory figure. I also had some very fine Alaskan wares such as sealskin boots white people called mukluks and Eskimos called *kamuks*, finely carved statuary made from walrus tusks, and high quality sketches on ivory that are popularly called *scrimshaw*.

This type of carving is now a well-known Eskimo craft, but there is an argument about whether it was traditionally Eskimo. A search on the Internet reveals statements like this one from www.scrimshaw.com: "Scrimshaw is the indigenous art form of the American Whaleman," and this from Wikipedia.org: "The making of scrimshaw began on whaling ships between 1745 to 1759 on the Pacific Ocean, and survived until the ban on commercial whaling." However, Eskimo artists deeply resent the use of the word *scrimshaw* for their art because they were doing sketches on ivory before the Australian sailor named Scrimshaw may have applied his name to the art of sketching on walrus ivory. Scrimshaw is a verifiable British surname, but most "authorities" on scrimshaw typically say the origin of the word is unknown. I finally found one Internet source, www.scrimshaw.net that upholds the Native Alaskan view. Scrimshaw.net artist Mark Thogerson, also a biology professor, says, "Scrimshaw—painstaking etching on ivory or bone—is one of only a few indigenous American crafts. Practiced for centuries by the Inuit and other native groups along the Northwest Coast, it was adopted by the Yankee whalemen of the early 1800's."

Whether you credit the Native Alaskan or not, the whalers' story goes like this: Eighteenth century whalers hunted whales in the daylight, and in the evening whiled away the time carving pictures on the bones of teeth of sperm whales and the baleen of other whales. They traded with Eskimos for walrus tusks also for material on which to carve these drawings. They put lampblack into the lines they carved to make the image stand out. Eskimos stepped up their production of carvings on ivory as a way to make money by selling it to white people after white people disrupted their fishing and hunting and took over their traditional hunting grounds. The carvings became in greater demand after Alaska became a state. The Marine Mammal Protection act forbade the importation or sale of whalebone after 1973, but native Alaskans could legally continue to carve these materials. I had to get a certification from the State that guaranteed that my scrimshaw and ivory carvings were made by Native Americans. I displayed a great deal of fine Alaskan art and a lot of people saw it for the first time at my booth in those sports shows.

We had crowds of visitors to our booth in Kansas City, who admired our crafts and were curious about our Native Alaskan artist. I rather quickly realized we needed a little book about his people. So I wrote a small book, *The Alaskan Eskimo*, with Robert Mayokok's by-line, and he illustrated it. It explained such things as that Eskimos didn't live in igloos but built them as shelters on fishing trips on the ice. One chapter of the book described the driftwood and sod homes with their tunnel entrances; other chapters described Eskimo clothing, food, hunting and fishing. Robert signed and sold this little book, and I let him keep the proceeds, which were very little.

In Kansas City people asked us a lot of questions about Alaska. After answering literally thousands of questions about the state, I wrote a booklet about travel in Alaska titled, "How is Alaska and the Highway?" and containing such information as these nuggets.

- The Alaska Highway begins at Dawson Creek, British Columbia, and extends some 1527 miles to Fairbanks, Alaska….
- Gasoline stations are seldom more than 35 miles apart…About half of the stations remain open all night….
- Many gasoline stations do provide sleeping facilities.
- Gasoline prices reach as high as 60 cents a gallon in Canada, but the Canadian gallon contains five rather than four quarts.
- The Peace River Bridge collapsed in the fall of 1957. However, there is a detour seven miles south of the bridge, which makes use of a railroad bridge.
- It is not necessary to travel in convoy as so many people have erroneously been led to believe. Thousands of single cars make the trip every year.

There was enough interest in my Alaska booth at the Kansas City show for the mayor to present me with a key to the city. I brought with me to the Chicago show a gift from the Mayor of Anchorage to the notorious Mayor Daley, last of the big city bosses. I made the presentation to Mayor Daley in his downtown Chicago office. I was finally well known in Chicago because of my swimming in Lake Michigan. I remember the Chicago mayor as a little pudgy guy about my size but not in as good shape. He acted bored but he did give me something in return to give to the mayor of Anchorage, which I did upon my return home.

We spent a lot of time and money disseminating knowledge about Alaska and Eskimos, but we lost money and learned hard lessons. First, don't believe what promoters of shows say about their shows. Don't believe that Americans will buy anything Alaskan. Don't think curious people around your booth mean good sales. We had fine examples of Eskimo crafts, and people looked at them as they would look at things in a museum; they didn't buy them. We had the same results in Chicago and Minneapolis. I didn't take Robert to Minneapolis because, while he attracted lookers, he didn't attract buyers, and his travel expenses were costing me money. If you'd told me I'd ever be selling on the road again, I'd have said, "No way." We went back to our little log cabin and tried to make that business thrive.

A Rough Start

I'd been on the road with the Alaskan crafts booth ever since Lydia and I married. Two weeks after I left, Lydia had to go back to Germany for some business. When she returned, I was in Chicago at the sports show there. My cousin Gordon Briggs picked her up at the Chicago airport and took her to the hotel where I'd been staying.

When I joined her there, she wouldn't let me touch her. She wouldn't tell me why. "I'm not in the mood," she'd say. She was totally pleasant but cut me off. What's going on? Sure, maybe women are just that way, but for ten days in Chicago, after two weeks in Germany!

Many years later, in a true confessions situation, Lydia decided to tell me she'd found the letter from Little Tina, arranging the tryst. In the hotel in Chicago, right off the bat Lydia had sent me out to the drugstore for something she wanted. She'd set me up. While I was out, she'd gone through my clothes and found the notorious letter in that coat. If she'd confronted me any time soon after our marriage, I would have told her that letter was old news, and I'd married her, hadn't I? We could have worked all that out. But she didn't tell me what was the matter. She stayed mad and I stayed rejected.

Back in Anchorage, I guess she said to herself, *I do love him. I'll make the best of it,* because we settled into running the Eskimo Shop together again, buying our crafts, developing a market, and getting along pretty well.

But I began to pay her back for rejecting me. She began to drink because of that. It took only a very small amount to make her drunk. She was a different person when she was drunk. She went into a rage. That made me unhappy and I'd go out with another woman. We went back and forth this way, hurting and retaliating, bringing out the worst in each other.

Finally I got so I didn't want to be around her. I said, "I think we should get a divorce." She said, "No way. I like being Mrs. Harry Briggs." She did. This was the stability she was looking for. It was far from perfect, but it was a step in the direction she wanted to go.

As a compromise, I said something like, "I won't be out looking for women, but if one comes along and I have an opportunity with her, I'll have an affair with her. And to be fair, you can do the same with a man. But not in Alaska." I wanted to protect my reputation there.

We had that understanding, but she didn't like it. She never took advantage of her freedom, but I did. She loved me. But I wasn't sure I loved her.

So our marriage got off to a bad start. We were pretty good business partners, however, and we threw our energies into our businesses.

Stocking the Eskimo Shop

Lydia proved to be great at developing inventory; she wrote personal letters to the Eskimo women who spoke English in every village, telling them of our marketing efforts and inviting them to offer their goods for sale through our shop. She also invited them to stop by our shop if they ever were in Anchorage. Some did. Many wrote replies to her letters; it's a very touching collection. Lydia was a very good person, sincerely interested in helping the Eskimos we dealt with. It embarrassed her to be praised, but she was an innately kind, caring person.

Lydia Briggs with the Alaskan crafts in the Eskimo Shop.

There were actually seven major language groups of Native Alaskans, each with several different tribes and cultures. The Eskimos were one of the larger groups and the best known; at least the name Eskimo was the best known. The largest population of Alaskan Eskimos lived in Nome in northern Alaska. Many barely survived on government subsidies, having largely given up hunting and fishing, and too often being dependent on alcohol. The Eskimos who lived off the sea, making their living from fishing and hunting sea mammals tended to live in small villages of 20 to 60 people. The native Indians lived further inland and hunted elk and moose. The Aleuts lived on the Aleutian Islands much more primitively.

One interesting group of Eskimos called the Inupiat, said to mean "real people," were descendants of Nunamiut who strayed long ago into the interior of Alaska, where they established a village called Anaktuvuk Pass, just south of the Brooks

Range. They lived off caribou herds. They built their houses Indian style using caribou hide. They were then called the last of the independent Eskimos, meaning they still led an independent nomadic life. I contacted some of them at the Pass, where I learned that they made very lifelike masks from the hides by pressing wet caribou skins on wooden molds. They sent me a sample and I was so pleased that I ordered a dozen. They didn't have a dozen ready, but they sent me what they had, maybe seven or eight. We advertised the masks on the radio and collectors began to come in. After a while, their production caught up with my need. This led to an article in a trade magazine mentioning that an Alaska businessman, Harry Briggs, had started a business venture involving these masks.

That brought the famous actor Sir Charles Laughton into the shop. He was appearing in America, sponsored by a woman's group. He did a one-man show all over the country including the recital of poetry. He was also a mask collector and had heard about our masks, so he came to see them. He had a reputation for womanizing, and he lived up to his reputation at our place. I came home after doing a TV show that night and noticed through the window that was a man in the front room of the shop. When I came in the back door, Lydia asked me if I wanted to know who was out there. I did. "It's Charles Laughton," she said, "and he's a real creep. He made a move on me, which I naturally rejected." She could have handled him easily but decided to keep him there for me to meet. I went back to Sir Charles and introduced myself as the pretty lady's husband. This obviously spoiled his day. He bought three masks and took off. I have a picture of Sir Charles, published in the *Times*, holding the masks without identifying our shop.

On my first trip to the far North to trade with the Eskimos, I learned a lot about native crafts and tried to explain to them about our shop, wholesale and retail pricing, and other points of discussion. It was hard for them to grasp from their distant perspective.

One of the more exciting acquisitions took me to the Diomede Islands in the Bering Strait between mainland Alaska and Siberia. When the United States bought Alaska from Russia in 1867, Big Diomede remained Russian and the U.S. got Little Diomede. The two islands are about a mile apart but the boundary between Russia and the U.S. runs between the two islands, as does the International Dateline. When it's Wednesday noon in Big Diomede, it's Tuesday noon in Little Diomede. Both islands consist of a high rock plateau with a little toehold of land down by the water. Little Diomede is a half-mile across with a little village on a narrow strip of land under a rock cliff on the Russian side of the isle. For eight months of the year, the island is covered in solid ice.

So on my second trip to Nome, I chartered a plane for a trip to the Diomedes. We could look down and see the dog teams as the Eskimos were going out to do some fishing. The population of Little Diomede was at that time about 60 people. They knew I was coming, and they were happy because I was bringing some oranges for them. They wanted oranges and booze. I only brought oranges. The pilot said, "I can't promise you I can get you in. We'll have to use skis." He saw the

Eskimos out there waving. He said the landing would be tricky and it was. We landed on the ice pack, maybe 300 yards from the village. The pilot said, "I'll come back in two days, but I can't promise I can get in." When the wind blows hard, landing safely is just not possible.

To build their homes, the residents of Diomede at that time took whale ribs and stuck the ribs upright in the dirt; then they stuck additional ribs horizontally into the cliff and covered the angle formed by the ribs with skins. You crawled into a narrow passageway into the main room where they had a fire. It was nice and cozy. I spent two nights there, listening to them tell stories. They were all related to people on Big Diomede so they had sometimes gone over to Big Diomede to see their families. The Soviets arrested them for illegal entry. The people from Big Diomede could come to Little Diomede without any problem. My hosts had their people in jail over on the Soviet island. They didn't understand why they couldn't go over there. They were telling me all this as if I could do something about it for them. They had a little school and a teacher. They had a contingent of the Alaskan National Guard, just a symbolic force. They showed me a couple machine guns and a few rifles. So much for the Cold War.

I wanted to get a whole walrus jawbone with its two tusks from Diomede. You see them hanging behind bars in clubs in Anchorage, and I wanted one for atmosphere in our shop. One Eskimo on Diomede had a fresh head of a walrus. All I wanted was the tusks and the jawbone, I said. He said all he had was this entire head and didn't want to cut it apart. So I got the entire frozen head. In the cargo section of the airplane going back, there was no heat so the head didn't defrost. In the hotel in Nome, I put the head out on my balcony and the dogs sat down below and barked at it. When I came back from Nome on a commercial plane to Anchorage, the walrus head was defrosting. The other passengers weren't too pleased. I took a taxi home and we put the head on the back porch for the night. Then I took it to the taxidermist in Anchorage, who couldn't handle it, so it went down to Seattle where they managed the job. I had it in the Eskimo shop for years. There weren't too many walrus there so it attracted people. Unfortunately, one time when we had it at the Eastern States Exposition, it fell down and broke its tusks.

I really enjoyed learning and collecting native artifacts. It's hard for me to believe that I, a banker's son from Massachusetts, was becoming an expert on Eskimo culture and trading with Eskimos.

Lake Michigan Again

The summer of 1959, I was training for my second marathon swim on Lake Michigan, and it was going well. Then the week before the big swim, I'd done a practice swim on Lake Winnebago, Wisconsin. It was ten miles across and there was no record of anybody having done it; so this was a first. A ten-mile swim a week before the main event was too long—but live and learn. I pulled a tendon in my right knee in that practice swim. It was feeling much better by the time I went into the water at West Beach in Michigan City, Indiana, on August 2, with Johnson Motors dealer Dick Thede in my nearest boat out of the seven boats that accompanied me. I was supported by Johnson Motors Dealers and by the Chicago Daily News, which gave me an inch and a half tall headline the morning I'd started at 3:05 a.m.

The Chicago Daily News was also sponsoring its 28th Daily News Regatta later that day and expected 100,000 people to be there to greet me when I was predicted to arrive at the Adler Planetarium about 36 hours later. The water was 69 degrees, the wind just 15 M.P.H., and I felt good, although 69 degrees is really too cold for a 30-mile attempt.

About four miles out, however, my knee was giving me trouble. I adjusted my stroke because I couldn't get a good kick on that side. I had started out doing about 50 strokes per minute, and now I could manage only 44. At about noon, I called my boats together and we conferred. I said I had no kick, just my arms, but I wasn't tired, and I was going to keep on. The afternoon edition of the Chicago Daily called this discussion with my escorts a "watery press conference" and gave me one and a half inch headlines saying, "BRIGGS SWIMS ON, DESPITE BAD LEG." However, I had to give up in the face of too much pain and too little progress after swimming 22 miles of the 34-mile challenge.

I didn't have much time to lick my wounds because there was the Eskimo Shop to attend to—fixing things around our cabin, enlarging the main room, where we displayed our goods, by taking down a bedroom wall, and my several outside activities to take up again and one new one.

AAU Boxing

At the end of September 1959, I was appointed as representative to the Pacific Northwest Association of the Amateur Athletic Union (AAU). I wanted to bring AAU-sanctioned events to Alaska, as these are well-run and prestigious competitions for all age levels. First, I wanted AAU boxing. According to regulations, any AAU event must be sponsored by a local nonprofit. I was eager to get started, so I offered the sponsorship of the Anchorage Hockey Leage, of which I was president. The first AAU-sanctioned boxing match was held on October 31, 1959. We had some sections of this competition, which were classified as exhibition fights, not AAU events, because some of the most popular young boxers were ineligible, having had some minor professional experience.

The next day I was elected to the Board of the Anchorage Boys Club as vice president. I quickly arranged for the Club to sponsor the second AAU boxing event, which took place on November 21.

I didn't neglect my actual paying jobs. I was just fine teaching at the University of Alaska at Elmendorf AFB. Some days in the spring, I'd sell hot dogs at my concession stands at Goose Lake Beach in the afternoon, then do my 5 p.m. sports show for Channel 2, and then teach a political science class at Elmendorf in the evening. Sometimes the same young people who bought my hot dogs in the afternoon were in my class in the evening. Just as one thing flowed into the next for them, it flowed together for me.

People look at my resume and ask how could you do all those things at one time. I said, "I was busy." The truth is none of these activities got the amount of attention it deserved. I worked on whatever was on the table in front of me at the moment. If it was a class, I taught it. If it was a hot dog, I put on mustard and sold it. If I'd concentrated on any one thing, I'd have been very good at it. Even so, I've been very good at a few things: swimming, organizing and promoting, and teaching. Maybe that's enough. I don't quote poetry much, but I guess my life was like the poet's candle burning at both ends, "it gives a lovely light." Unlike the candle, which would not last the night, my candle has lasted for 90 years.

Chapter 19

Expanding

My entrepreneurial nature was working overtime. As I brought sports programs into Anchorage and promoted them, and training awareness increased, athletes and those aspiring to fitness needed a place to work out. The boxing tournament, for example, brought to light the need for facilities in which to train. So as a profit making business and also a facility that I myself needed to better promote my sports interests, I bought the Anchorage Athletic Club in the spring of 1960. A really nice guy named Fred McKenzie had started the fitness center in a basement space on Fourth Avenue, but he wasn't a good businessman and the business was floundering. The Elks Club sponsored the Boys Club, and the boys used the Athletic Club facilities, and I was on the Boys Club board; so it seemed a natural enterprise for me. I bought the name Anchorage Athletic Club, rented the space, and bought the exercise equipment. I soon put in a permanent ring for boxing, and I was in business.

The club not only provided workout equipment but it was an important part of the whole sports scene in Anchorage, with athletes, coaches, and promoters coming here for sports related meetings. Another bonus was that, with the deal, I inherited Pop McEwen, the hardworking manager. Pop had helped start the Boys Club. The Club proved to be successful, and that helped my overall financial picture.

As I moved forward with entrepreneurial spirit, I learned as I went. As I dealt with cash flow, credit, taxes, and the bottom line, I learned solid lessons in finance, especially that you can't have what you can't pay for or foresee being able to pay for through a realistic business plan. I began to see how all of the federal programs that I'd thought were so wonderful in my idealistic youth were demanding more and more federal revenues and promoting dependence on a welfare state. In the meantime, excessive taxes and regulations on small businesses that kept our nation's economy going constrained private enterprise and deterred entrepreneurs. I went from being a New Dealer to a conservative pretty quickly, and I began to appreciate my father's and my Aunt Letitia's political views, and even those of Dr. Shoop at Western Reserve, who had moved me out of my preferred Ph.D. program in political science to a different field because of my liberal ideas. I began to pass on my new political philosophy to students in my Political Science classes, a field of study where a professor's political viewpoint is almost impossible to hide, even if I'd wanted to.

Back to Lake Michigan

In the summer of 1960, I was training for my third swim on Lake Michigan with Johnson Motors and the Chicago Daily News again as sponsors. Johnson Motors used their Johnson Dealers Association to carry out the sponsorship; both the parent company and the dealers got good publicity.

Some new wrinkles were that two of my key people, namely Dick Thede my "coach" or technical man, and Al Leason, the captain of my lead boat or navigator, were Johnson dealers but were not members of the Dealers Association. Association members had asked them to join, but they were not willing. Still as key people in my swim efforts the previous year, they got credit and publicity the same as the sponsoring Association, which provided boats, motors, and manpower. That arrangement didn't seem fair to the members of the Association. So I was asked to select a new coach and lead boat captain, if at all possible. In the end, I managed to keep my coach and navigator, because I trusted them 100%, the point being that a marathon swim includes dealing with all sorts of situations beyond the swimming itself.

Another wrinkle in the plan was that a Ford dealer named Jim Moran wanted to stage an event in mid-summer that would result in the first person to make the big swim across Lake Michigan. He wanted me to participate in his event, but I was happy with my own deal. The contest was a qualifying swim on July 19, which would include 25 contestants. Those who succeeded in swimming ten miles would qualify to make the full crossing on August 2, to take advantage of warm water and thus to preempt my swim. Each contestant would receive $100 per mile completed. I should have entered because I could use the money!

As it turned out, 18 contestants failed, of which six ended up in the hospital. Ten miles is about the breaking point for most amateur swimmers because that is about the point where the mind starts telling you that you can't stand any more. The contest qualified seven swimmers from the 10-mile trial. I had decided that, if any one of these qualifiers made it across the lake on August 2, I would attempt to swim from Nantucket to Cape Cod in the Atlantic off Massachusetts instead of Michigan. None made it.

It seemed to me that my endurance had increased every year since my first swim in 1956, but my speed was decreasing—not surprising for a 39-year old. Speed didn't matter to me except that the longer I was in the water the more body heat I'd lose. I was quoted as saying at the time, "The chances of crossing Lake Michigan are very slim. To make it, a man has to have training, endurance, excellent weather, and lots of luck." I had the training and endurance.

Because I had been missing the New England landscape, I had done some of my training in New Hampshire, including toughening my legs on Mt. Washington. Climbing mountains is a great way to gain leg strength, but I didn't repeat my Matterhorn mistake of doing too strenuous a climb too close to the main event. I did learn a few things from experience.

Wednesday in my final practice swim I did six miles in Lake Calumet. I had two fairly large boats lined up to serve as a guide and five smaller boats including an outboard lifeboat with my coach Dick Thede aboard. I was to leave Michigan City at

3 a.m. Saturday in order to arrive in Chicago at the time of the Chicago Daily News regatta for maximum welcoming crowds and publicity.

Friday morning at 8 a.m., 19 hours before my swim would begin, a 23-year old former Navy frogman named Martin Mogk went into the water at the Chicago side headed for Michigan City in the opposite direction in order to beat me in the crossing. He had two boats with him. He lasted ten hours. The idea that I was the man to beat had caught on.

The wind was light when I went in the water in the dark of Saturday morning. I remarked at the time that I'd conquered the psychological barrier of this swim and all I needed was the right wind or no wind at all. The wind picked up at about 20 miles, pushing against me. I ended up completing 26 miles, the same distance as an Olympic marathon run on land. It was the longest swim anyone had done on Michigan, but it wasn't all the way.

The Anchorage Daily News welcomed me home with the headline, "Harry Briggs Returns; Brings home a Record."

As usual, I committed to another swim on Michigan and then switched gears and went back to attend to business in Alaska. I had the itch to expand, as each little venture I had started earlier began to produce income.

Ninilchik

I had discovered a little hamlet called Ninilchik, located on the Ninilchik River on the west side of the Kenai Peninsula just a little bit upstream from the east coast of Cook Inlet. It had been an Athabaskan lodging place, a temporary base for that group of Native Alaskans to hunt and fish. Then, well before the U.S. bought Alaska, Russian fur traders, the first permanent settlers of Ninilchik, had come in and built houses in the Russian style. They spoke Russian, of course, which became a unique dialect as they were isolated from Russia over time. When I discovered Ninilchik, most of the population of about 100 people, descendants of nine founding families of mixed Russian and Native Alaskan heritage, spoke Russian along with some native words, and I'm told a few of the older residents spoke Russian at home as late as 2008. Ninilchik's simple wooden houses were very attractive in their unique way, and the town was only 188 miles southwest of Anchorage via the Sterling Highway built in 1955. Ninilchik seemed a perfect getaway vacation spot, not yet developed enough to drive prices up. The market was perfect for me to invest.

I wanted to buy the four buildings owned by the Russian Orthodox priest but he was asking $6000 for them and I didn't want to commit that much. So, for our first investment, we settled on an old wood frame house owned by a different person, located on the main street. In 1961, probably December, I paid $2000 for it.

We were excited to have our new property and decided to tough it out for a weekend in 1962. Lydia and I drove down with our dog Gloria. The temperature had dropped down to 20 degrees below zero when we arrived that evening. We knew the house had a stove so we'd brought firewood and a can of gas to start the fire. We also had sleeping bags and blankets. Lydia and Gloria got into a sleeping bag while I began to light the fire. I got a newspaper ablaze and put it into the stove. Then I did something stupid. I just lunged with the gas can toward the open stove door to pour it in. A stream of gasoline came out as I had planned and reached the burning paper. What I didn't plan was that the flame rushed right up the stream of gas back to the can I was holding, and I dropped it. Some gas splashed up the wall and within seconds we had a full-fledged fire. I hustled Lydia and the dog out of the house and then moved the car so it wouldn't be consumed by the fire. This whole thing didn't take more than two minutes. By the time I finished moving the car, I expected the flames would be coming through the roof. Surprise, surprise. There was a lot of smoke but the flames had stopped. It was so cold in the house that the walls were covered with ice and after the gas was consumed, the flames couldn't make it through the ice to the wooden walls. Lydia at this point showed her spunk by agreeing that we could make it through the night with blankets and sleeping bags.

In the spring, I made numerous trips to Ninilchik and fixed up the building both inside and out. I had found that Ninilchik resident Waldo Bishop was a great handyman. Between the two of us, we had the shop looking great. I brought down a bunch of gift items and opened Ye Olde Harbour Shoppe in June. I hired Wally's daughter to keep the shop open on specified hours. The only gift shop in town, it began to do quite well as day trippers from Anchorage and summer vacationers increased in number. We did well enough that we wished we had bought the four buildings from the Russian priest for $6000.

New Hampshire

Having done some training for the 1960 Lake Michigan swim in New Hampshire, I realized again how much I loved the region, and I wanted to retire there eventually. I intended to train there again for my fourth swim on Michigan and went back in the spring of 1961 on a mission to find a house. My requirements were that it be cheap, in a university town, built in traditional Cape Cod style, and have business potential. I didn't care a lot about its condition because I had discovered that I was good at fixing houses up.

I ended up looking seriously around Plymouth, New Hampshire, because there's a college there. I looked at a wonderful place with 35 acres, a barn, and seven fireplaces, for $3000. However, it had no business potential because it was at the end of a dirt road. On the way back from there, I saw a Cape Cod cottage. The realtor said, "You don't want that. It's on the edge of a cliff, and it's falling down." I thanked the agent for his service and then, without his knowledge, I returned to the dilapidated old house. There I met the Green family, who lived across the street, including Mel Green, who had lived there for many years with his wife Abigail, and his deaf mute son Robert. Both Mel and Robert worked at the local mill, which owned much of the real estate in the area. Although the mill paid very little in wages, it did rent homes to the workers for very little money. The Greens paid $2 a month for the house without a toilet or bath. The mill management finally put in a bathroom and raised the rent to $5 a month, which the Greens thought was extreme. That gives you an idea of property values. But the countryside around Campton, the village in which this house was located, was ski country in winter—or rather I could see that someday ski resorts would spring up—and foliage tours in the fall would surely be on the increase.

I paid $1200 for the falling down house and two acres with frontage on Route 175. The house backed up to a beautiful river and an amazing waterfall. I rushed to a phone and called Lydia about it. She was excited. I was the man! We worked out the deal by letter. With the $1200 payment we acquired the property in December 1960. I have now owned the property for over 50 years.

We opened the New Hampshire property in the summer of 1961 intending to put it to use while I trained for my fourth Lake Michigan swim. I arrived at Campton in the evening and slept in the station wagon. In the morning I was excited to explore my new property. I went through the house, which was in terrible shape. Then I went down to the river and followed it along to the falls. It was there that I decided to climb up the vertical bank to the top and then walk back to the house. I was about ten feet above the river when I grabbed a root to pull myself up. Unfortunately, the root wasn't strong enough to hold and it broke off, and there I was suspended in space with the root in my hand. In a split second I realized that if I went straight down, I would land on my head or back, so I flipped over, thanks to learning how to do back flips at YMCA camp, and landed facing the cliff. My left foot came down okay, but the right foot was caught between two rocks, which meant that it remained in place but the leg and knee kept on going. The result was a destroyed knee. Blood was gushing out. I was in a state of shock but ultimately got a hold of myself and managed to get out of the river somehow. I reintroduced myself to the Greens, who suggested I go to the hospital. The doctor there put some stitches in my knee and recommended that I admit myself to the hospital. I avoid hospitals. In fact, I almost never see a doctor. So I hobbled out.

I was obligated to Johnson Motors to swim again from Michigan City, Indiana, to Chicago in a few weeks. I went to a phone at the general store and called the people with Johnson Motors who had sponsored me for four years. That was the end of the road for them and me, they said.

I went to my tumbledown house with a sleeping bag and spent the night. In the morning, I was worse, but I didn't go to a doctor again. A Unitarian minister who had bought the house down the long road, a neighbor named Don at the general store, and another neighbor helped me until I could get around.

Don had overheard my call to Johnson Motors and figured I must be a really good swimmer. Later he said, "How about swimming Lake Winnipesaukee?" I said, "I'll never swim again." He said, "Just think about it."

Over the winter, I did think about it. The next year, 1962, I told a guy on local radio that I'd swim Paugus Bay, which was about five miles. If that went all right, I'd think about doing something longer. I developed a brand new stroke because my damaged leg was not good, a sort of a trudgen alternated with a crawl. On Erie, I'd started out with a crawl for the first half of the lake, then slipped into a trudgen for the second half, but now I was alternating one crawl stroke with one trudgen.

I did well at Paugus and felt good, except for my left leg. So I promised a 19-mile swim from Alton Bay to Weir's Beach on Lake Winnipesaukee, and I made it. People treated me like a star. So I said I'd come back the next year for a world's record, swimming Lake Winnipesaukee from Alton Bay to Wolfeboro to Center Harbor, then to Weir's Beach. So folks at Weir's Beach were backing me. At some point, I'd decide whether to do the whole lake.

Aunt Letitia

Also in 1962, I went down to Boston to take a plane somewhere and, after a brief visit with Aunt Letitia in Rockport; I left my car at her house. After my plane trip, when I went back to get my car, I found Aunt Letitia had had a stroke and was in the hospital in Gloucester. I went over to see her, afraid she might not recognize me, but she did. When she saw me, she burst into tears and just sobbed. I thought, *This isn't the Aunt Letitia I know.* She had always been very tough and never showed emotion, but a stroke breaks a person down.

34 Miles

As planned, in 1963, I returned to New Hampshire counting on a major swim on Lake Winnipesaukee from Alton Bay to Weirs Beach, but not swimming directly across the lake, rather going along parallel to the eastern shore from Alton Bay to the end of the lake, then up the western shore to Weirs Beach. It is important to understand that the Weirs Beach Tourist Association was promoting this event. And it was necessary to give them something for this. They had arranged to have a big crowd at the beach to see me finish. So naturally it would be good for the food stands. Thus the swim must end at Weirs Beach and certainly before ten o'clock in the evening.

With this goal in mind, we had two plans:

Plan A: if things went well, we would go from Alton Bay to Wolfeboro, then the 15 miles from Wolfeboro to the islands which surround Center Harbor, and then the three miles past the islands to the docks at Center Harbor. At this point, we would have gone from Alton Bay to Center Harbor, the length of the lake, which—if it had been a straight line—is 22 miles, but the length close to the shore by way of Wolfeboro adds another ten miles. Then we would turn and swim the three miles back from Center Harbor past the islands again and the seven more miles over to Weirs Beach. This would total 42 miles.

Plan B: if things didn't go as well, I'd swim from Alton Bay to Wolfeboro and then the 15 miles to the islands and then forget about going to the end of the lake at Center Harbor and swim straight across to Weirs Beach.

Halfway between Alton Bay and Wolfeboro, it was night. Somebody on the lead guide boat wasn't paying attention and for the second time in my career they lost me. I could see my guide boat drifting farther and farther away. I was a half-mile from Barndoor Island, so I was not in trouble. I could see boats and lights around the island. So I swam very slowly along the shore of the island for four hours. I never tread water. They finally found me at daylight.

I swam on to Wolfeboro and then headed for Center Harbor. A stiff wind came up and was blowing whitecaps into my face. If you try to take a breath and there's a whitecap in your face, you are in trouble. Because of this very choppy water—about the worst of my career, and that's saying something—and the time we'd lost at Barndoor Island, it was time for Plan B. So I skipped six miles by not going to Center Harbor, and I went on to Weirs Beach. We came into Weirs Beach at about 11 pm. A huge crowd had remained waiting for me, and we had given them 34 miles, a bit more distance than on Lake Erie, and with a gimpy leg. This was the longest swim ever made in New England and probably still is, but no world's record. Moreover, to "do a lake" you have to swim the full length, and I'd done 34 miles on this 22-mile long lake but, by not going to Center Harbor, I hadn't "done" the lake.

It was at the end of this swim that I pondered whether I wanted to do this anymore or not. In 1964, I tried to do some promotion for Belknap College, a small college in Center Harbor that existed from 1963 to 1974, and I swam as a fundraiser from Weirs Beach to Center Harbor to Wolfeboro, which is 22 miles. This has now been done a few times since then, but nobody else has done over 30 miles that I know of. By that time, I was 43, and Lydia wanted me to end the swimming because of its physical risks and also so I would concentrate on our businesses. To tell the truth, I had lost the desire; it had become work and suffering. So that was the end of my swimming career, at least for a while. In the next 30 years, I didn't swim ten strokes.

Ninilchik Again

A couple years before my swimming career ended at Winnipesaukee, in 1962, the year after my first purchase in Ninilchik, I'd bought the four additional buildings from the Russian Orthodox priest. I now owned one end of the village and planned a charming little resort, recreating an important part of Alaska's past but with the comforts tourists require.

We'd gotten a few antique Russian chairs for the shop. When we were back East during the fair season, Lydia even got something from the Russian prince she'd lived with for six months. She went into his brownstone in New York City, while I waited outside. I figured she'd be out in a minute because his wife would be there. But the wife was out, and she was there for 30 minutes and came out with a beautiful Russian icon, which came back with us to Ninilchik. Sales in Russian goods in this Russian village were satisfying.

Also in 1962, encouraged by the healthy sales of Russian crafts in our shop in Ninilchik, we expanded the Eskimo Shop in Anchorage by adding an international room in the garage behind the cabin, where we sold goods from Lydia's native Germany as well as Austria, Holland, Israel, and other countries.

About this time also, a trapper who spent much time with the Indians, asked Lydia if she would like to have an authentic Athabaskan Indian totem pole. We had bought a

Lydia shows off new eastern European wares in the International Annex.

few Athabaskan artifacts from him before. Lydia said, "Yes," but didn't tell me anything about it. I saw it for the first time when I came home in the evening from the TV station. Lydia had wanted to surprise me with it, and I was surprised! I complimented her for another imaginative marketing move, as the totem pole soon became a landmark in Anchorage.

The Flying Cossack

Some sections of Cook Inlet have the second fastest and highest tides in the world. This is the reason that Anchorage is not a great port. During the four to five hours of the tidal change, either in or out, you can see logs and other debris rushing upstream into the Knik Arm or westward toward the ocean. The water moves so fast that it would be virtually impossible to maintain adequate docks in Anchorage, although there are a few docks for barges. Freighters and barges come up from Seattle and go into the port of Seward on the other side of the Kenai Peninsula; the containers then go aboard the Alaska Railroad, maintained by the Department of the Interior, through a two mile tunnel cut through a coastal mountain and then into Anchorage, about 100 miles, and then on to Fairbanks, another 400 miles. Cook's Inlet tides reach high and run fast up the river to Ninilchik. One of my buildings was a log cabin, half of which went out on pilings over the Ninilchik River, where there is about a six-foot tide that sometimes reaches the cabin.

At low tide, you can find tremendous amounts of coal deposits the water has left on the beach. At every low tide, you can walk out on the dirty beach and pick up big chunks of coal. Thus, except for the long winters, a person could live on the beach, building coal fires to keep off the chill and to cook fish and game. Huge amounts of salmon run in the Ninilchik River and dozens of moose graze in the fields.

The plentiful supply of salmon made me want to venture out on the sea. In the spring of 1963, Lydia and I invested in a boat. We, with the help of friends Waldo Bishop and his wife, were going to make $50,000 a month catching salmon. The Bishops were the only other English speakers in Ninilchik. I went down to Seattle to buy the Bristol Bay double-ender along with fishing gear and nets. We named it the Flying Cossack to reflect the Russian tradition of the little port at Ninilchik, where she would be harbored.

The boat was brought up on a barge to Seward where I would take over the helm for the trip around the Kenai Peninsula to the Cossack's ultimate home. Seward is on the southeast side of Kenai Peninsula and Ninilchik was on the northwest side. To get the boat all the way around the tip of the Kenai Peninsula to Ninilchik was a 300-mile trip, and I would have no ship-to-shore communications. Waldo didn't want to be out there without ship-to-shore, and Lydia had prevailed on me not to bring my dog Gloria, so I set out alone.

The first attempt lasted about one day. Approximately 30 miles out of Seward, the distributor stopped functioning. I was maybe six miles off shore and envisioned the wind blowing me against the waiting cliffs. Fortunately, the wind changed and blew me right back out to sea. At that time of year in southern Alaska, there is never total darkness; the night amounts to about four hours of twilight. As the sun came up, I could see that I was many miles, probably 30, from the snow-capped mountains that fall off into the ocean.

By the law of the sea, a ship is not allowed to ignore another ship that is in trouble. Thus, after failing to attract the attention of several passing fishing boats, one finally came over to see if I was adrift. The captain and owner threw me a line and towed me all the way back to Seward Harbor, where with a little more help, I made it back to the dock. Waldo, a sometime mechanic as well as all around handyman, came over from Ninilchik and put in a new distributor. I was all set for my second attempt, a solo trip again

It was wonderful! Unless you have been there, it would be difficult to understand the vastness and wonders of that great state. For example, for the first few hours, I must have witnessed a half dozen whales rising up in the sea as if to take at look at the Cossack before splashing back below the surface of the water. I remember huge towering rock islands, which extend maybe a thousand feet into a bird-laden sky. Although I didn't have charts, it seemed safer to pass through the water between the rock islands and the mainland. During one of these passages, I encountered the biggest flock of birds that I could possibly imagine, tens of thousands of puffins with the striking black and white markings on their faces and especially their big orange beaks. There were so many puffins in the sky that it appeared to be twilight much too early.

About noon of the second day, I finally passed the last rock pinnacle at the tip of Kenai and turned northeast into Cook Inlet. I could see storm clouds gathering to the north. After passing English Bay, a then uninhabited trapping village, I noticed that there was a killer whale swimming parallel to me. This was easy for the whale because the Cossack's maximum speed was only about eight knots per hour. Although I hadn't seen any fishing boats since the first day, it wasn't long before there were dozens of the smaller, black and white mammals following me as they often follow the fishing boats. They were perhaps looking for a handout or maybe just curious. Gee, a city guy from the suburbs of Boston seeing all this!

I was soon offshore from Seldovia, a remote village of about 30 people on the southeast coast of Cook Inlet, and I had to make a decision. Do I follow the coast of Cook Inlet and turn into Kachemak Bay, an arm of Cook Inlet that poked 40 miles deep into the southeast shore of Kenai Peninsula? Do I hug the coast all the way in and all the way out until I reach the safe harbor at the town of Homer on the other side of the Bay, where I'd still be 50 miles from Ninilchik? Or do I sail straight across the open mouth of Kachemak Bay, the much shorter route to safety at the town of Anchor Point, much closer to Ninilchik?

My fuel was running low, so I opted to run straight across the Kachemak Bay to Anchor Point—only 20 miles from Ninilchik. I knew that if I went down into the icy water that I wouldn't last much more than two hours. Not a happy death. If I should run out of gas or lose my power on the longer route, I would smash up against the rocks. The shorter but still 40-mile crossing seemed the best bet. By the time I'd committed to the direct crossing, the winds had picked up and I was about to have some of the worst hours of my life. A Pacific Northern Airlines plane apparently spotted me as it descended to go into Anchorage International Airport about 60 miles away. It circled me once and dipped its wings as if to let me know someone knew I was there or perhaps to warn me to go back to Seldovia since the pilot had better knowledge of the size of the storm.

Large swells on the sea soon became 20-foot walls of water surrounding me. As the Flying Cossack and I were lifted to the crest of a giant wave, the engine sputtered a bit before we were dropped into the trough that followed. Then up again, then down. I gripped the wheel turning the Cossack to face each wave head on to avoid being tipped over sideways. I didn't have time to give a prayer of thanks after surviving one wave before the next one hit.

I was desperate to get to within a mile of the coast in the Anchor Point area. The seas were so high that we were not going more than two or three knots per hour, and the engine wasn't working well. The boat took such a pounding that I was surprised it didn't break up in the first few minutes of the storm. I'd tied my boots around my neck in case we did break up and I had to swim. I'd have them when I reached shore. I was glad for my work pants and heavy brown flannel shirt, which would keep me warm.

Finally I made it pretty close to Anchor Point. I could see the lights of the town from about two miles out, but there was no way to dock. Cliffs came down to the sea except in the small opening to the harbor, and I'd wreck getting through. I managed to get an anchor down but the anchor was dragging. All night I spent at the wheel, clutching it, fighting the seas. I wasn't fighting for me, I was fighting for the Cossack and our dreams that rode in its hold.

Then the engine stopped and I was totally at the mercy of the storm. I don't know how long this lasted before the Cossack suddenly flipped over and I was relieved to find myself in the water. This is where I could take charge of my destiny. I started to swim.

There was never any question in my mind that I'd be all right. The long steady strokes of my marathon swims went by the wayside as I dogpaddled that piece of Cook Inlet that remained between me and the shore. I took it slow. No doubt I'd make it. The hard part began when I reached shore. Waves crashing onto rocks, sucking back with a roar. Where to make a scramble for a toehold of land?

I finally managed to clamber up on a rock between two huge, long, slow waves. Out of their reach, I looked back and saw the capsized hulk of the Cossack blowing to shore. If I'd stayed with it, I'd have been brought to shore. How much safer I'd felt in the water, as cold as it was, and as fiercely as it crashed upon the shore.

Among all my swims, I guess this was the most important swim of my life. Maybe the good Lord intervened, knowing that Lydia would need me for many more years.

When I managed to crawl onto the rocks, I faced a 100-foot bank. Above the rocks, it was like a landslide. Two steps up and one sliding back. Finally at the top, I put my boots on and started out to find civilization. I walked through the woods for about an hour. I passed two moose in an open field. They looked at me and strolled away. Soon I came to a dirt road I was sure would lead me to Anchor Point, which I was fairly certain was to the left and north of me. However to the right I spotted a station wagon with a lady and two children standing outside. Ah! Help at last. I headed toward her but, when she spotted me, she immediately collected her children and drove off, probably frightened by the apparition of a shipwrecked seadog standing there.

I turned and went back the other way and, within a couple miles, walked into the General Store at Anchor Point. They knew me there because of my swimming activities and they offered their phone for me to get in touch with Lydia back in Anchorage. She'd seen the storm, which was the biggest storm of the summer, and she'd heard that a barge had broken loose in Anchorage and two sailors had drowned. And she hadn't heard from me in much too long. She was having a fit. When I got her on the phone. She said, "What's going on?"

I said, "I'm all right, but I lost the boat."

"You lost the boat!" she cried. She was understandably dismayed to lose our biggest investment that we thought was going to make our fortune. However, she didn't pay quite enough attention to my brush with death to suit me.

Lydia liked being Mrs. Harry Briggs because I worked hard and was ambitious. She hadn't bargained for my being an intrepid risk taker and sometimes using bad judgment. We had insurance for $5000 to cover the boat, but we lost the equipment. I was just glad to get out alive. Needless to say, that was the end of my career as a salmon fisherman.

Chapter 20

Earthquake

One day Pop McEwen, my manager at the Athletic Club came down the stairs and said, "Come up. I want you to see something." I was busy. "What for?" I asked. "Just come up and see," he said. It must be really something, so I went up. There was a taxi parked out on the street with a big sign on its side with my picture on it and the words "KENI Channel 2. Harry Briggs." I found out that all of Anchorage's 100 taxis had my name and picture on them for about two months. Lydia loved that. She really did like the publicity I got for my sports reporting and the fact that I was known all over town and beyond. It was not like me to be surprised by the sign on the taxi and not know who was responsible. I'm guessing Bob Winslow made it happen. He owned Anchorage Cold Storage and he bought more advertising than anyone. I bought only his products for my concession stands, so he was always pushing for me. The job with KENI was a great job in many ways.

My reporting went well beyond sports later that year when President John Kennedy was assassinated on November 22, 1963. KENI normally went off at midnight, but during those weeks, we were on the air with breaking news twenty-four hours a day. I was terrible at first at this kind of reporting, and I knew it and was embarrassed. I just kept at it, did a self-analysis, and improved. I'd try to cut out my "y'know," and all of a sudden I went from terrible to pretty good in two months. Then I got relaxed. As I went along, I got stronger and gained confidence. I ended up doing a job that made me proud.

Another on the air learning experience involved a second Jackie Robinson interview. I normally did sports on what we called the Big 60. My 15-minute sports news was broken down into five minutes of local and ten minutes of national sports. One day a man called saying, "You don't know me but I've been to quite a few of your sports events. And I'd like you to interview Jackie Robinson on KENI. He'll only be giving one 15-minute interview and I'm giving you first chance. Do you want to do it?" I said, "Absolutelyl."

Robinson had gotten some gray hair on the side and he was more poised than when I first interviewed him in Puerto Rico at the beginning of his Big League career. He said, "What do you want to talk about?" I said, "I'll tell you something about yourself that most people don't know. You played four sports at Pasadena Junior College before you transferred to UCLA. Most people don't know you didn't play your whole college career at UCLA." So he said, "You're right. How did you know?" I said, "You told me when I interviewed you once before, in Puerto Rico." He didn't remember that interview, of course.

I had a habit, not a good one. I answered my own questions too much. I asked Jackie Robinson a question and I gave the answer. On camera, he said, "Now you asked me a question and do you want me to answer it or are you going to answer it yourself?" I was embarrassed, but I made some joke back. I'd been good at wisecracks ever since way back in high school. At the break, they told me to just keep this going. The telephone lines were lighting up. Forget the time limit. Jackie said, "I hope you weren't offended. You were pretty good for a local guy." Then he put his hand on my shoulder and said, "You're okay." We went back on the air and we did a good show. That was a highlight for me. Lydia watched me every night. She said, "You opened your big mouth again. But you learned and that's the best interview you ever did."

I was hotter than a firecracker by 1964. The Eskimo Shop was doing so well in its location in a residential area on East 3rd Avenue, thanks to my advertising on the air, that I opened another one downtown on 4th Avenue, where doctors' and lawyers' offices and the federal government building might provide lunch time foot traffic. I expected a different kind of customer there, and I wanted both. This Eskimo Shop did even better than the original. The Anchorage Athletic Club, three blocks away, was also bustling, with 50 by 150 feet of workout space for men and another 50 by 150 feet of space for women. Ninilchik was growing. Alaska was booming. I was promoting a sports stadium for Anchorage where big events could be held. I envisioned myself promoting events at this arena. I knew everyone in Anchorage, from the Police Chief to the Mayor and the Governor of Alaska. And everyone knew me or knew of me. I'd even been approached to be a candidate for governor. I thought about running.

Lydia and I were getting along pretty well, even though she had terrible outbursts when she drank, which was not all the time. I admired her more and more for her character. She was hard working and determined and had a great sense of values. However, taking her out of the clubs didn't take the club culture out of her life. The girls she knew at Guys and Dolls were the people she was comfortable with. But she was a star among them with more kindness, dignity, and good character. And I loved having her on my arm when I went out because she was a knockout but I could see beyond her beauty to her good heart. I don't know if I felt the kind of love for her that I'd felt for the girlfriends I almost married, but we were building something between us.

We'd made it in Alaska….together.

Earthquake

I had flown to Seattle to look at some merchandise for my shop and planned to go home by way of Juneau. When you have business in Juneau you need to book your flight to arrive a day or two before you have to be there because the city has terrible weather, as it did this time. We flew out of Seattle on March 26. We circled Juneau a few times before we were instructed to return to Seattle because the weather wouldn't allow us to land. I flew again to Juneau on March 27 and landed without problems. I was very tired, so as soon as I checked in, I went to bed—it was about 2 o'clock in the afternoon—and slept. The next day, I was going to talk to people in the State Legislature about getting funds allocated for building the sports arena in Anchorage.

Late that afternoon, Alaska Time, I heard sirens and bullhorns in my sleep. I am a chronic sleepwalker so I thought it was a dream and went on sleeping. Pretty soon I heard the sounds again, so I put on clothes and went down in the lobby, where I was told that at a little after 5:30 there had been a terrible earthquake in Anchorage, which might cause a huge tidal wave or tsunami in Juneau. Everyone was saying, go to higher ground, but we were already on the side of a mountain with no place to go. My first concern was for Lydia. I was really worried about how well she was holding up. It was my job to take care of her and protect her, and here I was far away. There was nothing to do but to get involved where I was.

I knew that KINY radio, sister station of KENI in Anchorage, was located next door. I walked into that office and identified myself. The reporters there were delighted to see me because they didn't know anything about Anchorage. So I took over! As soon as I did, I took a phone call from a radio station in Seattle, I gave them as much information as there was available including several locations which I considered to be vulnerable. By this time, I was getting a faint signal from newscaster Ty Clark with KENI in Anchorage, where KENI had the only generator that was working. KENI was sending signals to Fairbanks and Fairbanks was sending them on to Juneau. I don't really know how they were doing it. Juneau had only radio, no TV station. Juneau's radio station KINY was owned by the same person, Al Bramsted, who owned KENI, so they were working together. Reports were coming in about this street or this building or that area of town and I had to make sense of it, knowing the layout of Anchorage.

Ty Clark was from Haverhill, Massachusetts. We'd become fairly close while working together. When I got the faint signal from Ty in Anchorage. I asked, "How bad is it?" He said, "Pretty bad. The National Guard has moved into downtown where looting is a problem." I asked him, "Is there any way you can find out about Lydia?" Our log cabin was about a block from the commercial area, and the Athletic Club and downtown Eskimo Shop were right where the Guard would be. He said he'd try.

Of course, I was terribly worried about Lydia, but I went ahead and reported. In fact, I made the first broadcast about the earthquake that actually came out of Alaska.

Finally, word came about Lydia. "She's okay," I was told, "but she's in a state of shock." Boy, was I ever glad to hear she was okay. I couldn't wait to get back to comfort her. I also wanted to know about the Club, which at the time of the earthquake was always full of people.

However, the representatives in the State Legislature in Juneau were the only people allowed to go back to Anchorage for three days, so I had to stay in Juneau. I don't remember much of anything about those three days, but I know I was plenty worried.

When I finally was free to go, I took a flight into Anchorage. When I saw the control tower spread out on the ground, I got an idea of the destruction. It was something to see!

The cab driver at the airport knew me. "We're not supposed to go in downtown," he told me, "But I know where you live, and I'll take you there." So I was home.

Lydia was really, really glad to see me. She was glad to pass on to me the responsibility for dealing with the problems caused by the earthquake, but I have to say she did her part.

The log cabin was in good shape. The wood frame structures stood up better through the vibration of the earthquake than the many cinderblock buildings that just disintegrated. Our merchandise flew off the shelves and we lost a few Eskimo carvings, but not a lot. However, by the time I got back to Anchorage, looters had ransacked the newer shop downtown, and we lost all our merchandise there.

The building that housed the Anchorage Athletic Club was built on the side of a hill. The Club was in the basement, with the women's workout area in the back deeper into the earth than the men's area in the front. The two areas were on the same slab but separated by a wall. Later I heard from the sole woman who was in the Club during the earthquake, working out on a stationary bike. She told me it felt as if she were on an elevator going down; the entire women's section suddenly lowered seven feet, while the men's section stayed at its original level. She found the two feet of overlap and crawled up through it into the men's section to safety.

The Anchorage Athletic Club was lost. Fortunately for us, we didn't own the building, but the equipment ruined was all ours, and the lives of our customers were in disarray. Later we found that the highway from Anchorage to Ninilchik was

US government photos

broken up, effectively cutting our little Russian village off from tourists, even if any potential tourists existed anymore. I don't believe you deserve success if you don't pay your dues, but we had paid our dues in Alaska. Life, it seems, isn't fair.

Damage

Many suffered far worse than Lydia and I did. Alaska lies along the northern portion of the Ring of Fire and is the most seismologically active state in the union. This earthquake of magnitude 9.2 was the worst in North American history and of greater magnitude than the 2011 earthquake in Japan. The disaster killed 131 people and did $538 million in property damage, which in 1960s dollars is a lot. Most of the deaths were from the tsunamis, especially the first tsunami, which occurred about 20 minutes after the quake, sweeping away the whole port of Valdez, Alaska, and the people working there. Some of the property damage occurred during the four to five minute shuddering of the quake. The rest was caused by avalanches and landslides triggered by the quake.

Here are just a few examples of the devastation in Anchorage: The 1200 L Street Building in Anchorage, a fourteen-story reinforced concrete apartment building, was shattered during the earthquake. The five-story Hillside Apartment Building was so badly damaged that it had to be razed. In the showroom area of the Fifth Avenue Chrysler Center, the roof T's rested on reinforced concrete columns, which completely collapsed, dropping the roof T's onto the automobiles below. Landslides crushed whole subdivisions like the Turnagain Heights subdivision, and the terrain became unrecognizable.

I'm telling this story in the weeks after the 2011 earthquake and tsunami destroyed whole towns in Japan with thousands of lives lost. Alaska, not as densely populated, did not suffer as badly, yet when I see the Japanese looking at their destroyed homes, I have tremendous feelings for them. Those people are tough. I know how they feel, and I think about them a lot.

Toward Recovery

With the Club lost and no income from our shops, I needed to move quickly. I was desperately looking for a place, when a suitable building appeared out of the blue. A building owned by a man in his eighties named Mr. Edris was available. He'd left Anchorage and had been renting the building to the Anchorage Police Department. The police had moved out, and now the earthquake had crippled the town, so Mr. Edress wanted to sell his building for a reasonable amount of $80,000 with $15,000 down. It was not listed with realtors but somehow he knew to call me. I said, "I don't have any money right now for the down payment." He'd seen me on TV for years, so he said, "I know you. I'll let you buy it for no money down, just start making payments." So with that arrangement plus a 10-year mortgage for $65,000, I bought this building on what was now the main drag quickly and with little hardship.

The next job was to move the equipment from the old Athletic Club into the new one. No one was supposed to go into the damaged buildings, but I knew the people in charge and so got permission to do the move from midnight to 2 a.m. I had a friend with a truck who would help. Lydia pushed me; I might have been slower without her. She said, "Come on, let's do it." So we got the equipment moved in two hours. Then we had to transform a building suited for a police department to a facility with a steam room and plenty of open space for work outs.

I figured I needed about $20,000 to do that so I applied for a Small Business Administration (SBA) loan. What an experience! I had long taught my political science students about the red tape involved with the bureaucracy of the federal government, which I had learned first hand in my three federal government jobs, but this was the worst. We applied and several weeks later the people in Washington turned me down. They said that, because I didn't own the facility in which the club operated and only rented it, I hadn't really lost anything. I had just lost my largest source of income! Since the steam room was the biggest reason to join the club, I decided to concentrate on the steam room in my next application to the SBA. I used the loss of income argument, and they agreed to loan me $10,000.

I took this to Clyde Lewis, a plumber and good friend as well as an Athletic Club member. He said that to do the job right it would cost $15,000 but for $10,000 plus a lifetime membership, he would do it. It took him about five weeks. In the meantime, I brought Waldo Bishop up from Ninilchik to help me remodel to meet the requirements of a health club. We reopened in mid June. A few people who worked out regularly, our best customers, were back on track that summer, but it was rough for us because most people were more concerned with rebuilding their homes and businesses than with working out. By this time, I was really broke. Fortunately, the Goose Lake food concessions were starting up for the summer.

We also planned to move the Eskimo Shop into the new building along with the Athletic Club and turn the log cabin into a home again.

Aunt Letitia

Another loss in 1964 was Aunt Letitia's death. She'd had a succession of strokes since her first one and finally lost the ability to speak intelligibly. No one really knew how much she understood. During that time she spoke as if she were making sense but what came out was not even recognizable words. Then suddenly she had a moment of lucid speech. Mary reported that suddenly she said perfectly clearly, "Oh, would that I had died." This was not the way she would have wanted to live or die, and it was finally her time.

I was very tied up with the losses in Anchorage and had not seen Aunt Letitia recently, so nothing concrete seemed to change for me when she died, but I'll have to say that she had been an emotional mainstay for me for many, many years, and shared her home and table with me on many, many occasions, and generously gave me money when I really wanted to do something for which I didn't have the funds.

She was never fun or playful or even openly affectionate, but she was a rock of stability in my life, and her death saddened me.

I also admired her tremendously as a physician and as the head of her household. How respected she was in Boston had been impressed on me in a funny way many years before when I'd just gotten back from the Pacific. I got a call from people at the Veteran's Administration to come see them. They asked me, among other things, if I had a discharge. I said, "Yes." They told me I needed to see a doctor and asked if I had one. I told them I had one, my aunt Dr. Letitia Adams. They said, "She's your aunt! Oh, she is the best doctor in Boston!" It took me a while to figure out that my honorable discharge from the Marines was not the kind of discharge they were talking about, but I sure knew my aunt was famous!

Getting Out of a Mess

By marrying Lydia I ended up with some connections I didn't care for. B-joints were a big industry in Anchorage. Lydia had wanted to get out of the unsavory environment. When she married me, we were pretty successful, but those B-girls from the old days hung around my place. Lydia enjoyed them. She'd been a top leader in that industry and those girls looked up to her. Did I get her out of that? No, they came over to the house. These were the people she was comfortable with. Anchorage had 1000 doctors and lawyers there in a town too small for that number. Did she feel comfortable with any of them? No. So Lydia and her girlfriends were hanging around and I'd sit with them. I felt comfortable with them, too. The difference is that I felt comfortable with a lot of different kinds of people, but I was raised in a different world from Lydia's.

Before the earthquake, I'd discovered I had another kind of problem. Well-known mobster Blackie Robinson had just been let out of prison in Illinois, and he was going to be strong in Anchorage in organized crime and in the joints.

One day, when I was out of town on a swimming trip, a well-dressed woman came into the shop, and Lydia had reason to believe she was a shoplifter. The woman had a taxi waiting. Lydia watched her until she took something. When she left the shop, Lydia grabbed her by the arm and the woman slipped out of her coat and ran to the cab. Lydia caught up and jumped in the cab with her, and they drove off. The woman finally escaped from the taxi, but Lydia saw where the woman lived and called the police, who went to the woman's home and found the stolen goods. The shoplifter turned out to be the wife of Blackie Robinson, the guy sent up to Anchorage to run the mob in the city. She was charged with theft.

Blackie didn't want to have trouble right off. So Blackie got Frank Maroney, who was the boss of the Anchorage underworld for years, to ask Lydia to go easy on this mobster's wife. Frank Maroney one night had murdered a man in one of his clubs and was sentenced to serious time. While he was out on bail during his appeal, he was helping Blackie take over the job, so keeping Blackie's wife out of trouble was his business. Lydia said, "Nobody steals from me and gets away with it." I said, "This could get us into trouble." She said, "I know that, but I'm not letting her off easy."

Frank then skipped the state, went to California, and was eventually murdered while trying to horn in on someone's territory. This was big news in Alaska. I knew about these guys. In marrying Lydia, I'd stolen their biggest moneymaker from the clubs, which was my first offense, and now there was the Blackie Robinson situation.

I'd been on one of my swims, and when I returned, Lydia told me about Robinson's wife. I argued with Lydia to get her to just drop the charges to end the story right there. She wouldn't budge. Then the mobsters began to contact me. Fast Freddie Fergone, a club manager they sometimes used as a hit man, contacted me, saying, "Drop the charges." I said, "I want to, but Lydia won't." After that meeting with Fast Freddie, they began to apply the heat. They'd come around at night and shine spotlights in our windows. They would make threatening phone calls giving us several days to drop the charges or they would do something terrible. The police sent somebody to stay in our house for three days to see if anyone might come or to overhear the conversation. Someone in the police department must have tipped the mob off because during that three day period there were no calls. As soon as the police left, the harassment started again. I think Lydia finally just got sick of it all. When we did go to court, Lydia didn't appear and it blew over. I think she worked something out because the harassment finally stopped and she officially dropped the charges.

It wasn't just Lydia. I got myself into something similar with the same guys. I got involved in professional boxing because of the Athletic Club. I had the Boys Club, and I had a ring, and then the older boxers showed up. Pop McEwen handled the ring. I was pretty naïve. I thought I was a man of the world, but in this case I wasn't. Joey Lopez, a good fighter from Seattle, appeared at the gym one day wanting to work out. Jimmy Nelson, a handsome young man, was a local boxer. I had a perfect match there: Joey, the champion from Seattle, and the local Jimmy Nelson. I arranged a feature fight; we drew a lot of people for that. It was a natural. I promoted at least eight cards including the Alaska Golden Gloves and the Boys Club. I'd have little kids with big gloves, a great show. That lasted maybe two or three minutes. Big laughs. I got a few nonprofit matches for free, and I'd pay the pros and get my share from the gate.

I interviewed both boxers on the air. I also said in the press that I thought Lopez would win though Jimmy is a great fighter. I would announce the fighters, then go to the TV cameras to report the fight, and then I'd go up into the ring to announce the winners. What I didn't know was that there was heavy betting going on, and my prediction played a part in it. The gambling was done on the side, Mafia style, and the police were in on it.

Jimmy Nelson absolutely killed Joey Lopez. The seasoned pro was on the ropes; he collapsed. What a terrible beating Lopez took! I realized later that they had it all fixed. I don't know how they got Lopez to do it. They brought in all that money, thousands of dollars, for Lopez whom I and the press had predicted would win and then they rigged it so that Jimmy won. The Mafia loved me. I provided fights and they cleaned up. They were using me, and they got respectability because I was Mr. Clean.

After that a bunch of bad people started hanging around the Club where the kids were training. Pop McEwen was there and Lt. Heaton, a good cop, and some unsavory people. Heaton said, "You have to do something about this." What? These bad guys were selling drugs in my place and to the kids, too. Joey Lopez was doing most of it. I told Heaton, "Go into my office and be there, so it's not just me." Then Pop went out and brought Joey into the office. I told him not to come into my club any more. He was on drugs. He went down to Freddie Fragone's strip club. Freddie called me and said, "You'd better get out of here because Lopez is on the prowl."

The next day at noon, I went down to the Eskimo Shop in town to relieve our employee as usual. Several minutes after I'd taken my place behind the counter. Pop came rushing in, saying that Joey Lopez had been at the Athletic Club looking for me. Pop and I were talking about what to do, when all of a sudden there was a terrible noise of breaking glass. In stormed Lopez, after putting his big foot through the glass door. I tried to keep my cool. To get behind the counter or out you had to squeeze between the counter and the wall. I looked right at Lopez and squeezed through. With Pop looking on, I stepped out from the counter. Pop thought I was going to be killed. Rather than make a move toward Lopez as both Joey and Pop both expected, I made an abrupt right turn and went out the door. My heart was pounding but I didn't run. I walked the two blocks to the police station where I told what had happened. The police sent a man over to enter a police report.

I called Fast Freddie and said, "Joey just broke in my glass door." Freddie said, "Yes, he hates you. Maybe I can handle him." We had a meeting that night, with a couple of guys there to keep Lopez from attacking. I told Lopez again, "You have to stay away from my place." Lopez said, "I will blow up your house." I was scared. Lydia was embarrassed that it was her people. It was my fault for getting into boxing. I came up with an idea. It was a time to get Golden Gloves down to Seattle. I said, "Joey, would you like to accompany the boxing team to Seattle? But no drugs." He said okay and he was no longer an immediate threat, but it was an uneasy three days for me down in Seattle.

Then the earthquake happened and we lost the Athletic Club. The earthquake got me out of that mess.

I still had my book selling business and I was on the Parks and Recreation Commission, and these guys, Lydia's people, still had their claws into me. There was a lot of stuff like that going on. When people ask me why I left Alaska, I often say because we lost our business in the earthquake and never recovered. That's the truth and a quick answer that satisfies them, but really Anchorage was getting to be unhealthy, and it seemed time to leave.

However, it took one more disaster to get us to pack our bags

Chapter 21

The New York World's Fair and a New Career

The New York World's Fair was held April to October in 1964 and the same again in 1965. Representatives from the State of Alaska asked me to exhibit our state's products at the Alaska Pavilion in the second year of the Fair. I'd essentially done something similar at the three sports shows in 1959 where I'd learned that people were interested in Alaska but didn't buy what I had to sell. But it had been six years and I'd gotten over the frustration of that experience. Besides a World's Fair is a big deal, and my market for similar goods in post-earthquake Alaska was suffering. So I reserved two booths for Native American displays and selected some Eskimo goods for sale.

The Alaska Pavilion. What a farce! There were twelve booths in the Alaska Pavilion. I had my two Native American booths, and a guy named Dave had two spaces for some reindeer and a black bear he'd been keeping on a busted up animal farm in the Pocono Mountains of Pennsylvania. He was a nice guy and he liked animals, but he was a poor businessman operating on a shoestring. He must have tied his bear up with a shoestring, too, because once he had the bear in Manhattan where it escaped in Columbus Circle. He had to call the police to help capture it. The Alaska Pavilion rounded out its stellar representation with a booth selling Eskimo Pies, those blocks of vanilla ice cream covered with chocolate on a stick, made by a company in Richmond, Virginia. The rest of the booths in the Alaska pavilion were occupied by whoever would rent them, souvenir shops of all kinds.

My booth had the only authentic Alaska products in the Alaska Pavilion, the scrimshaw and carvings, the sealskin mukluks, Alaskan jade, and again the fine Eskimo artist Robert Mayokuk with his work. Again we had lookers but we were selling nothing. Apparently, I hadn't learned the lesson from the shows six years before, but this was the World's Fair! I'd expected a world-class crowd. Then something happened to turn things around.

Princess Wah Nese Red Rock

Robert fancied himself good with women, which was a surprise to me because he was old and ugly. One day he showed up with an Indian woman in her mid-forties, who was classy and beautiful. Princess Red Rock, born in Fairbanks, Alaska, had a great resume as a concert singer having studied at the Eastman School of Music and been a soprano in the St. Louis Opera Company and later the San Francisco Light Opera. Her signature song was "Indian Love Call," the song Jeannette MacDonald had sung to Nelson Eddy beside a Canadian log cabin in the 1936 movie *Rose-Marie*, only Red Rock sang it better. Red Rock was the Indian girl dancing on a drum in that film. She had also performed at the inaugurations of both President Franklin Roosevelt and President Truman as well as at the dedication of the Florida Everglades, the opening ceremonies of the Bobby Maduro Miami Stadium, and sundry other occasions. Princess Red Rock was the real deal.

Red Rock recognized that I was the man in charge of our booths, and she dropped Robert and grabbed on to me. So I had to take her to dinner that night. She told me, "You're doing it all wrong. Forget authenticity. Go buy children's trinkets like rubber tomahawks decorated with feathers and made in Japan." And this was from the daughter of the last chief of the Ojibwa totem! "You need jewelry," she declared. "Not Alaskan. I can sell it." So we went into New York City and bought fake tomahawks and Indian headbands with feathers dangling. She got all kinds of inexpensive jewelry including plenty made of hematite, which is iron oxide, the same as rust except in mineral form. It's even a waste product from iron mines, so it's cheap. It also polishes up beautifully and makes quite stunning jewelry that looks a lot like silver. So we brought all this back to the Alaska Pavilion and Princess Red Rock not only attracted a crowd, she sold our stuff. Though only part Native Alaskan, with her shiny, long black hair, and her Indian costume, she sang in her native language, while brandishing the rubber tomahawk. She was a tiny woman, but she had a great presence and dramatic flair. She really turned it around for me. We made a deal and we were in business together.

Tom Pallister

I met another person at the World's Fair who would become a fun and infuriating part of my life. Tom Pallister managed three booths and the hat check stand at the restaurant Top of the Fair for New York boss Arthur Stirmac. Stirmac's booths weren't doing much business either, so Tom was underfoot. Tom let me know what a capable businessman he was. He'd also been a Captain in the Army with over 35 missions over Germany as a navigator on a bomber. Sometimes we'd eat supper together and we'd talk about the war and all his missions. He had me snowed. I was impressed with his military service, but a few details of his missions didn't seem likely to be true to me. He already had me in trouble before I figured out that he was a pathological liar, a swindler and one of the biggest losers I'd ever met. At the time, I really believed in Tom.

In midsummer, after watching the paper maché Empire State Buildings and the bobbing heads sell in other booths, and then seeing that those guys were moving out early, I asked them, "Why?" They said, "For more sales." I asked, "Where?" They said, "At the state fairs." So I left my booths at the World's Fair for a while in the care of Robert Mayokuk , Tom, and Red Rock to test some other waters. I went to the Plymouth State Fair in New Hampshire near my home there, and the booth rental was only $30 for four days. I got a Miss Alaska runner up to go with me. She was a hit! I did $1000 of business in four days there, compared to $500 from my whole stint at the World's Fair. Vendors at the Plymouth State Fair said I should go to the Eastern States Exhibition and the Deerfield Fair, where I would do even better, but they added that the vendor lists were full there because these were such desirable fairs. I'd never get in, they said. That was just a challenge for me. So I went to Deerfield where they had a town meeting, and I made a pitch and got one space at the fair. Then I called Eastern States and sure enough, I was told, "We're booked." I said, "I'll bring either Princess Red Rock, famous Indian singer, or Miss Alaska." They changed their tune: "We're booked but maybe we can work something out. Sometimes there's a cancellation." So I went to the Eastern States Exhibition where I rented a booth for just $300 and took in $5000.

I called Lydia and said, "I think I've found a way to earn a living." I didn't actually know how then, but I soon began to learn. I sent Lydia $1000 and I told her I'd be back in Anchorage for the month of December. She was glad for both. I then booked the Cleveland Sports Show and the New England Flower Show.

To earn a living at this work, I'd need some help because setting up and running a booth is physically demanding; fairs operate all day and long into the night. After the World's Fair closed, Stirmac was probably going to lay Tom Pallister off. Tom was in charge of closing down the restaurant, where he sold all the furniture which didn't even belong to Stirmac, and pocketed the money, but I didn't know that yet. I figured he knew his way around New York City and was a great businessman, so I approached him to help me move my good quality, authentic but unsold Alaskan wares from the World's Fair to New Hampshire to be the nucleus of an Eskimo Shop I'd set up in my house there. I could just see my white polar rug with its head lifted greeting visiting tourists into my shop in Campton.

So I started my new career as a carney. If I was going to be a carney, I was going to be the best carney I could be. I decided to go back to the New York Sportsman's Show, one of the best. Tom and I went to the manager of the show. I did the talking about our recent success and reserved some space for early next year. I told the manager I'd send him a check for $300 to reserve the space as soon as I got to Alaska, where I had time and space to attend to my accounting. So I left for Anchorage. I sent the check to Tom in New York, where he lived in a little apartment, to give directly to the New York Show manager.

I was still up in Alaska when I was reconciling my checkbook, and I noticed the $300 check was cashed and endorsed by Arthur Stirmac. How in the devil did that happen? It was a mystery then, but the mystery soon became clear: Tom still worked for Stirmac, who said something like, "Ever hear from Harry?" And Tom said, "Yeah, in fact I got a check from him today." Stirmac figured they could double the money at the racetrack so Stirmac cashed the check for Tom, signed and deposited it. He took the cash to the racetrack and gambled it away. I'd never heard anything from the New York Sportsman's Show about my space. So when I contacted the manager of the show, he was upset. The missing $300 would have been just the deposit on the space, and he needed the full $600 now. I had to handle that, and then I got the authorities involved and finally got my money back.

I was just beginning to get the picture of who Tom really was. I confronted him, really gave it to him. He said, "I've never done anything like that before in my life. I don't know what came over me." He even cried. I said, "I'll give you one more chance." So we signed on for the New York Sportsman's Show to be held the winter of 1967. We did the Cleveland Show and the New England Flower Show, and I knew he was siphoning off some of the proceeds, but I needed him so I put off dealing with that. We made a little money anyway. What actually upset me more than the stealing was all the details he'd told me of his flying missions over Germany during the war. I'd had flying lessons myself and knew a good bit about our German campaign, so I recognized he was making too many mistakes; I didn't believe he'd even been an aviator. I couldn't forgive him for that when so many of our boys died on such missions. But I needed him now.

Lois

Jumping ahead a bit, Tom was 45, a year older than I was, but he looked 60. He was bald and his teeth were yellow, and I don't know what women saw in him. But he was such a convincing guy that he attracted a woman named Lois. He exaggerated his importance and his business acumen. He pretended that he was the owner of my business and that I worked for him. I never contradicted him when he was doing one of his spiels. Lois was impressed and settled in with him in his tiny apartment in New York; they were talking about marriage. They were together about a year, and she began working for the business, too. She was really good at it and was very independent. She'd tell me what to do and how to do it or get out of the booth. I got out and left it to her because she was the best operator I have ever known. Her romance with Tom didn't last, especially after he borrowed money from her and she never saw it again, but she's stayed with me in my business ever since.

That was the team—me and the three musketeers, Princess Red Rock, Tom Pallister, and Lois.

A Year at the Fairs

Soon I was working the fairs almost full time. At first Lydia was sending me money from the Eskimo Shop, and I was struggling. Later she was struggling and I was sending her money, a situation I found a lot more rewarding. It was a hard way to live, but we had to get back on our feet financially.

I started separate fairs in January 1966. The whole year took me through the sports, flower, and home shows, beginning with the great New York Sports Show, and from San Diego to New Hampshire.

While I was doing the fairs, Lydia was holding on in Anchorage. For the summer of 1966, I sent Princess Red Rock to Anchorage to run the Eskimo Shop so Lydia could run the Athletic Club. They didn't like each other. They were both boozers, but they both could drink at night and run the businesses by day. Lydia had started drinking over our agreement, however reluctant on her part, that we both could date others when out of state. Now she was drinking heavily every time she suspected me of straying, and her suspicions were rather frequent. Lydia thought I'd had an affair with Red Rock. Absolutely not. I'd had affairs but not with Red Rock. I'd not do that with an employee. Not good business. She suspected Lois and me, too, and another woman who had worked for me for a while. These were business associates and friends, almost part of the family. No way I had affairs with any of them.

It was strange to go back and see my wife late in the year after a bad summer on the road. She said, "How long are you going to be here?" About two months, I told her, and I got busy working on the club, doing plumbing work, installing paneling and other improvements that would cost a lot of money if I paid someone else to do it. All of a sudden I could do this stuff. I never did this as a kid. I could replace the windows and fix the plumbing. Lydia thought that was pretty great.

A Decision and a Disaster

For the rest of 1966, I was trying to fix up the club and fix up my marriage. In the winter of 1967, I came down to the New York Sports Show I'd manage to book in spite of Tom's shenanigans.

In February 1967, someone made us an offer for the building the Anchorage Athletic Club was in. We'd paid $80,000 for the building just a year before and still had a mortgage of $65,000, and we were offered $150,000 for it. I was no longer KENI sports director, a job I'd really loved but had to give up in order to tend to my business out of town. I said, "Let's take the money and run." Lydia said, "No! The building and the business will be worth a lot more later." So we talked about divorce. Seriously. I made up my mind to split. She said, "I'm holding on to this club and you can have the rest." I said, "You're right. This building in this location will appreciate. Okay, I'll do the shows and send you some money, and you think about it."

I went on the road to New York and Boston, then to the Southwest. Between shows in Dallas and Houston, I went to Mexico where I picked up some contacts. One day I got a telegram from Houston. Call home, it said. I called. Lydia said, "We lost the club about three days ago."

"What do you mean, lost the club?"

"We lost the club in a huge fire."

Thank God, Lydia was all right. Thank God, the firemen saved our dog Gloria, too.

It was determined that the fire started in a clothes dryer in a back room where we laundered the towels from the Athletic Club. There was no sprinkler system to contain the fire to that room, and the whole building went up in flames. Lydia discovered it about 1 a.m. and called the fire department.

Two months earlier, we'd had the offer for $150,000 and turned it down! And now we lost it. This was my fourth major disaster; the fire at Limerick, the shipwreck, the earthquake, and now this. I thought the good Lord was angry with me.

I'd just set up my booth for a show. If I left it, I'd lose the $2000 rent, and they'd never let me come back. Lydia said, "Stay there," and I did. I asked her, "Have you heard from the bank?" No. With a mortgage and the fire, the bank had a stake in this and should get in touch.

The insurance company claimed the insurance was not valid. I'd given Lydia money for insurance, and she used the money for something else. The bank was the second mortgage holder. As such, the insurance company had an obligation to notify the bank, which in turn would have contacted me, the owner, and demanded that I pay the insurance premium, which I would have done immediately. The insurance company's failure to notify the bank meant the insurance was still in effect.

So as soon as I could get back to Anchorage, I went to my best friend, Gene Williams, an attorney who used to be the city attorney. Gene verified that the key was: Did the insurance company notify the bank? If not, the insurance company was derelict in its duty. I asked at the bank, "Have we paid the mortgage for the month?" Yes. I said, "Are you aware that this building burned 19 days ago?" The person I was talking to went to get a higher authority. So Mr. So and So came and said, "I read about it but we weren't notified." So the insurance company was indeed derelict in its duty.

The insurance appraiser came and said to Lydia, "This wasn't worth much anyway." He wanted to demoralize her. It wasn't a good building, true, but it was a great location, and it was our source of income. I know his assignment was to make us accept very little. Then the insurance company noted I hadn't paid the taxes. They were slightly delinquent: $5000.

So here's where things stood:

First, the city was owed back taxes:	$5,000
Second, the city required that I demolish the building:	$12,000
Third, I owed for new merchandise bought on credit:	$25,000
Total:	$42,000

I didn't have any money for all that, but I was more concerned about taking care of my debt to Mr. Edris. I suggested to him that I deed the property back to him and I would attempt to get a settlement from the insurance company, which would compensate for the loss of the building and would also pay off the $25,000 second mortgage. In return for this, Mr. Edris would not move against me for the log cabin. He accepted that offer. I then sued the insurance company. It took three years, but on the day before it was to go to trial, the insurance company settled for just a few dollars less than the coverage.

Mr. Edris ended up with the vacant lot and almost $80,000 from which he'd have to pay the taxes and demolition. He came out rather well. That was as it should be.

Lydia and I ended up with the log cabin, but we had a $25,000 inventory bill. I had just bought $25,000 worth of goods including $15,000 of sealskin boots bought on credit from a company in Quebec. These were in the building, destroyed, all unpaid goods. I intended to pay for them, but how? This was the biggest problem in my life. Could we survive? I put aside the whole idea of divorce. I said, "We'd better hang in here together." She said, "Tell me what to do." I said, "I have to protect my business down at the fairs. And you stay here and see this through."

I'd built Lydia the new shop in a room in the Athletic Club, which wasn't officially open at the time of the fire as we'd just gotten our inventory. I said, "We'll have a fire sale and you can sell as much as you can and reopen the Eskimo Shop in the log cabin." I started buying stuff to sell at the fire sale, stuff from elsewhere.

In the meantime, my creditors were looking for the $25,000 bucks to pay for the inventory we'd lost. In particular, the boot manufacturer in Canada to whom I owed $15,000 for boots was after me. I had every intention of paying off the debt, not going bankrupt, but I couldn't do it instantaneously. I had to keep my businesses open on the road, and I badly wanted to keep the Eskimo Shop. My lawyer told me a subpoena would be served on me in a couple days. In Alaska, it had to go the actual person named on the subpoena or a spouse. So I said to Lydia, "Grab as much real Eskimo stuff as you can carry in two suitcases and take the midnight flight to Seattle. Until then, don't open the door."

I sent Princess Red Rock to Anchorage again to run the original Eskimo Shop in the log cabin. She was born in Alaska, raised in Ontario, the daughter of the last chief of the Ojibwa-totem, and now she was going back to the land of her birth to stay. It seemed fitting. Lydia joined me at the Minneapolis State Fair where I was trying to keep my booth open. Red Rock and Lydia passed in the night, which suited them both just fine.

We'd been out of Alaska for a season and Red Rock was running the shop. I felt morally obligated to Red Rock. Before the New York World's Fair she'd been living in a little apartment in Brooklyn, a boozer and washed up star. She'd helped me out and I'd put her in business, and now she was part of the family.

When Lydia said, "Let's get rid of the Eskimo Shop, we're out of Alaska," I said, "No, that's where Red Rock is going to live out her days." I felt obligated to her; she'd taught me how to make a living. She took care of our doggie in Anchorage. She used to go around bars in Anchorage and sing "Indian Love Song." She was pretty famous around there. Her fame along with her sales ability worked together. The Eskimo Shop had a reputation but no promotion, although there was occasionally an article about Red Rock personally. I had to pay taxes of about $2000 a year to keep her going. It was a problem, but I was determined that as long as she was alive I'd provide a place for her to live. Red Rock said she was only two years older than I was, although she looked older. I envisioned taking care of her in her old age while I'd live forever, and that's so far how it worked out.

So Lydia and I were together again. I had a busted up van that we slept in when we were on the road back east, and we had the New Hampshire home to crash in. It was a struggle to survive, but our business and our marriage finished the season.

Chapter 22

The Carney Life

Beginning with the lessons I learned at the disastrous Worlds Fair in 1965 and moving on to success in fairs in the east, I was confident I could make this business work. I needed income quickly to avoid bankruptcy, bad credit, and the loss of the Eskimo Shop. I had lost too much already. I was determined that my creditors were not going to ruin me. The boot manufacturer to whom I owed $15,000 for boots joined forces with my other creditors to put pressure on me for a total of $25,000. There was nothing to do but to begin earning that money as quickly as possible, and this was the enterprise at hand that seemed most likely to allow me to survive financially.

The business of being a carney became a 45-year career and counting. There were many highs and lows, and the highs came later. One of the lows happened shortly after I moved in at the New York Sports Show. We had union trouble. We both intended to spend the night at Tom's place in New York City. A guy came to the door and said, "Who do you have watching your booth tonight?" I said, "The Fair provides the security. It's part of the booth rental." The guy said, "Who will watch the security?" Then he added that everything would be gone from my booth in the morning if I didn't hire additional security from him. I didn't give in to this shakedown. Instead, I slept in my booth every night of the show and nothing happened. People later told me I was lucky to survive. I learned from that, but I never rolled over for the union.

Later, at the Detroit Boat Show, I lost the whole season for not holding my tongue. Unions made it impossible with their rules and extra fees for everything. Teamsters were supreme. I wised off to one of them as we set up, and everyone knew I was a non-union guy, so Monday morning I came in and found I was wiped out. All the tables were gone, the merchandise, everything. I went to the show manager. He said, "You learned your lesson, you don't mess around with the union."

Like a lot of vendors, I soon began to avoid the union run shows. The unions eventually killed the shows. What's left are the fairs. An exception is the Harrisburg Sports Show in Pennsylvania, the best show of all, and it's non-union.

Low Points

I had Lydia with me in New Hampshire and, wanting to earn my way out of debt as fast as possible, I decided that we could nearly double our income if both of us were on the road, each of us running a booth at a different fair. I already knew this was an extremely difficult business. I asked, "Lydia, are you tough enough to do this?" I knew she was. She was as strong a woman as I ever knew, but I had to ask the question because I felt I should be protecting her, not sending her out into such a rough industry to make a living.

Lydia agreed. So when I did the Wisconsin fair, she did another fair. I wanted all the money we earned to pay the debt to the providers of goods I'd bought and lost. I said to Lydia, "Send me all the money." She said she needed some personal money and she'd send me only part of her take. So we had a blow up. I finally said, "I'll pay all the bills, all the costs in Anchorage, and all the taxes with what I earn, and you can keep all you earn and you support yourself and buy food for you and for me when I'm home." Our partnership that had grown closer in the crises of earthquake and fire was strained, but we set new limits and carried on as a team in other ways.

I did fabulously well in the Cleveland show and Tom was doing the Boston Flower show, where we did fairly well in spite of Tom's siphoning some money off the top. Booking agents were trying to get me booked into local home shows, and I did a few to fill in gaps. I lost everything at the home shows that I'd earned at the good shows.

I made plenty of mistakes. Again I listened to people who were in other markets. What you can sell definitely depends on the market. I cannot make a sale to locals—fudge and hotdogs, yes, not a Delft plate for $45 unless it's right before Christmas. Traveling people are the only ones who buy gifts. I had gifts, so I had to go where the travelers go. I also learned that people in the South are slow to buy. They say they'll think about it and come back, but they don't come back. Up North, they make up their minds quickly and buy. So I cut out my southern shows except Florida.

I listened to other people too much in the beginning. At some fairs there are big tanks of water for log-rolling contests or canoe or fly-casting demonstrations. People told me that customers flock to these things, so I gave it a try. After a demonstration was over, lots of people came from the tank and walked by my booth, looking at my stuff. Then it became a trickle. Traffic was never constant. A guy who sold Jeeps across from my booth in one fair said, "You should come to Tallmadge in Ohio." Someone said, "There's a frog jumping contest in California," and I drove 3000 miles and they didn't have my space saved. They said, "Go to Chowchilla." In Chowchilla, they said, "Go to Pomona" or "Go to the Del Mar Fair." I drove all the way to Del Mar in San Diego County to book a space. Then from there I went back to the Talmadge Festival in a suburb of Akron, Ohio, my old stomping ground; there the people just hung out but didn't buy. A total disaster. Then I had to go back to California for the fair in Del Mar because I'd booked there.

A guy in Del Mar came up to say he was from the sales tax department. I had $3 in my pocket and was sleeping in my camper. He said I had to give him $50 in advance for sales tax. So I wrote a check. I did okay not great. I had $1000 in my pocket at the end but hadn't paid for inventory. Even so I was a lot happier going east with $1000 in my pocket than west with $3.

The next time this happened, I had $1500 in my pocket and felt pretty strong. The collector came and demanded $50. I said, "What would you say if I said I won't pay?" He said, "My boss said I have to get $50." I said, "Tell your boss to come and sit in my booth and count every dollar I take in." The guy said, "How about $40?" Then $30, then $20. We settled for $20 and they repeated that same amount of $20 the next and last year. They know no one is paying the right amount of tax so they use an illegal method to get an average amount from everyone.

The same issue came up at one show where a judge was on the take. You had to pay the judge to get the best booths. A fair official was even killed in that town and the judge went to jail. There you had to pay sales tax every day. I took in a reasonable amount and paid a reasonable tax, but they called me in and said it was too little. I said, "You can sit and watch my booth all day, but you can't assume my intake." Two hours later, there was a guy standing there clicking off the number of people buying at my booth. I don't mind paying the right percentage of sales tax, but I don't want to be shaken down for everybody who's cheating on their taxes. As Lydia said, "We may not have made much money but we never took any shit from anyone."

One of the lowest points I recall in this business was during those first couple of years on the road. I booked the Tallahassee fair, as I did every year except three out of my whole life on the fair circuit. On this particular trip to Tallahassee, I had a beat-up van full of Indian moccasins. Lydia had gone to help Tom at a little fair somewhere, so I was alone.

I'd headed south down the east coast and was about 30 miles west of St. Mary's, almost to Florida but about 300 miles from Tallahassee out on the panhandle. My gas tank was almost empty and I had a flat tire. I didn't get the van all the way off the road, and so the vehicle was a bit in the highway; I was trying to save the tire. A state patrolman stopped by and told me I was supposed to get off the road when I had a flat. The road was virtually empty; my van would not have been a problem. Not a good enough excuse for the trooper. He saw the moccasins in the back and he tried to get me to offer him some as a bribe saying, "Mighty fine moccasins you have back there," but I didn't take the bait. So he said he'd call the sheriff. The sheriff said, "Ordinarily we put people like you in jail, but if you can pay a little money maybe we can talk." I had $40. I thought I'd get to Tallahassee on that. So I said, "All I have is $25." He said, "I'll tell you what I'll do." He took the $25. "I'll give you one hour to get this car out of here. Or I'll put you in jail." When he left me, I started walking for help.

I soon saw a red light in this house, the real deal, a whorehouse. The mistress said, "Can I help you with anything at all?" Wink, wink. I told her the sheriff told me I had to be gone from the county in an hour or I'd go to jail, but I don't have any tools to fix my tire.

The girls didn't like the sheriff because they had to pay him regularly to keep the business open. The girls got some tools for me and said, "Forget about bringing them back because the sheriff will be here soon." I changed the tire but the car was running badly and I was afraid I'd break down. I looked for a place where I could hide and I found a spot down a little road and hid. The sheriff didn't find me. In the morning, I had a race because I had $15 and was losing gas; gas was filling the carburetor and the engine was not acting right. I bought gas all the way to Tallahassee and arrived broke. A friend there lent me money to eat. I had no money and a van full of moccasins. I sold them and got a little money but the fair was not good enough to go back next year. That night in Georgia was the absolute low point for me.

Once I was In Atlanta at the Boat Show because my first cousin Frederick Briggs, who lived in Georgia, Uncle Fred's son, told me Atlanta was really hopping. A booth in Atlanta cost about half of one in the northeast, but I had a few pathetic shows in Atlanta, so I quit coming. I remember one amusing occasion there, however, in about 1968. Lester Maddox was Governor of Georgia at the time. I was wearing one of those arrows that looked as if it went through my head; they were novel then. I stood there in a business suit with an arrow through my head. Lester Maddox's PR people came by and saw it and thought it was the funniest thing ever. They asked to have the arrow for the Governor. I refused because it was my last one and my wearing the arrow in my head attracted people to my booth. Later the Governor himself came by. I told him the story about the Georgia state trooper who tried to shake me down and the Sheriff who took my money. He said, "Yeah, we have trouble with them. If you have any more trouble with our police, call me." I gave him my arrow and his people gave me a number to call, if I ever had another problem in Georgia. I never did.

Low points in this business were very discouraging in the first few years. Later a bad show was just a bump in the road. I put up and broke down my booth in hundreds of venues across the country, and Lydia did too.

Making a little here and a lot there, losing a lot there and a little here, still within about three years, I had that $25,000 paid off. I thought I'd really accomplished something. The creditors thought I'd go bankrupt, but now they had the whole amount I'd owed and they got none of my possessions. The paying off of my creditors was one of the highs in my business, one that kept me going in this means of livelihood. Once out of debt, I could put my money to other things like our home or just to have a night in a motel instead of the van occasionally. I guess the lows had their value, too, as opportunities for honing survival skills in this business.

How the Business Worked

The work that I did was tough. I'd go on a two-month tour, sleep in my van to avoid hotel costs, carry in lumber to set up my booth, stand at the booth all day and late into the evening, do the inventory after the fair closed, a 14-hour day. That schedule was common for me year round. I didn't want to go out for a big meal after the fair shut down. I just wanted to sleep. Family members like Frederick in Atlanta or Gordon in Chicago would hear I was in town and say, "Why don't you stop into see us?" I didn't have the time. I had to drive to the next fair. I might occasionally have had a day off between fairs, but if I visited people, I wouldn't have a day off. So mostly I didn't tell people when I'd be in town. I can't imagine any tougher work for 45 years. At first, it was to survive, later to improve a house, finally, to put a little money away.

We carneys helped each other out. For example, I had a concession over at Fort Bragg in North Carolina selling my stuff; Robert, the guy in the next booth, was a wire bender. In the evening, I'd tend his booth and mine so he could go home. I couldn't bend wire but I could take orders for his wire creations. He'd watch my booth so I could take an occasional break. We became good friends.

One day we were standing there while the guy on the other side of me was demonstrating a special kind of bottle stopper that went in the bottle and locked, keeping fizz in carbonated drinks and air out of wine. This guy was good and his demonstration got passers-by excited. When he finished his demonstration, he asked, "Who wants to buy one? Let's see your money." Nobody said anything. Just then a guy came in, making a path through the people so everyone could see and hear him. He said, "How much?" A dollar. "Give me three." So then everyone started buying, and the money came in, maybe $20 total from the group. The crowd dispersed. In a few minutes, the guy started up another demonstration for a new crop of people walking by. When he said, "Let's see your money," in came the same guy, calling out, "How much did you say it was?" One dollar. "Give me three!"

By the third demonstration, when the same guy came in to buy three, I'd figured it out. So I learned. They worked in pairs and the guy who comes in is called a shill.

You never want to be next to a demonstrator. They take your entire crowd. With seniority as a vendor, I slowly built a good space at my regular fairs, near the wall on the right side of the entrance because people turn to the right, and in a place with no demonstrators near by. If you complain about demonstrators nearby, they just turn up their mikes.

If I get someone to watch my booth for me, I can go to the men's room. On the way back, I occasionally stop by a demonstrator and watch the show. I've even been a shill sometimes when I was walking by a vendor. I'd say, "How much is it?" and I'd buy a couple of whatever the vendor was selling. These vendors would later say, "Thanks, Harry," and I'd give them the gizmos I'd bought, and they'd give me my money back. One time, I just went up to a demonstrator and volunteered as a shill. When I went back to get my money, he said, "No money back. You bought 'em." So there are all kinds of people in the business, and you learn which is which, often the hard way.

I carry a line of jewelry, gold chains and ankle bracelets made of gold electroplate. Hundreds if not thousands of people have come up to my booth saying, "Is it real gold?" Once I was training a new operator and I saw a mother and daughter coming up. I said to my trainee, "She's going to ask if it's real gold. Just wait and see." The pair got to my booth and the daughter asked, "Is it real gold?" My trainee thought I was psychic. To the question, is it real gold, I say, "No, but it's plated with 8 mg of gold." I try not to fool anybody.

Gold filled is better than electroplate, but this line holds up well, too. I wore one of my herringbone necklaces myself to see how long the gold finish would last. That jewelry is for people with money who can afford it but don't intend to wear it all day and all night. Some people wear solid gold to bed and in the shower. If people say, "Can I wear it to shower?" I say, "This is not for you." On the other hand, an old woman came up to me at the Rheinbeck Fair. I recognized her. I thought, *Jeez she's going to complain*, but she smiled and said, "I'm back for more; it holds up so well."

This year, 2011, an 18-inch herringbone chain about a half-inch wide, factory guaranteed, will cost me maybe $3. I put it on my stand and if I put the normal retail markup, it would sell for $6. That doesn't look right. People think, if it's any good, it should cost more, and they don't buy it. So I mark it up to $25 and they buy it. So I play around till I get the right price. It's different for every market, every place. Also, people don't buy jewelry from a guy wearing a tee shirt with mustard on it. I dress well and look respectable.

The factory guarantee will replace chains where the gold came off for a service charge of $5. I know that $5 just pays for a new chain and a couple dollars profit. So I don't say I guarantee it, I say the manufacturer does. I try to talk someone out of buying if someone is poor. I've even said, "Take it," sometimes, if a person really wanted it but I could tell didn't have the money. It might be marked $25, but it only costs me $3. It's a play-it-by-ear business, and buying cheap allows a lot of play.

We've always done great in Harrisburg selling jewelry. People say, "At a sports show?" Yes, people like to take home gifts to the little lady. Or if it's a woman, she is tired of looking at fishing gear, and she says, "Oh, look, jewelry." Her husband thinks she's going to pick out something that costs $500 but she likes something that I've priced at $25 and he says, "Buy it, buy it." All this I had to learn in the early years.

We had fun sometimes, joking around with others in the trade, but most of the high points had to wait a few years. We learned as we went. There was a lot more to come, but this is what got me started.

Chapter 23

Home—New Hampshire, Florida, and on the Road

I've always loved New Hampshire with its White Mountains and wooded valleys, crystal clear lakes, and rushing streams. As fascinating and wild as Alaska is, I was happy to be back where I knew the paths and the peaks since boyhood. Just four or five years ago, I accompanied my niece Letitia to the mountains and took her down a steep path to where a waterfall dropped like a ribbon into a pool below. On the way back up, I bounded up a shortcut I suddenly remembered from my youth and I felt like a boy again. I felt at home in Campton, a small town between the lake country and the mountains, with a rushing stream behind our house and, in the spring, a torrent of snowmelt roaring over the waterfall, my waterfall.

When I bought the house in Campton in 1960, I intended to use it as a base from which to train and make my swims as well as eventual retirement. When I stopped swimming, we were happy to have it just as a second home, and I made necessary improvements gradually. Beginning with the New York World's Fair, I also used the property to store inventory. After Lydia also left Alaska, we used the Campton home between fairs in the Northeast. After we paid off our debts in Alaska, we had some money to build a 50-foot addition to the original house including an apartment over the new living room, a garage, and a swimming pool.

In 1972, I put up a Bavarian type log cabin; the cabin cost $2000 and the basement and putting the cabin up cost another $1000. It took me two more years to finish the inside. We opened the New Hampshire Eskimo Shop in 1975 using Harold Matthews, a carpenter who had helped put up the building, and his wife Janet to run the shop for the summers of 1975 and 1976. Lydia herself opened the shop on Mother's Day, 1977. One of the first "customers" was a shoplifter, actually two people working together. Lydia knew their tricks but they escaped with quite a bit of merchandise. Lydia was so upset by this that she locked the shop and we were closed for quite a while except when I'd open it for a friend between fairs.

We'd quickly tired of the Eskimo theme, having answered the same ten questions about Eskimos about 1000 times and, even more tiresome, listened to ten people a day tell us everything they knew about Alaska from their week-long vacation there. We were ready for a different theme. We made our collection of Eskimo works of art (the ones that hadn't been shoplifted) into an exhibit to be viewed only by invitation.

We turned the cottage into an antique shop called The Chalet. Lydia had known nothing about antiques, but she began to read books on the subject and took a renewed interest in the shop. I admired her willingness to reinvent herself along with the business.

The antiques business was new to me also, although I'd been surrounded by antiques in my parents' and my aunts' homes. I learned a lot from a "picker" named Don, whom I met in 1986. Don and I combed through yard sales together until he figured out what kinds of things I wanted, estate jewelry and anything good. "Good" meant what would make money in the shop. Don finally said, "I'll get antiques for you, but I want the jewelry for myself." I agreed.

He had a spiel: "I'm looking for jewelry and I pay the best prices in town." The average old woman on Social Security needing a bit of cash might have a ring that originally cost $700. She'd think, *I don't really need this ring*, and she figured it would still be worth $700, at least $500. The woman would bring it to Don. He'd look at it and weigh it on a scale. Then he'd say, "I'll give you $7 because old jewelry like this is only worth the melt down value." Of course, he didn't melt it down; he knew people who wanted to buy the ring. He'd buy good jewelry and sell it for twice as much; the ring would bring him maybe $15 or $20.

It's a dirty rotten business. It starts at the bottom, the desperate person who sells the ring for $7 and then the buyer like Don who sells it to a retailer for $20. That's a good deal for him. Then the retailer may sell it for $500. The worst scam in the world is "Old jewelry is only worth the meltdown value." I was glad not to be buying jewelry from scammers like that, but I used the knowledge of antiques that I'd learned from Don to great advantage.

Our antiques business did well enough, and combined with our sales on the spring and fall fair circuit, we had our heads above water and were putting some money away. But I was eager to do more.

Family

We enjoyed our combined home and business. We built a patio and put in a small swimming pool where we could relax and listen to our waterfall. People could come here to visit us, and it seemed a good way to live. My cousin Frederick Briggs, his wife Marjorie, and their children came occasionally and enjoyed my waterfall as much as I did.

My cousin Gordon Briggs had attended Norwich Academy, a four-year college in Vermont, the first private military school in the country, now Norwich University. He served on its board and came by my place in Campton when he was in New England for a board meeting. Lydia was quite charmed by him. Gordon's son Robie and his terrific wife Susan also came to visit us there.

Letitia and her family stopped in once when I was gone to a show but Lydia was there. Her brother Tom Lavender Jr. also came a few times or stopped by my booth at the Deerfield Fair. He spent his whole career in Boston but retired with his wife on a little farm in New Hampshire, not far from my place and close to Deerfield. Eventually, my sister Virginia came to live with Tom much later in her final years, and they came down to visit.

But don't get the impression that I was close to my family. I was not close in the way that many families are. I didn't keep in touch, remember their birthdays, attend their graduations, or send post cards from far away places. Mostly they came to me; I didn't come to them. I was happy to see them when they came, I was happy to hear their news when they sent Christmas letters, and I wished them well, but after my parents and aunts died my feelings for family, feelings of affection and loyalty, were mostly reserved for those who had been with me on the road through thick and thin.

Also, don't get the impression that Lydia and I were living happily ever after in our little cottage. That came much later. For now, we were living mostly to make a living. We didn't have much of a romantic life, and Lydia was drinking. She didn't drink all the time by any means, and she was nice when she wasn't, but something would set her off and she'd go on a toot. One night about 1 a.m., she was drunk and went swimming naked in Perch Pond, and I had to go get her out of the water before she drowned. When she drank, she really lit into me. One time Lois was there and she cried, "Get that woman out of here!" But I was a lot more patient than Lois. I appreciated the difference between the Lydia I admired sober and Lydia drunk.

Florida

In the meantime, as much as I loved New Hampshire, I realized that the ski lodges I'd anticipated in that region hadn't materialized or that we were too far off the beaten path. We also had too short a tourist season, and like snowbirds we needed to follow the sun. During the winter in 1971 we started contracting with McCrory's, a national retail five and dime chain like Woolworths, in West Palm Beach. We'd have a stand in the store and give McCrory's a percentage of our sales.

In West Palm Beach we had no place to live at first, so we rented a busted up trailer in a beautiful trailer park. The park was beside the crystal clear waters of an inland waterway with dockage, beautiful. I always wanted to be by the water. I asked the manager, "How much?" He said $500. I thought I was buying the waterfront lot. It turned out the $500 was just to rent the beat up trailer. Then the whole park was condemned, and we couldn't come back.

The next year during the winter season, we contracted again with McCrory's and rented an apartment in town. Our adopted stray kitten Cleopatra used to run up and down the curtains, and our landlady saw it once and complained. We couldn't wait to have our own property. This is when and where I had to make one of the biggest decisions of my life.

It was clear by now that Lydia wanted a home in Florida for the winter months and New Hampshire, which she loved, in the summer. In order to accomplish this, I realized that I must make a decision. I was not totally committed to a career on the exhibition circuit. I could do many things—journalism, radio and TV, coaching and athletics administration, other kinds of collegiate administration. However, if I took a job in any one of those fields, I'd have to spend 12 months a year in that location. I told Lydia that we could have a house in the North and a house in Florida but only if I continue to do what I was doing on the road. She chose the road, and I have been doing it ever since. There's not much prestige that goes with what we did, but as Lydia said, "We may not amount to much, but we never took any shit from anyone."

The next year, 1973, we bought a 38-foot travel trailer, the largest allowed on the highway without special equipment. The price was cheap that year because there was a gasoline shortage and people weren't traveling. We had finishing paying off the debt in Anchorage so we were ready to buy a piece of property to put the trailer on. I went downtown in Palm Beach to a realtor and asked to see lots of five acres or more. I learned that five acres cost $50,000 and I was planning on $5000. So I had the trailer and no place to put it. Eventually, we found a trailer park five miles from the ocean, with a nice pool, for $150 a month. So we had a home but owned no land.

IN 1974, we'd had a good summer in the northeast, so we planned on buying a $25,000 house somewhere in Florida. Lydia had spent a Christmas in Naples one year and liked the area. So we planned three days on Florida's west coast from Tampa south. The first two days we looked in Sarasota, Venice Beach, Englewood, and Fort Myers. The third day we spent time at Fort Myers Beach, Estero, Bonita Springs, and finally Naples. We made one last attempt in Naples Park to find a house before we had to go set up our booths and start selling. We had engaged a realtor but didn't see anything we liked for the money we had. The last day in Naples Park, we passed a house on a double lot, beautifully landscaped. We left the realtor and went to ask about it. The asking price was $25,000, an estate deal that seemed to have our name written on it. We spent that night in a motel and settled the next day. Was I ever happy for Lydia! I personally didn't care all that much for Florida, but she really wanted this.

We both worked in Florida through that Christmas 1974, Lydia at McCrory's in Palm Beach. I went over to Fort Myers to a McCrory's there. The company would take a vendor any time of year, but Christmas was the best. I set up my stand by the front door and sold jewelry just like at a fair. McCrory's got 25%. I made $35,000 one Christmas in Ft. Myers. I also did a dozen Walgreens in Florida over the years. At least one store manager would demand a fee for himself for allowing me in, though the company washed its hands of this practice, and the percentage went up to 30% over the years, but this kind of selling was mostly good for us. In my best season I made $55,000.

We lived in our house in Naples in the winter for nineteen years. The only bad thing that happened there was that we arrived from the northeast one year, hoping to relax for a few days before I went up to Charlotte to do a show. We walked in and found that the flat roof had collapsed and half the roof was open to the sky. It was disgusting. We'd just put in new pine paneling, and now the water had wet the walls almost up to the ceiling all the way around. Our insurance didn't cover that loss. I had to go to a fair and leave Lydia with that problem. We spent many thousands of dollars to build a whole new mansard roof. It ended up very nice looking.

I'd lost my home in Maine to a fire, my fishing boat to a storm, my downtown building in Anchorage to an earthquake, the fire in the Athletic Club, and now this. There was nothing to do but rebuild and move on.

Red Rock

All this time, Princess Red Rock maintained our Eskimo Shop in Alaska, not making any profit but fulfilling my desire for her to have a home. In 1982, I got a call from my friend Gene Williams, by then a district court judge, notifying me that Red Rock didn't have the shop open. I found out that she'd had what you might call a nervous breakdown. She'd tried to reach me and couldn't as I was on the road. She'd then called her son. He apparently told her to pack up her things and come to his place in Los Angeles. She perhaps didn't secure the door well. In any case, when I went to Alaska to check on things, I found people had broken in and trashed the place, smashing the display cases, and leaving it a wreck. I did what I could, secured the door, and went back to take care of my business back East.

After a while Red Rock didn't get along with her son too well and wanted to come back. I told her, "This is the end of the line for the Eskimo Shop. We're going to sell the cabin. You can come down and live with us in New Hampshire, and I'll build an extra room for you in our house in Naples." She said, "I don't want to do that, Chief." So she went to live with friends in California. In 1983, I sold the cabin in Anchorage for $135,000. I was sad, thinking that would be the last I ever saw of the cabin, but it was not.

We lost touch with Princess Red Rock for a few years, and then she called us again in distress. We took her to New Hampshire and took care of her, helping her get back on her feet. Lydia had compassion, and, even though she wasn't fond of Red Rock, she agreed to take care of her. But after Red Rock got some money from us for running the shop in New Hampshire for a season, she took off and lived with neighbors down the street for a week before she went back to Alaska. I think she and Lydia had a fight. I never heard from her again. It disappointed me that she no longer stayed in touch with me. I really tried to do right by her. She died in 1988 and was buried in Anchorage.

Tom Pallister

Tom managed some booths for us on the circuit and we paid him a percentage of sales. On a couple occasions we stayed with him in his New York City place, and while he was out, Lydia found two sets of his books, one set of figures we took to be accurate and another set that Tom reported to me to get his percentage. Tom would lie and cheat and steal this way and when I said we had to get rid of him, Lydia would say, "Oh, no, we can't do that." And when Lydia got fed up and said we had to get rid of him, I'd say, "No, no, we can't do that." We jokingly called him our son, this big old bald guy. We'd always have him around even though he was the worst liar I've ever seen. The truth was he was a lot of fun.

When Lydia and I had a few free moments and asked each other what we should do now for fun, Lydia would say, "Call Tom." And he'd come over and we'd have a good time. I never called him on his pathological lying in front of other people. We kidded him about some of his grandiose stories though. Once he was dating a woman in Florida who thought he was really something. One day she came to our house and asked for him. We said he wasn't there. She said, "Well, where's his yacht?" After that, we got him a Captain's hat and called him Cap'n Tom. Before that he was the Bomber or Tom the Bomb because he bombed at fairs so often.

We did eventually change our business relationship. Beginning with the summer of 1970, I set him up with inventory one last time and paid his rents for the summer and that was the end; he was on his own, no longer part of our business. However, he spent the winters with us in Florida, working at McCrory's from the winter of 1968-69 until December 1974 when we bought the house in Naples. He never saw that house.

Lois

Lois runs an operation on the circuit better than I do. She once had a husband but she drove him nuts. She'd drive anyone nuts. She'd set up her booth just so, and it was perfect. If you moved anything, she'd move it back. If you put a glass down on a table, she'd complain. She nagged and criticized and complained worse than anyone I've ever known. I couldn't stand to spend time with her but I love her like a father. She was serious about her obsessiveness, but she could take a joke when she figured out it was a joke. We pulled a few stunts on her just to see her go bananas until she figured it out.

I said, "Lois I'll leave you $100,000 when I die," and I've set it aside. She's in her mid-sixties and I would like her to have some retirement. I'd already set her loose. She was on her own in the business because I had been providing transportation and she'd hear a little noise in her car and she'd take it to a mechanic. She couldn't stand any little noise. I was paying $2000 a year in mechanic's fees. I finally had to say, "Lois, get your own car; I can't stand this any more." So she went on her own and pays me a percentage. She's lived in a little place in Pittsburgh on less money than anyone I know—less than I do, and that's saying a lot. She's too old now to set up the booth by herself so I help her when we have a booth at the same fair.

These three have been my family. Of course, there have been other employees, partners, and friends along the way.

I had an acquaintance in Charlotte I'd known over the years when I was doing the Christmas and the spring shows there. Sonny Taylor was a short order cook at a fast food restaurant next to the Convention Center. In his time off, having discovered selling products with me, he set up in a fairly large flea market where he sold sportswear seconds and T-shirts. In the spring of 1993, after the spring show in Charlotte, I picked Lydia up in Naples and we headed for New Hampshire by way of Charlotte. Lydia was impressed with what Sonny was doing, and Sonny thought he'd like to try the fair circuit so we three set off in three cars. Sonny did so well the first day of selling and Lydia liked the idea of clothing. Thus I ended up looking for goods in the garment district of Manhattan to buy cheap and sell at the shop in New Hampshire. I had switched my booth inventory to imports from the House of Holland and the Black Forest in most of the shows, so I had plenty of European wares to go along with the clothing. In the summer, when I wasn't at a fair, I looked for antiques in flea markets to sell. It's incredible what I could find to buy cheap that had value in the antiques market. We ended up having a very diverse inventory in The Chalet.

Expansion

As we were picking our markets better, we increased our earnings.

I'd go to a fair for ten days renting a booth for under $1000, take in $12,000, and have $8000 profit. We'd buy an item for 50 cents and sell it for $10. You need to mark up an item by at least ten times. So to sell at prices people will buy, we had to buy cheap stuff. When we'd learned how to do it really well, we began to expand our business. At one point, I had five crews in the United States working fairs and shows. And I started going to international shows in England and Scotland both for a change of scenery and because the home shows in the United Kingdom are widely attended, very classy events, where I should be able to make a good profit.

The first year that I did the Daily Mail Ideal Home Exhibition, I was all set up for the opening, my merchandise was laid out on display, my supplies were under the table. I came in on opening day and everything was fine. I made my first sale, and then reached under the table to bring out a replacement item and there was nothing there. Someone had taken all my merchandise overnight. I had paid $5000 to rent the space and I had nothing to sell.

I had better luck at the Ideal Home Exhibition in 1983. It was the Exhibition's diamond jubilee, and there were over 400 exhibitors. A magnificent display in the show room featured a 40-foot balloon, a replica of the ornate balloon built in 1783 by two Frenchmen, hanging from the ceiling. The backdrop was a replica of a chateau with a French water garden flowing out into the middle of the show room under the balloon. It was grand! Royal visitors came before the crowds were allowed in. Princess Michael of Kent came by my booth. The *Daily Mail* noted this visit, saying that the princess was "enchanted by Eskimo jade statuettes" and she accepted my challenge "to try the Eskimo yo-yo, two weights at the end of thongs, which have to be whirled in opposite directions." That was correct. However, the newspaper said I was Canadian—perhaps they thought Alaska was in Canada—and that I'd run a store in Anchorage for almost 30 years. I was getting my Ph.D. in Ohio 30 years earlier and selling hot dogs at hockey games, but no matter. Any press is good press. I did fine that year.

Between big shows, I warehoused goods in Cheltenham. For years, we had a kiosk in Rackham's, a prestigious store in Birmingham in the same conglomerate with Harrods. I had a bunch of people working for me in the US and the UK. I also went to Ideal Home Shows in France, Brussels, Stuttgart and other locations.

The last year I went to the Ideal Home Show in England, I was upstairs in a relatively small room where the central exhibit was the Chinese booth. On opening day, Queen Elizabeth came in with Prince Philip. The queen spent an hour in the Chinese exhibit. I could see her talking a few yards away. Prince Philip was outside the Chinese Booth near me. He was checking his watch and pacing the hall. Finally she came out. As they passed by my booth, Prince Philip said to me, "Alaska! I didn't expect to see Alaska represented here. Are these things all made in Alaska?" I replied, "No, it's a scam. It's all made in Providence, Rhode Island." He laughed and went on, saying, "That's a funny little guy," and he laughed again.

I had to do something to entertain myself. Anyway, I was interested but not too excited by meeting royalty. Sports greats were another matter. However, even with star athletes I was never an autograph seeker or publicity hound. Giving them privacy was a matter of respect. A high point in my career as a carney was having Ted Williams sit in one of my chairs for days, even though I never spoke to him.

Ted Williams made a lot of money in the off-season. Ted and his buddy Jack Sharkey, heavyweight boxing champ and a fisherman, were paid by fishing equipment companies to hold casting contests at fairs. I went into the Harrisburg show, the best sportsman show in the world. I had Dutch imports in that sports show and some fairly expensive casual patio furniture with hunting and fishing scenes on big pillows. I had about four pretty good years doing that. This particular year, Tom was running the furniture booths for me because there was little cash involved. One day Tom said, "Guess who is sitting in one of our display chairs." I looked and there was Red Sox heavy hitter Ted Williams sitting in my chair. He and Jack Sharkey were right across from us near the big arena where they did fly casting, and when he wasn't performing, Ted Williams would be sitting there in my chair. I didn't bother him because he was a star and everyone was trying to get to him. I knew he found that annoying.

Tom, however, wasn't shy, and he made friends with Ted. Ted said he didn't want to be bothered by people, didn't want to do autographs, so Tom ran interference for him. One day a guy came up, and Tom said. "No, you can't talk to Ted now." The guy said, "I know he's in the dressing room. Tell him Irish wants to speak to him." So Tom did and Ted said, "Irish? Send him in." Ted hit 521 homeruns and had the highest batting average and on base record ever, even though he gave five years of his career to serve our country—three years in World War II and two years in the Korean conflict, in which he flew 39 combat missions. Irish had been his maintenance man on his plane in the war, so Irish got in to see Ted.

Ted Williams had three loves, the Marines, baseball, and fishing. All this time I was at that show, I saw him sitting in my chair and I didn't want to risk spoiling the memory of the night he called me after my first swim on Lake Michigan. When Ted asked whose furniture it was, Tom said the owner didn't want to be known. Tom was in seventh heaven dealing with the great slugger. He really didn't want me to identify myself because Ted probably would have spent more time with me as a fellow Marine Reserves Officer. If it hadn't been for Tom, I might have stepped forward. As it was, I quietly watched the great ballplayer and loyal Marine sitting in my chair for about ten days, preserving unaltered the memory of that long phone call I'd had with him.

That's a good memory to end on.

Chapter 24

The Blissful Years

Through all our years of marriage, Lydia and I were living under the conditions I had set early in our marriage. She and I both could have affairs with others. She was never happy with that arrangement and only took advantage of her freedom once that I knew of, and she told me beforehand that she was going to do that. I, on the other hand, had seven affairs during our 32 years of marriage, which is not really very many considering my proclaimed freedom. I didn't tell her about any of them, but somehow she found out about every one of them. She would start drinking at her first suspicion of an affair, even the ones I wasn't having, and she would go into a rage. By now, her drinking had become her escape from many discomforts, not just my affairs. How she was when she was drinking made me very unhappy at home and all the more likely to find comfort elsewhere. I am very sad for this pattern in which I participated.

In spite of my infidelities and her drinking, we'd had fun. We'd laughed a lot. We'd built a small fortune together and lost it together. We had taken care of each other, and we had helped each other. We knew each other with all our flaws better than we knew anyone else in the world, and I admired her more and more with this knowledge.

I really loved her now, in a way I'd never loved any other woman I'd been with. It was not about romance but something more. And I believe she loved me, too. As this was becoming clearer to me, one day I said something momentous to her, "If you give up booze, I'll give up women."

She said, "I'll stop drinking when I want to." So I went out with a woman, and she got awful and drunk. This went on.

I'd offered her the hardest thing I had to give, but I offered it easily and sincerely, and it hadn't worked.

Some time later, I tried again: "If you give up drinking, there'll be no more women because you're the only one for me." She didn't say anything.

It took years, but she ultimately did begin to drink less. I noticed, but she wouldn't say she was trying to quit.

Then we began to play tennis together. I was 70 then, on top of my game. We played tennis every day, go, go, go. She only drank once after we started playing tennis. I credit the sport. In the seasons when the shows were not good and in between shows, we played every morning at public courts in and around Naples Park. We'd play for two hours before it got hot. Then we'd have lunch and go to the beach. I wasn't crazy about the beach. I liked the water but not the sand. I'd go out with her to the beach because she wanted to. But playing tennis, we felt totally together. That is why, since then, I have raised money for tennis scholarships in three different college programs. I wanted to honor what brought us such pleasure together.

When I was convinced that Lydia was determined to give up drinking, even though she hadn't told me her commitment, I called the woman I'd been dating in England, where I'd been going for shows, and told her that there was no more us.

The next four years were wonderful. Lydia and I just had fun. Of course, we worked at the business all over the country and in Europe. But work was different. Everything was different. We didn't need anybody else in the world; we just enjoyed being alone together.

Bonita Springs

Lydia had never owned anything of her own. Over the years, I'd owned a lot, but because of the rocky start to our marriage and my old fashioned idea of marriage, the property was always in my name. She earned her own money but she'd never owned a home. One summer, while I'd been on a swimming trip and she was running the Athletic Club, a lawyer member asked her if she owned the log cabin. She said, "Yes, because Harry and I are married." He explained that she needed to be on the deed to acquire the property, in case of my death, without going through probate. Upon my return she challenged me on this immediately. I didn't like the challenge and said I needed a couple days to consider the matter. Naturally, upon consideration, I realized that the only equitable solution would be to put her on the deed, which I did. A few years later, I put her on the deed for the New Hampshire property. We also owned together the properties in Ninilchik, the new Athletic Club, and in Naples, Florida. Lydia was happy to officially own something.

She was always working beside me to acquire and preserve what I had bought. She was convinced I knew what I was doing. When I'd bought the whole end of the village of Ninilchik, she thought, *this guy is all right.* She said, "Don't ever do anything big without consulting me," and I'd agreed. And we'd get something going, and we'd say, "We can do it," and then the dream was shattered. But we kept plugging away.

Now, while living in Naples, Lydia said, "Why didn't we get waterfront property?" I said, "Because it's too expensive." I wanted to make her happy now, to make up for the years when we'd been less than a couple. I'd always wanted a marriage that was exceptional, and ours wasn't. It was okay sometimes, but not exceptional. Now it could be.

So I went out and looked at waterfront property nearby. I saw a 50-foot lot priced at $50,000. Then I heard about Bonita Springs up the coast. I saw an ad for a waterfront lot there for $1000. I went up to see it and got an agent. The lot was a big field with tall grass and no trees. The agent explained that when it rained the lot filled up with water. I looked at other places in Bonita Springs. The agent showed me some lots for $5000 that were not appealing. But he had a new listing for $8000, he said. "Too much, but I'll look," I said.

This lot was in a subdivision, where a cul de sac ran out near the end of a peninsula. I looked straight down the length of the peninsula and saw a big expanse of water. On the water was the prettiest lot I'd ever seen. I went home and told Lydia about it but said I definitely couldn't afford it.

"How much is it? Let's go see it," she said. We came around a corner and there was this gorgeous expanse of water at the end of the road. She said, "I want it. Find the money."

"Are you willing to contribute?" I asked. "Yes. We have to have the lot."

So we bought it and we found we needed a seawall. I spent $5000 more on the seawall and a dock. As long as we had it, we could sit on the wall or the dock and enjoy it. The sky was full of birds: pelicans, blue heron, and bald eagles. We owned a piece of heaven.

The biggest problem with owning a piece of heaven was that we had to mow the lawn even without a house on it. The neighbors called the county about my grass, when it got too high, and I was fined $400. So one day I was cutting the lawn at Bonita Springs, and a woman offered me $150,000 for the lot. I took her number and I told Lydia. She said, "If it's worth that much, why don't we build on it?" So we did, a gorgeous little house with a covered pool. The sale of our Naples property, which included a couple lots adjacent to our house there, almost paid for the new house.

When we ended up with that beautiful home in Bonita and I'd bought her a brand new Cadillac she said, "You're the man." It was her dream house and my dream for her to have it. She was the woman for me, the love of my life. And though she had never declared she was giving up alcohol, she was sober.

Lydia and I lived in this blissful state in our dream house in Florida all spring. In the summer, we went back to New Hampshire for the 1991 fair season. The best day of my life was the one in which she called me from kitchen to where I was in the TV room, and she said, "Haddy...." Lydia had been determined to learn perfect English from the moment she arrived in this country, something else I admired about her, and she had, except for mastering the *RR* in my name, and so "Haddy" had become almost a term of affection. This time it was the opening words to an announcement. She said, "Haddy, I want you to know something. I have this alcohol 95% beat, and I'm going to make it." I was joyful beyond measure. It was official: She had committed herself to our marriage.

Saying Goodbye

A few weeks later, I had gone down the steps I'd built from the house to the river. I took my tools down to hook up the pump to bring water from the river up the steep bank to fill our pool. Lydia went down with me several times and made several trips up and down to bring me more tools. On her last trip up, she told me that the water was running into the pool. Success! She yelled down that she would have supper ready in fifteen minutes, but that she felt a little sick.

I spent a few more minutes wrapping up the job, and then with bloody knuckles from the work and in my dirty work clothes, I came wearily up the stairs. When I came around the corner, I could see Lydia sitting in a porch chair slumped over. I thought she was mocking my exhausted posture, and I didn't appreciate that, after all I'd accomplished. As I came closer, I saw that she was really in trouble.

"Lydia, you've had a stroke!" I cried. I straightened her up. She was talking to me but it made no sense. I had to get her to the hospital in Plymouth. I started talking to her about the plan, just keeping on talking so she'd know what was happening and just so she'd hear my voice. I was saying, "Now I'm going to get the car….and everything is going to be all right." I couldn't find the key to the Cadillac and she could see them through the door of the house and she pointed to them, so I knew she was thinking straight. I grabbed them and ran up the hill and got the car and brought it around for her.

I carried her out to the car. It's amazing and terrifying how hard it is to get an adult into a car without that person being able to help. I talked to her about everything. "Now I'm going to put you down on the ground for a second and then I'm going to put you in the other way around and then…." I got her into the car and took off for the hospital in Plymouth. All the way, I told her how much I loved her. She tried to move her left hand over to take mine and couldn't. I took her hand, and she smiled.

When I got to the hospital, it was maddening. I pulled up to the office and ran in and told them I had my very sick wife in the car. They acted like I was the stupidest person alive, and they said I had to go to the emergency entrance. I didn't know where that was. Finally someone came to help me. I was still talking to Lydia, "Now these people are going to take care of you; this doctor is going to help you."

They took her into a room and did all kinds of tests. In about a half hour, the doctor came out, and said I could go in to her. When she saw me, she smiled the most beautiful smile. She tried to talk but I couldn't understand her. In a few minutes the electronic stuff that was hitched up to her began to go crazy. Another doctor came in and said that Plymouth Hospital was not equipped to handle her situation and I would have to choose whether to take her to the Mary Hitchcock Hospital in Dartmouth or to the Concord Hospital, each about 50 miles away. I chose Concord. They told me to go on ahead and they would probably pass me. I drove slowly and nobody passed me, and I arrived at the Concord Hospital alone. The emergency room was full. I waited for about ten minutes until I could see the blinking lights of the ambulance. I heard my name called and met with a doctor who said that I must make a decision immediately.

He said she'd had a massive stroke, that he could operate and maybe extend her life a few days, but she would not be able to communicate. Or we could consider her terminal, in which case we'd not give her any life support except those measures required by New Hampshire law, and she'd live less than a day. Lydia and I had talked about such things before and we both agreed we would not want to live like that. But still it was a terrible thing to have to commit to right this minute while the doctor stood there waiting for my decision. I finally said I'd decided not to operate. I was in such shock and despair.

The doctor also noted the blood on my hands from working on the pump at the river. He said he'd have to make note of that blood in his report. That didn't help my grief any.

Then a nurse came who deals with people in terminal situations like this. I resisted this help at the beginning, but she was so great that I allowed her to minister to me. She really helped and calmed me down a lot. They then moved Lydia from the emergency room to a "terminal room" where she was made as comfortable as possible. I was told that she would survive long enough for me to go home and clean up, so I drove back to Campton, bathed, and put on a suit. I was back at the hospital in a little more than two hours.

For the next 12 hours, I stayed with her, talked to her, and held her hand for hours. The nurses were wonderful. They told me that, after years of observing such scenes, they were convinced that Lydia could hear me. I'll have to say that Lydia had a look of defiance on her face, and she appeared to be angry.

Lydia was raised a Catholic in Germany, but I can tell you she was a confirmed atheist. When I'd called Tom with the news, he was stunned. He said we needed to give Lydia last rites. He said it was important to a Catholic even if she was an atheist. So I asked for a priest, and he gave her last rites, which was all in Latin, so I don't think it did her a bit of good, but it didn't hurt her.

It was a little after one o'clock the next day, June 14. Lydia had not been breathing regularly all this time, but suddenly her breathing changed and became even more irregular and difficult. I went out in the hall and got the nurse. She and at least one other nurse came in and remained with me until Lydia's breathing stopped. I said, "She's left me, hasn't she?" The nurse nodded and began to arrange Lydia's body and took all the tubes out. Then I was left alone with Lydia.

The next time I looked at her, her eyes were wide open and she was smiling. In a few seconds, she had gone from looking angry to looking at me with the most angelic smile I have ever seen. That smile is one of the main reasons I believe in an afterlife.

For the next few minutes, it was Lydia and Harry together for the last time. I tried not to cry because she wouldn't want that. I held her hand, touched her face and hair, and took one final look at that angelic face. I started out the door. Then I remembered my last moments with my mother, so I returned and gave Lydia my best Marine salute, and this time made it through the door.

Chapter 25

After Lydia

Though devastated by Lydia's death, I knew I needed to be as active or more active than before to manage my grief and to keep my life going. In the months following her death, I tended my booth at the New England fall fairs I had booked.

When winter came, I headed back to Florida. Our dream house at Bonita Springs seemed empty and sad now, but I did the best I could to carry on. I not only took up my sales routine there, but I also went back to one of my pleasurable pursuits of the past. In the spring of 1992, I got a job as an adjunct professor at St. Leo University at Homestead Air Force Base. That brought back the satisfaction of teaching young people and stimulated my intellect in a way that had been missing for several years.

I started an athletic scholarship for tennis players at St. Leo in memory of Lydia because I believe tennis, the first sport Lydia had ever played in her life and at which she proved to be very good, was a big key to her recovery from alcoholism. It served as an emotional distraction from her addiction and a physical healer. Our playing tennis together with such pleasure was a huge step into our blissful last years together. The first scholarship was awarded in 1994.

In late summer 1993, I returned to Alaska to settle some things. In 1983, after Princess Red Rock had died, we'd sold the log cabin in Anchorage for $135,000 to a man who subsequently used it as a gambling joint and house of prostitution, judging from what I'd heard. The man didn't pay the taxes on the house and he stopped making payments to me, so I'd gotten ownership of the cabin back.

In early 1991, I'd engaged a realtor to sell the cabin again, and a woman named Wadeen Hepworth made an offer, but Lydia wouldn't agree to accept the offer, and I deferred to her.

Now with Lydia gone, I wanted to close the Alaska chapter, so I flew to Anchorage to sell the cabin. I remembered that Wadeen Hepworth had a real estate license, and since she had seen the charm underneath the mess two years before, I figured she might find a way to sell it now. However, when I called her, she said she didn't want to list it because she still might want to buy it herself. We met at the cabin. The grass needed cutting and I could see that there was a hole six feet in diameter in the glass wall that ran along the porch. Wadeen said some vagrants had gotten in a fight and did that damage; she'd been keeping an eye on what happened to the cabin. The inside was worse. The bathroom was a horror story. The water in the bathtub couldn't be shut off. The toilet was no longer in existence, but the bathroom had been used as a toilet anyway by some intruders who had never cleaned it out. Logs had rotted in the corner of the dining room near the floor and kitchen cabinet doors were off their hinges. All the heating vents had clothes and personal items stuffed in them; the windows were covered with rags and there was junk and dirt everywhere.

When I walked in and saw the horrible condition, I cried. The combination of all the memories I had of this cabin came flooding back: Our first morning when Lydia and I woke up there after we were married, and how happy Lydia was to live in this cabin, how Lydia and I had struggled here with our marriage and our livelihood, and now—to have this place so defiled—I couldn't bear it. If anyone should have this place now, it should be Wadeen with her vision and enthusiasm for it. Still I thought she was nuts to think of buying it. We decided to meet in an hour for coffee at Peggy's Café to talk it over.

Wadeen came armed with a book where she'd recorded her previous offer. She said she still wanted to buy the house. I tried to talk her out of it because I thought she didn't know what she was getting into. She agreed the house was a disaster, but she said it still had charm for her. She'd decided to buy it and right there we sealed the deal. Even so, when we went to the closing the next day, I still asked the title person to please tell Wadeen she shouldn't go through with it. She insisted she could fix that house up because she had loved it and talked to it for the two years after her first offer as she passed it everyday on her way to work at Alaska Railroad.

Since Wadeen had insisted on buying the house, I told her I'd help her clean it up. I borrowed a lawn mower and cut the grass. It made a big difference in the appearance of the cabin from the street and lifted my spirits. That was the easy part.

Just as I hated for my elementary school teacher Miss Barstow to go into the stinky boys' bathroom, I couldn't let Wadeen face this bathroom job herself. I gagged as I scooped human waste from the bathtub. I also removed and disposed of 30 one-gallon cans of urine that had been stacked neatly in the hall. I wanted to protect this nice and gutsy woman from the worst consequences of her foolish decision to buy.

What neither Wadeen nor I knew and she told me later was that the house had been slated for condemnation by the city. When she found out, she went to the city code enforcement department to try to get a reprieve. Lou Ellis, who was in charge of the department, said he wanted to see the house for himself before he gave it a final condemnation because he wanted to save it if he could. The plumbing inspectors, the building inspectors, and the electric inspectors crawled all over that place, determining what had to be done to save it. Lou gave Wadeen grandfather rights to allow her to use the house. With a hard won loan of $45,000 from Anchorage Historic Properties, she began the process of rehabilitation. I admired her determination at every step.

In the next few days, when I saw that she was serious and capable and that the cabin was going to be livable once more, I decided to bury Lydia's ashes there. While for me, I think it doesn't matter what happens to the body after death, for her I wanted her ashes to remain where she'd been happiest in her life. I'd already buried a portion of her ashes at Bonita Springs and another portion at our place in New Hampshire. I'd brought with me the third portion of her ashes in a little metal lozenge box, and with Wadeen's approval, I buried them under a large May Day tree in the backyard. Wadeen promised she would plant a lily garden under the tree to honor Lydia who had once been "Lily the Silver Serpent."

For many years, I didn't see how the restored cabin turned out. Much later, when Wadeen in turn moved and had decided to sell the house, she sent me pictures. I was really happy to see the cabin in such good shape. She said she wished she'd sent the pictures sooner but she'd made a few changes in the house and was afraid the changes would make me sad. To the contrary, I was just happy that the place Lydia's ashes were resting was being kept up and that someone else was living happily there. In the end, however, Wadeen didn't sell the house; she let her daughter live in the cabin while she herself is living nearby. I am satisfied that it is in good hands.

The restored cabin

The Come Back Kid

Four years after Lydia died, I was on my way home from playing tennis and stopped at Dunkin Donuts in Campton where I was reading the *Laconia Citizen*. The paper said that a guy from Toronto was going to try to be the first to swim Lake Winnipesaukee because "no serious swimming attempts" had been made on the Lake. So loyal fans of mine from way back phoned the editor. Later I called him and when I said my name, he said, "Yes, I know who you are because so many people have called me about your swimming the lake." He was a nice young fellow, and he apologized for his error. So he came to see me and by way of retraction did an article about my swims, including a photo. I found I enjoyed revisiting this phase of my life. The swimmer from Toronto came and did the Lake, swimming its 22-mile length. I went and met him for an interview we did together on the radio. He announced in that interview that he would do the lake both ways the next year. The next year he came and tried. The first 22 miles were fine but he only did a couple miles of the return trip. It's a mind thing; retracing your route instead of going forward is hard. I began to wonder if I could still do that stuff.

My wondering soon turned to eagerness to see what I could do. I knew very well how to work college public relations resources, so I contacted the PR guy at Concord Technical College; he was a Marine. I said, "I'd like to make a comeback now. I'm

74." He publicized my swims as I went over to Squam Lake, which was where the movie "On Golden Pond" was filmed. Little Squam Lake and Big Squam Lake are connected and together are ten miles long. I did Little Squam for a warm-up, then Newfoundland Lake, which is five miles long. Next I did the ten miles of the Squam Lake system. I found I had slipped in physical strength but I hadn't lost my mental toughness, which is the difference between me and the guy from Toronto.

The next summer, I did Lake Winnisquam, which is 11 miles. The Marine from Concord Tech had moved on, so this time I partnered with Plymouth State College. The 11 miles were easier than the ten miles the year before, so I was headed in the right direction. The next summer I switched to Tilton School, where I had first been a student back when Tilton Academy also had a junior college. I got better PR there, as an alumnus. With Tilton, I swam Lake Sunapee, which is only eight miles, but it was tougher for me. My stroke was off somehow. Then I realized there were no more long lakes to do in the vicinity of my home.

The following year, May 12, 1998, I was inducted into the International Marathon Swimming Hall of Fame, an affiliated unit of the International Swimming Hall of Fame, based on 45 marathon swims, defined as ten miles or more, and my being the first to cross Lake Erie. (I haven't described here every swim I did, for fear of boring you.) In the first group of marathon swimmers inducted into the newly formed Marathon group was Gertrude Ederle, first woman to cross the English Channel and my early inspiration from the passenger ship to Europe when I was 16. The induction ceremony was held at the Hall of Fame in Fort Lauderdale. It was a wonderful occasion with speeches, dignitaries, and famous swimmers. And there my name, with all the other marathon swimmers, is inscribed in the Hall, which was on the site of the former Governors Club, where I had been hired as a lifeguard and tender of the pool before I went into the Marines. I'd gone from pool boy to Hall of Famer. So bits of my past were fitting into my older age like puzzle pieces in the big picture.

Before I get too nostalgic, however, I need to say that the celebration that should have been a highlight of my life became a personal disaster. I had a lady friend who really wanted to go with me to the induction ceremony. At the last minute I agreed to take her. Because the organizers had me down for one seat up in front of the room with other inductees, they weren't prepared for her and had to seat us at a long table with other guests, the nearest of whom included a former Olympic swimming champion and a Frenchman who had donated the wine for this event and his wife.

I knew my friend was a heavy drinker, but I'd never had any trouble with her. There were cocktails before dinner and the French wine with the meal, and before I knew it, my friend was saying loudly, "Harry is the best swimmer in the world." At first, I was just embarrassed that she was boasting in front of an international gathering of best swimmers in the world and I was countering what she was saying with modest objection. Soon she began slurring her words and getting out of hand. I tried to calm her down and that only made her worse. When my name was called to get the award, I was really mortified. Like the other inductees, I'd prepared a few words and, as a former sportscaster, I'm usually pretty good at a podium. But this time, I was terrible. I fell all over my words and sat down as quickly as possible. Then my companion got even louder and began to be belligerent. She used the F-word and said some other bad things. I took her by the arm and said, "You're leaving with me right now." She wanted to stay. You can imagine this scene. The Frenchman's wife said to me, "I understand what you're going through. I've had some of this kind of trouble in my own family." That was a kind and comforting thing for her to say, as I hastily escorted my date out of the Hall of Fame.

Eight days later, on May 20, my 77th birthday, I swam by far the toughest swim of my come-back, the seven miles across Tampa Bay, from a beach on the east side of the Bay near the town of Apollo Beach to the St. Petersburg pier, crossing tidal currents going two miles an hour. It took me 14 hours.

I had a Florida marine patrol boat with me and the swim coach from the University of Tampa. The University of Tampa was sponsoring me and had been very good to me, getting me publicity before the swim and accompanying me for a four-mile practice swim in the Bay. However, the University of Tampa baseball team, which wasn't expected to do much, had a great season that year and unexpectedly went all the way to a big national tournament at the end of the season. The athletic director and the sports PR person took off for the baseball tournament right before my swim. So when I went in the water, there was no one there but the swim coach and my guide boats. But this swim was for me, not for the publicity—not that I'm shy about publicity—so I went into the Bay enthusiastically.

At one point a freighter was coming into the Bay, and we radioed to ask the freighter if it would slow down to let a swimmer pass. "A swimmer? No can do," was the reply. So the coach told me to tread water for 45 minutes. I have never been able to tread water well. It is more exhausting and boring than swimming, and I lose my rhythm. So I swam back and forth until the freighter passed and then I went on.

I ran into difficult waters then, with wind blowing and whitecaps. I was heading towards St. Pete when the tide changed and was taking me past the St. Pete pier almost to the bridge. I thought, *I can't make it.* Then my job was to drive those thoughts out of my mind. That ability was my strength. The wind died down finally, but we'd had to give up the St. Pete pier. Still the swim would count as crossing Tampa Bay, if I made it to the Coast Guard Station. I swam for 30 more minutes with the current heading back to Tampa at two miles an hour—about the speed I was swimming—so I was soon farther away than before. So I reconsidered the pier, and we headed for the big sombrero, the lighted stadium. For the first time in too long, I made progress. Each time I took a breath, I saw the lights of the city up ahead. I was moving up on it. Again the current was so fast, I might miss the pier. It was now completely dark and the water was black. My hand touched something solid moving through the water, a bit unnerving, but I chose to think it was just a dolphin. A quarter mile from the pier, the boat left me so my guide could go in to ask if it was okay if we landed at the pier. Yes. A good thing.

The only press at the end was a reporter from Naples, who had heard about the swim and had come up but couldn't find my people, who had gone to the baseball tournament. He went around to the planned landing place, and that's where I came in. It was nice to have someone to record my success.

I've made a swim of some length a part of almost every birthday since then. When I turned 90 in 2011, I swam two miles on beautiful Kincaid Lake near Alexandria, Louisiana, and then celebrated with the wonderful folks of Northwestern State University and other friends at a banquet at Tunk's Cypress Inn.

How I got to Northwestern is another story.

"Johnny's So Long at the Fair"

As a child I often heard the 18th century English nursery rhyme that goes, "Oh, dear, what can the matter be, Johnny's so long at the fair." Well, oh, dear, I was so long at the fair. I continued my business at shows and fairs ever since my first one, when I was living in Alaska; it has been my main livelihood most of my life. With costs of booths rising and times changing, I can't really make any money at it any more, but I've done it every fair season, alternating with teaching a semester in the off season, because that's what I do. It's in my blood now, and I help out Lois and I see people I know, and I just enjoy making use of the skills I've learned over the decades. It's not good to quit what you've always done. You lose motivation.

To complete my story, I should also include one more person along with Princess Red Rock, Tom, and Lois, who have helped me or partnered with me in the carney business and then gone on their own but remained closely connected. I met Margaret at a show in England and saw her from show to show. She was good company and we had some fun and that was it. Like the others—like us all—she is flawed. Her flaws arose out of a very difficult childhood situation in England. She married a guy I respect and admire named Roger, who is a Mormon priest, and they were living in California. When Margaret heard through the carney grapevine that Lydia had died, she came east to see me. To make a long story short, she and Roger ended up living in my house in Campton, New Hampshire, running The Chalet, and keeping an apartment for me to live in when I do the fall fairs in the Northeast. Somebody had to live there because the snow or ice in the winter makes the roof leak and the property needs care. Margaret couldn't put up with Tom Pallister and sent him packing. I never saw him again. Margaret has been there 19 years and made decisions about the shop; it's hers, really. She keeps whatever profit she can make. It's in my will to leave her the property. Margaret and I are not getting along so well right now, but I reward people who have helped me and, especially, I keep my word. The White Mountains still call to me, and my waterfall still thrills me, but the house no longer feels like home.

Leesville is now one of my homes. It was in the carney business, selling goods at shows and fairs, that I happened to come to Leesville. I still have my good friend Robert Barber, a wire bender, who has made his living running a booth at the post exchange (PX) at military bases, where he bends gold-filled wire into a customer's name or a message like "Joe loves Susan," and it becomes a pendant or a pin or whatever you want. I wanted to do a rodeo in Texas so I said, "Robert, do you want to come with me? You do ten foot of gold and I do ten foot of my stuff." "Ten foot" refers to the width of the booth. Robert agreed, adding that he'd never done Fort Polk, which was on the way to Texas from where he was in Georgia. So we decided to meet at Fort Polk.

I'd been in the southern part of Louisiana a few times; I'd driven Route 10 outside of Baton Rouge through a swamp where the road is a causeway. This time I came by way of Jackson, Mississippi, and the land looked like I expected Louisiana to look flat—but when we came out of Alexandria, there were hills. I said to myself, *There aren't any hills in Louisiana*. But there are. We were on a 200-foot plateau then we go up and down until all of a sudden it turned into forest, like New Hampshire without mountains. I was amazed.

I got to Fort Polk and was looking around. I went into a building looking for the PX and asked a Colonel for directions. I also said to the Colonel, "This looks like an education building. Is it?" And the Colonel said, "Yes." I said, "Do you need any instructors?" He said, "We don't, but there's a university about three miles down the road and they might."

Northwestern State University-Leesville/Fort Polk

So I went to the Northwestern campus and introduced myself. What a stroke of luck. Creighton Owen, a wonderful man, hired me to teach political science there. In that summer of 1998, I went to New Hampshire in early August, where I swam the 11 miles across Keyser Lake in North Sutton, New Hampshire, which had never been done before, for the benefit of Tilton School. Then I went to the fairs in New England and then Wisconsin, and was back to do the fall classes at Northwestern for the first time. Creighton Owen unfortunately died of cancer several years later, a really good guy. He was replaced as executive director by Larry Monk, who also became a great support and a good friend.

I was teaching a couple 8-week terms at Northwestern, alternating them with my business on the fair circuit. In late July 2008, at the end of my teaching duties in summer school, I was getting ready to leave for the fall fair circuit, and I stopped by the university to say goodbye. All the women were crying and the men were stunned. Larry Monk had died suddenly the night before in his sleep. What a loss for the school and a personal sadness for me.

Now Joe Pope is doing a great job as executive director. The staff has continued to be helpful to me in many ways. Thomas Tilley, who is responsible for over 200 computers for Northwestern's Leesville campus, in particular has been wonderful to me. He cut my grass when I was very ill one time and has filed my handwritten grades for me because I never learned to use the computer. He's done a lot of things for me that have made my life easier. I've also had many promising students at Northwestern and many rewarding exchanges with them. Even with an occasional illness and my age (remember 90 is the new 70) I'm proud that I have only missed one class in the 11 years I've been teaching in Leesville, and that one absence occurred when I took the Mardi Gras holiday on the wrong day. We New England/Alaskan boys don't keep good track of Mardi Gras the way Louisianans do.

Since I only was teaching here for two eight-week terms a year and had my residence in Milton, Florida, I bought a rundown house in Leesville for $8000 to fix up enough to live in for the teaching terms. When the hurricanes destroyed my home in Florida, I unexpectedly found the rundown house here was my main home, so I got out my toolbox and got busy. So that's how I ended up in Leesville.

Also, after several years, I began to teach political science classes also at Central Texas University at their Ft. Polk campus. The people there have been very helpful to me, and I consider them good friends, especially site director Phillip Schuster.

I feel fortunate to have come to Leesville where people have treated me with respect and friendship and given me part time employment. I have made some true friends here. Soon it began to feel like home.

Chapter 26

On the Waterfront

When I first came to Leesville, I still owned waterfront property in Florida. Lydia's dream house at Bonita Springs no longer called to me. I wasn't happy there any more. After a difficult and sad decision, I sold that house in August 2001. I buried a portion of Lydia's ashes there.

I'd also buried a portion on our Naples Park land; I had to ask the new owner for permission, which was graciously granted. So now her ashes remain in all the places we loved together, the two homes in Florida, the cabin in Anchorage, our place in Ninilchik, and now Bonita Springs. I still have a small portion that I have always intended to bury on Wendelstein Mountain, at the foot of which lies Lydia's hometown of Rosenheim in Bavaria, Germany. Lydia and I went there once together, and she showed me the home where she lived with her grandmother, one street down from Nazi war criminal Hermann Goering, and where her uncle defied Hitler. He was sent to Dachau, tortured, released to tend his farm and produce food for the army, and then disappeared to join the resistance until the war was over. This past is what I'd wanted to somehow erase or correct by giving Lydia a safe home, a better life than she had ever known. I'd hoped also to take her ashes back to the mountain she had loved.

After selling the Bonita Springs home, I was thinking about buying a place on Toledo Bend, a lake that lies on the border of Louisiana and Texas, not far from Leesville. I was also considering another house in Florida, and it had to be on the water, so I was looking for something on the panhandle, closer to Louisiana so I could go there for long weekends between the days I had classes. Driving a few hundred miles has never bothered me.

A realtor found me three adjacent 50-foot lots on the waterfront in Milton, Florida. On this land there was a mobile home, but it had a house built around it so that it didn't look like a mobile home. It had a beautiful living room. I didn't understand then the implications of having a mobile home, for example, the depreciation. Now that I've experienced it, I know. Also on the lot there was a concrete workshop 36 feet by 20 feet with plenty of room for my tools, and I could store my merchandise there. The realtor said the asking price for three lots with house and workshop were $74,000. "Do you want it," she asked. "Absolutely," I said. I built a 50-foot dock and I was very pleased with myself.

Ivan, Dennis, and Rita

In 2004, Hurricane Ivan hit Milton head on and washed away my dock. The roof of the house was sagging and so much mold accumulated inside that the county condemned the house and I had to demolish it. The insurance company offered me 50 cents on the dollar because I had a depreciated trailer, not a conventional house. At least I still had the workshop. Then in came Hurricane Dennis the next year, a category 3 hurricane. The winds came off the bay and got under the roof of the workshop, and there was nowhere else for the wind to go, so the whole thing collapsed, absolutely collapsed. This was only seven months after I lost the main house.

Then in September 2005, there was Hurricane Rita, another category 3 that hit the coast of western Louisiana. When I came back to Leesville from being on the road, I found a tree had fallen on the roof of my house here.

A Little Black Cloud

It's normal that 90 years of living will bring a lot of loss. Even so, it seems that I've experienced more than my share of losses and misfortunes while doing more than my share of effort. I'd lost my home in Limerick, Maine, to fire; then I lost my new fishing boat in a big storm in Alaska; then we lost our businesses in the Great Earthquake. We bought a building, relocated there, and after three years of struggling to rebuild the business, which was going to be our fortune, the building burned. We lost our property in Ninilchik after the earthquake killed the business and hippies moved in and wrecked the place. I finally sold the property to a friend and got my money out but all our dreams for that little place were dashed and we were gone.

All of this was nothing compared to losing Lydia. I'd finally given her the home she really wanted and she got to live there only one spring before it was all over.

After Lydia's death, there was a landslide in New Hampshire when all the earth under the swimming pool of our home washed down into the river. I spent many thousands of dollars rebuilding that to save the whole house from sliding down. I had homeowners insurance but about all that covered was fire. I thought I had insurance to cover at least the roof, but the insurance company said there was an exclusion; landslides were not covered.

I've made a lot of mistakes in my life, and I've learned from most of them, but my losses have not often been caused by my mistakes but by what insurance companies call "acts of God." And so it is natural and necessary that I find meaning in my life that compensates for some things that have gone wrong.

Real Love

I found meaning in finally making my marriage to Lydia work. In the beginning we didn't really love. To Lydia, love meant I took care of her and gave her what she needed: security, something to call her own, respectability. To me, love meant sexual attraction especially during the chase. I got what I wanted and grew tired of it quickly and wanted to give it up. She got what she wanted when we married and never wanted to give it up. In order to survive, we stuck together. Over time, especially hard times, I came to admire and respect in Lydia the characteristics that I valued—hard work, tenacity, and pitching in to help when the chips were down. She had also admired these qualities in me. We'd have the beginnings of a dream, and we'd say, "We can do it." The dream was shattered, but we kept plugging away. We had good times together and affectionate times as well as terrible times, but we didn't learn until late in life what love really was. All the trouble earlier in our marriage tested our relationship to the point where we were able to recognize real love when we finally had it.

My feelings for Lydia were and still are overwhelming. As I realized what a wonderful person she was, as I truly loved her in a mature way, it bothered me that our marriage was okay but not exceptional, but in the end it turned out to be exceptional. We had to overcome so much. Her greatest accomplishment, I think, was kicking alcohol. The greatest accomplishment of my life was achieving five blissful years.

I'm convinced that my mission in life was to provide for and protect Lydia, who had never been provided for or protected in her youth. What a wonderful way it ended! If this was my mission, I have been a success.

Teaching and Scholarships

I find meaning now in teaching and funding scholarships. In my classes, I have mostly good students. The few poor ones I try to encourage, and if they learn more than they came in with, I try to give them a decent grade.

When I teach students whose tuition is picked up by the military, I point out to them what a valuable gift they are getting from the taxpayers, and I remind them that their fellow students not in the military often struggle to pay for their education. I want my scholarships to benefit motivated students who are struggling financially to stay in school. To keep a student in school who otherwise couldn't pay tuition gives me great joy.

I have established four scholarships in addition to the tennis scholarship at St. Leo University. At Plymouth State University in New Hampshire, I established a fund in memory of Lydia that benefits the ladies tennis program. Through the American Legion, I established a scholarship fund in memory of my dad, Harry H. Briggs Sr., for three students each year in any department of Northwestern State University at Leesville.

Then I established a scholarship, now fully endowed, in memory of my aunt Letitia Douglas Adams, M.D. for students in nurses training at the Leesville campus. My aunt, Letitia Douglas Adams, M.D., graduated from Tufts Medical School and interned at the New England Hospital for Women and Children (later the New England Hospital) in Boston. She did surgical training and rose from assistant in surgery to being the chief of the surgical department at the New England Hospital.

She was elected to the American College of Surgeons in 1926. She always maintained a general practice and delivered thousands of babies. If a mother had lost more than one baby, she was lucky to be sent to Dr. Adams. My aunt was known for her great success in sending mothers home with healthy babies who had not previously been able to give birth successfully. A colleague whom she had encouraged to become an orthopedic surgeon wrote of Dr. Adams, "Hers is indeed a rare gift, for she is one of those who are naturally endowed with skill, humanity, and idealism that she is able to care for the whole person."

She was particularly supportive of nurses, and, on her retirement in 1950, the Nurses Alumnae Association of the New England Hospital for Women and Children expressed their gratitude by awarding her Honorary Membership. So you can see why I wanted to support a scholarship for nurses in her memory.

Last year and this year, on my birthday, I raised funds to benefit Northwestern State University nursing and radiology sciences students at NSU's Cenla Center in Alexandria in memory of my mother Dora Douglas Briggs. It's ironic, I suppose, to support nursing and radiology students in her name when she did not believe in receiving health care. However, I believe she would approve of this scholarship now.

Not all of these scholarships I've established are fully endowed, but I'm working on reaching the point where they are all permanent.

Home

I myself now live part of the week in my small house in Leesville that you would have perhaps called a shack when I bought it. Inside, however, I have paneled several rooms so that they look quite nice. More recently, I have put new siding on three sides so far, built a pretty back entrance and a porch, added a deck on one end, and put new siding, doors and windows on the workshop, so that it looks as nice as the house. I have always gotten great satisfaction from talking a rundown place and making something of it. I do not have central heat or air-conditioning and I drive a very old vehicle because I prefer to live on my social security and my pay for teaching in order not to spend my savings or sell my properties, which I've willed to several people who've worked with me over the years as well as put a portion of my estate into a charitable trust. Sometimes, I do worry about making ends meet, but I prefer contributing to the education of students than my own security. If security were my main motivator, I would have lived my life very differently.

My only regret about my home in Leesville is that it's not on the water. Ever since the hurricanes blew away my home on the waterfront in Florida, I've had my eye out for a place on the water in Louisiana not too far from my job and for the right price. In June 2011, on my way home from visiting my friend Robert, the wire bender, I came through the bayou country where I discovered a small cabin for sale on a bayou, a gorgeous cabin with a dock that runs out into the flowing water where alligator, turtles, fish, and birds abound. I could picture myself and a lady friend sitting on that dock in the evening under the stars. It seemed a perfect place to end my days. I bought the cabin for a modest sum, thereby preserving my estate, as the land is leased for a reasonable annual fee. I wanted a lease for 15 years, but the owner only gave me 10 years. When I reach 100, perhaps they will extend the lease. So now I plan to teach indefinitely in Leesville, staying in my home there for the part of the week when I have classes, and living on my bayou the rest of the week, on the water where I belong. I hope to get a canoe to explore the bayou. I don't really like boats; I don't care for their stability. I like the challenge of a canoe. I picture myself gliding on the dark water, slipping between the cypress and tupelo gum, almost one with the water.

In theory, I live alone, and I prefer to live alone, but in practice, I often have people sharing my home, people who have no home of their own and no means. Sometimes it's a person attempting to stay sober, and I give them a place to stay. Once it was a man disabled in his work, who had not been able to qualify for disability; he stayed with me while I helped him redo his paperwork to reapply and succeed in getting benefits. The fact that he left suddenly, taking at least $3000 of my cash with him does not deter me from taking people in. After him, I had a couple staying in a tiny room in my house who had been living in the woods in the winter rather than continuing to work for an abusive employer. Whatever it is, it's a condition far worse than mine and I cannot in good conscience leave such people homeless.

I share my home with people whom I don't judge as being worthy or not so worthy but who are in need and to whom I can give a break in life. A number of them don't treat me well in return, but I understand that; they didn't have the privilege of being raised in a stable home as I did, have the education I did, or the savvy to get themselves out of a pickle. They didn't all have a safe home. They didn't have a banker father, as I did, who not only gave me some background in financial affairs but who supported his family and other families through the Depression. They didn't have a mother who was a Christian Scientist who didn't believe in seeking medical help and an aunt who was a physician, representing two incongruous ways of living that have served me well. The people I have taken in didn't perhaps have the physical and mental gifts that I have been given through no virtue of my own. And so, when those I help behave badly, I am just grateful to my parents for the raising they gave me. Understanding the life of the down-and-out, understanding how they were raised, I understand their desperation and I do what I can for them without judging too much. I was once a liberal, now I'm a conservative, opposed to large government and crippling lifetime welfare for those who could learn to manage on their own. Helping others in my own neck of the woods is a personal commitment.

I plan on making it for a few more years without assistance. I have lived this long with very little medical treatment, going to a doctor only for injuries that require stitches, whether it's from falling off the roof while replacing some shingles, which happened a few years ago here in Leesville, or from a puck in the face, which happened decades ago. Even though I am leaving scholarships for nurses and wish them well, I do not plan to ever be in a hospital again.

I have never been what you would call religious and never belonged to a church though I have attended a service every now and then. I'm told there's a hymn that speaks of "earthquake, wind, and fire." I know about those. The lines by New England poet John Greenleaf Whittier go:

> Let sense be dumb, let flesh retire:
>
> Speak through the earthquake, wind, and fire,
>
> O still, small voice of calm.

The part about the earthquake, wind, and fire—I have lived it. The still, small voice—I think I have heard it. But I'm not yet ready to let flesh retire.

When the end comes in life's ever flowing stream, I don't know whether I will be with my mother and father, whom I have dearly loved, or whether I will be with Lydia again, whom I miss so much, but I am certain that what comes next will be something very, very good. While I'm holding off the final voyage and endeavoring to live the life of a younger man, I'm standing on the waterfront of the great unknown. I don't fear the water. The water is like gentle arms that buoy, even beckon me.

At home in Leesville, I have some of my scrapbooks, the ones the fires and the hurricanes didn't get.

Made in the USA
San Bernardino, CA
14 May 2019